T0277114

THE
WITCHES' CRAFT

THE ROOTS OF WITCHCRAFT AND
MAGICAL TRANSFORMATION

ABOUT THE AUTHOR

RAVEN GRIMASSI (1951-2019) is a Neopagan scholar and award-winning author of over twelve books on Witchcraft, Wicca, and Neopaganism. He is a member of the American Folklore Society and is co-founder and co-director of the College of the Crossroads.

Raven's background includes training in the Rosicrucian Order as well as the study of the Kabbalah through the First Temple of Tifareth under Lady Sara Cunningham. His early magickal career began in the late 1960s and involved the study of works by Franz Bardon, Éliphas Lévi, William Barrett, Dion Fortune, William Gray, William Butler, and Israel Regardie.

Raven was the directing Elder of the tradition of Arician Witchcraft, and together with his wife, Stephanie Taylor, he developed a complete teaching system known as Ash, Birch, and Willow. This system was the culmination of over thirty-five years of study and practice in the magickal and spiritual traditions of the indigenous people of pre-Christian Europe.

THE
WITCHES'
CRAFT

THE ROOTS OF WITCHCRAFT AND
MAGICAL TRANSFORMATION

RAVEN GRIMASSI

Chicago, Illinois

The Witches' Craft copyright © 2023 by Raven Grimassi. All rights reserved. No part of this book may be reproduced in any manner whatsoever without written permission from Crossed Crow Books, except in the case of brief quotations embodied in critical articles and reviews.

First Printing. 2023.
ISBN: 978-1-959883-47-0
Library of Congress Control Number on file.

Cover design by Blake Malliway.
Edited by Becca Fleming.
Typesetting by Gianna Rini.

Disclaimer: Crossed Crow Books, LLC does not participate in, endorse, or have any authority or responsibility concerning private business transactions between our authors and the public. Any internet references contained in this work were found to be valid during the time of publication, however, the publisher cannot guarantee that a specific reference will continue to be maintained. This book's material is not intended to diagnose, treat, cure, or prevent any disease, disorder, ailment, or any physical or psychological condition. The author, publisher, and its associates shall not be held liable for the reader's choices when approaching this book's material. The views and opinions expressed within this book are those of the author alone and do not necessarily reflect the views and opinions of the publisher.

Published by:
Crossed Crow Books, LLC
6934 N Glenwood Ave, Suite C
Chicago, IL 60626
www.crossedcrowbooks.com

Printed in the United States of America.

DISCLAIMER

Some practices, techniques, and rituals herein may contain elements that put the practitioner at risk for bodily harm and injury if performed incorrectly. The reader assumes responsibility for such risk and is not encouraged to engage in any activity that may cause harm to themselves or others.

To the Witches of the past. Know that there are still those among us who honor your memory and all that you endured to preserve and pass on the Old Religion to future generations.
You will not be forgotten.

CONTENTS

— CHAPTER 4 —
THE ART OF WITCHCRAFT 98

— CHAPTER 5 —
THE WITCHES' TOOLS 113

— CHAPTER 6 —
THE MAGICKAL ARTS 133

— CHAPTER 7 —
PERSONAL POWER   159

— CHAPTER 8 —
ALTERED STATES OF CONSCIOUSNESS   175

— CHAPTER 9 —
THE WORKINGS OF POWER   193

— CHAPTER 10 —
THE OLD WAYS IN
MODERN WITCHCRAFT   209

— CHAPTER 11 —
ANCIENT PRINCIPLES IN
MODERN CRAFT TENETS   236

— CHAPTER 12 —
THE WELL-WORN PATH   261

— APPENDIX —
THE DOREEN VALIENTE LETTERS   272

Wiccan, oh Wiccan,
'Neath the Moon's soft glow,
How is it you gather
And yet do not know?
How is it you dance
In the hush of moonlight
But your eyes fail to see
The thrice ancient rite?
Have you not felt
That the Old Ways are true,
And under the stars
That nothing is new?
Wiccan, oh Wiccan,
Where has your heart gone,
To the scholars and skeptics
Who say we are wrong?
There are things in the night
They can never know,
How a chant can bring magick,
To draw the Moon low.
Wiccan, oh Wiccan,
'Neath the Moon's soft glow,
How walk you this path
And yet do not know?

—Raven Grimassi

ℐNTRODUCTION

THIS IS A BOOK ABOUT THE OLD WAYS OF WITCHCRAFT. It is a serious and in-depth study of the art of Witchcraft. I have written this book for two purposes. First, I noticed a trend in which many authors have omitted time-proven methods, techniques, and concepts in favor of almost strictly self-styled and self-created material. For all that we have gained from this approach, we have also lost much ground. Many young people in the Craft community now have never heard of many things that were once the basic elements of practicing Witchcraft. When things are not passed on, they disappear. In this book, I hope to preserve much of what has been forgotten, misplaced, or tossed away due to a lack of understanding of its value.

Many modern books on Witchcraft will describe a technique or method of performing a spell or ritual and then go on to inform the reader that almost everything described is optional and that the prescribed items can easily be substituted with other things. This approach tends to lessen the effort on the part of the student and fails to teach the lessons learned when obstacles have to be overcome, frustrations have to be endured, and delays must be tolerated. This also fails to build character in the student, for there is no forging of one's metal without passing into and through the fire. I personally feel that the modern ambiguous approach to teaching Witchcraft is a disservice to the student, for focus and effort themselves are essential training stages for a new Witch.

As a balance, the material in this book is designed to strengthen the powers of the Witch by requiring self-disciple, patience, and perseverance. The material in this book also instructs the reader in time-proven methods and serves to help instill a sound foundation for the Witch to build upon. Once a student has confidence in the basics, then they can better explore and discern the alternatives.

The second reason I wrote this book is to respond to those who criticize Witches who believe in an authentic older form of Witchcraft, pre-dating modern Wicca. Today, scholars have turned their attention to modern Witchcraft, and many new books have been introduced by them that appear aimed at undermining and derailing both Witchcraft and the modern Goddess movement. In the following chapters, I will offer historical and literary references to counter the critical claims made by many modern scholars and skeptics.

Today, the Witch and the scholar often find themselves at odds concerning the truth about the history of Witchcraft, and whether or not Witchcraft was ever a religion in ancient times.

Writings about Witches and Witchcraft in Western literature span from around 800 BCE to modern times, and appear in each consecutive century in one form or another. The Witch figure has been infamous for over 2,500 years. Eventually, the widespread torture and killing of those accused of Witchcraft was sanctioned by both secular and ecclesiastical authorities. For a religion and a people that scholars say never existed, this seems amazingly remarkable.

What other parallel can we draw from history that encompasses so much literature over a vast period of time, and addresses with such intensity and tenacity a people that never existed, while at the same time resulting in the torture and deaths of thousands of real individuals thought to be this non-existent thing? There appears to be no match or precedence in all of history. Why have people believed in the actual existence of Witches since ancient times? Why are we still talking about them in the twenty-first century?

As this book will demonstrate, the ancient Greeks viewed Witches as practitioners of "illicit religion." If Witches did not exist in this era, why were they being referred to as people practicing illegitimate religion? If non-existent within society as a whole, why wasn't the Witch simply and strictly a creature of legend? Why do modern scholars dismiss the vast weight of literature accumulated on Witch-craft over the centuries as not having any relevance to an actual sect?

One of the major obstacles to discovering documentation of actual Witches and their religious practices during the Middle Ages and Renaissance periods is that no one was really doing any research or study on such a sect. Due to this factor, we have no direct docu-mentation separate from Witch trial transcripts, a few commentaries, Witch hunter handbooks, and so forth. Virtually all writings about Witches and Witchcraft were focused on Satanic practices, real or imagined. In other words, the focus was on Witchcraft as pre-defined by the Church and the "learned" of the time. Therefore, it is really no surprise that the evidence is not readily apparent for the existence of an old Witches' religion.

The lack of evidence for an old Witches' religion goes beyond not having searched one out. It is also due to ignoring what evidence does present itself. When the mention of a Goddess appears in the Witchcraft literature of these periods, it is dismissed as an illusion of the Devil and investigated no further as a genuine belief. This was the official position of the Church as noted by Regino, the Abbot of Prum, in 899. Regino refers to what is now called the *Canon Episcopi*, which addresses people who believe they ride with the goddess Diana at night in a great wild procession. The Canon states they are deluded into believing this by Satan. If Witches did worship a Goddess, and some of these Witches ended up in the hands of the Inquisition, it appears that no one seemed particularly interested in honestly pursuing any accounts of Goddess worship. Instead, the Inquisitors were interested in such things as how many times the Witch had intercourse with the Devil.

Despite this extreme tunnel vision approach to investigating Witchcraft, there still appears a backdrop of valuable information that may point to an actual surviving sect of authentic Witches. What I refer to here is the inclusion of the lore common to the era, as well as literary references to ritual tools and so forth, all commonly accepted as the contemporary knowledge of the Witches' Craft. But first, we must ask if any evidence exists that Witchcraft was ever viewed as a religion during the period of persecution. Such appears to have been the opinion of Francesco Guazzo, an Italian Ambrosian monk who grew up in the region of Tuscany and came to be regarded as an authority on Witchcraft. In his book *Compendium Maleficarum*, written at the request of the Archbishop of Milan (Frederico Borromeo) and published in 1608, Guazzo writes in great detail concerning the structure of the Witch cult in many regions of Europe.

In Chapters Twelve and Eighteen, Guazzo indicates that Witches gather in circles drawn upon the ground with beech twigs, and work with spirits of Earth, Air, Fire, and Water among others. Guazzo notes in Chapter Ten that Witches adhere to certain laws. In Chapter Six, Guazzo states:

> *"The infection of witchcraft is often spread through a sort of contagion to children by their fallen parents...and it is one among many sure and certain proofs against those who are charged and accused of witchcraft, if it be found that their parents before them were guilty of this crime. There are daily examples of this inherited taint in children..."*

Guazzo states that Witches *"read from a black book during their religious rites"* and he notes a religious demeanor among Witches in Chapter Eleven, where he writes:

> *"For witches observe various silences, measuring, vigils, mutterings, figures and fires, as if they were some expiatory religious rite."*

Guazzo's depiction of Witchcraft seems to indicate a rather structured and organized cult and is consistent with accounts from various Witch trial transcripts dating from 1310-1647. Folklorist Lady de Vere also describes an actively structured Witch cult in an article she wrote in 1894:

> *"...the community of Italian witches is regulated by laws, traditions, and customs of the most secret kind, possessing special recipes for sorcery"* *(La Rivista of Rome, June 1894).*

Folklorist J.B. Andrews later added:

> *"The Neapolitans have an occult religion and government in witchcraft, and the camorra; some apply to them to obtain what*

*official organizations cannot or will not do. As occasionally happens
in similar cases, the Camorra fears and yields to the witches, the
temporal to the spiritual" (Folk-Lore: Transactions of the Folk-Lore
Society,* March 1897*).*

As we can see, the idea that Witches existed as actual people and as
an actual sect is a long-standing theme in Western literature. Even as
late as the mid-nineteenth century, folklorists such as J.B. Andrews,
Lady de Vere, Roma Lister, and Charles Leland were investigating
what they believed were active Witch sects in Italy. Andrews and
Leland were among those that believed these sects were surviving
remnants of an old Witches' religion.

In the following chapters, we will look at the writings of ancient
historians, poets, and commentators that address the topic of Witches
and Witchcraft. We will also look at various cultural folklore and
ethnographical material that demonstrates surviving themes related to
the Witches' religion. In addition, we will encounter the older forms of
Witchcraft that have stood the test of time.

In the exploration of the various aspects of Witchcraft, particularly in the first chapter, we readily find what I term *the commonality
of the human experience.* What this addresses is the fact that rituals,
ideas about magick, and various methods and techniques appear
with great similarity within various cultures that had no previous
contact with one another. This is because our ancient ancestors
thought in similar ways, in human ways, and created many of the
same structures and concepts.

The idea of ritual tools is one good example. Today, we are familiar
with the four tools of Western occultism: pentacle, wand, blade, and
chalice. Many people believe these tools first appeared together in
a magickal or ritual setting sometime around the latter half of the
nineteenth century. However, in the ancient cult of Mithras, we
find these four basic tools along with the sword and scourge. These
are also the tools that appear in Gardnerian Wicca, but it would be
incorrect to say that Gardnerian Wicca is an offshoot of Mithraism.
This theme is explored further in Chapter Two.

Commonality appears to be the key to understanding the history of
modern Witchcraft. During my travels as an author, I have attended
many Pagan festivals and have talked with many Witches across the

land. Some of these claimed to be Witches from a long family line; others claimed to have been taught by hereditary Witches of the "old blood" lines. Of the Witches I spoke with, there were those I readily believed, and some I regarded with varying degrees of reservation.

In the final analysis, there were some constants I discovered in all the Witches that I believed came from old traditions pre-dating the nineteenth century. My belief in these individuals was based upon several things in general. One of the most important factors to me was that they did not truly care if anyone believed their claims, and were very light-hearted about the entire matter of disbelief. The second factor was that they all independently agreed upon what was new Witchcraft and what was old Witchcraft. Two primary examples of new Witchcraft were the Rede and the Three-Fold Law, at least the concept as it is taught by the majority of Wiccans today.

In my discussions with other Witches, the exchanges of ideas always came back to commonality wherever we spent time tracking down origins. One interesting theory arose called *morphogenetic fields*. The idea of a morphogenetic field has been popularized by a biologist named Rupert Sheldrake. The theory is that every organism is surrounded by an interconnected energy field, which transmits "information" in one form or another. Sheldrake suggests that the evolution of a species begins when members in one location are subjected to environmental changes, and members in a still stable environment receive the information that the need to adapt is required. This occurs through a relay of information through the morphogenetic field.

The theory of the morphogenetic field is similar to the basic concept known as the *hundredth monkey*. The idea here is that once a large number of individuals engage and maintain a certain practice because it is functional and effective; they reach "critical mass" and a new cultural awareness takes place. This new awareness is somehow communicated directly from mind to mind over great distances without any apparent connection, bridge, or known conveyance. Some people find evidence of Jung's concept of the collective unconscious in such phenomena and have used this observation as evidence that an ideological breakthrough occurs when enough individuals in a population adopt a new idea or behavior.

Sheldrake suggests that societies have social and cultural morphogenetic fields that organize behavior. In essence, these fields allow individuals to act as one unit in a commonality of action and expression. One example is how birds fly in formation and all turn and move together as though they were one organism. Sheldrake states that tests have been done on the reaction time to stimulus of individual birds. The tests found that the maximum reaction time of the bird was less than the time required to turn in harmony with the flock. In other words, the formation of birds turned faster than any individual bird in the flock could do on its own.

Sheldrake extends the theory of morphogenetic fields to the "hive mentality" and suggests that these fields allow the individuals of the hive to communicate with one another across distances and through physical barriers. Sheldrake also points to the so-called "mob mentality" in human society when crowd behavior commits acts that few if any of the individuals would do (or condone) on their own. Where Sheldrake's theories connect to Witchcraft lies in his ideas regarding ritual as a morphic resonance.

Sheldrake notes that the patterns of ritual acts are the same from one country to another. He sees such rituals as having the effect of evoking memory per their designs. Sheldrake theorizes that rituals create the right conditions for morphic resonance to occur between those performing the ritual at any given moment and those who originally (or previously) performed it. What Sheldrake is suggesting is that rituals reconnect the participants with their ancestors through morphic resonance and that this is a type of communication and memory recall. If Sheldrake is correct, then a case can be made that the rituals, beliefs, and practices of so-called "modern Witchcraft" are actually the manifestations of ancestral memory.

Scholars are not interested in such theories as they may apply to history; they are interested instead in what they can see before their own eyes. Unlike the scholars, Witches are, by contrast, believers in things that are unseen. There is an interesting connection between the English words "truth" and "tree" that may help us better understand the problem. Both words are derived from the Old English word *treow*, which meant "loyalty" or "fidelity." The word *treow* itself is derived from the Indo-European *deru*, which was applied to things that would endure and were trustworthy.

When we view a tree, there are actually two sections: that which is visible and that which is hidden beneath the earth. The trunk of the tree is verifiable upon examination, as are the branches and the leaves of the tree. The roots of the tree are not visible nor apparent, and cannot be discovered by the same methodology employed to survey the visible tree. The evidence is the outward sign, and using such evidence, one could argue that there is nothing to indicate the existence of something other than what is clearly evident. Additionally, the visible part of the tree can be reshaped as desired by cutting away the undesired segments, and the true nature of the tree can be altered through grafting. This is essentially what was done to Witchcraft during the Middle Ages and Renaissance periods.

To discover the roots of the tree, one would have to search for something seemingly unrelated to the visible evidence of the viewable tree. This would require a leap of faith, but since the "truth" of the tree lies in *both* the evident and the unapparent, such a leap is necessary if one sincerely wants to know the entire truth. This is where the scholar and the Witch part company, for the Witch is a dweller of both worlds.

The roots of the tree are the oldest parts and they remain hidden from view. The root system of a tree is vast and much larger than the visible portion of the tree, and yet it goes unnoticed because it is hidden from view. The tree itself symbolizes the two worlds of the seen and unseen. It also symbolizes the two modes of awareness, which are the conscious and subconscious mind. The conscious mind relates to the "natural" world and the subconscious mind relates to the "supernatural" or spiritual world. In ancient times, the two minds worked together in order to integrate the two worlds. From this mentality arose the myths and legends that have come down to us. These were the esoteric tales of how the worlds interact, which the mundane world later embraced as simple tales of entertainment or as conveyors of morals.

The Witches still dance around the ancient tree, and the entrance there into the enchanted world is still guarded by the Mysteries that the mind cannot unlock but which open freely to the heart and spirit. It is my hope that the following pages will take the reader successfully through the labyrinth of Witchcraft's history, and deliver up the secrets of the Witches' craft, which lie deep within the center of the maze. It is a treasure worthy of pursuit, but know that the Mysteries protect themselves until you are ready to receive them. Let us begin the journey.

CHAPTER 1

ROOTS OF THE OLD RELIGION

MANY MODERN SCHOLARS BELIEVE that Witchcraft as a religion is a modern construction largely credited to a man named Gerald Gardner who wrote books on the subject during the mid-twentieth century. In this chapter, and throughout the book, we will explore the fundamental aspects of the religious and ritual concepts of the Craft, demonstrating their antiquity and longevity. In doing so, it will become apparent that too many archaic elements exist in the religion of Witchcraft to have been a modern construction traceable to Gerald Gardner and a small handful of cohorts. It would have required the combined efforts of mythologists, anthropologists, folklorists, historians, and highly trained occultists working together over several decades to create the complex layers and inner connections that appear in just the published material on Witchcraft alone, not to mention the restricted initiate material that was available within a ten-year span of Gardner's writings. It seems highly unlikely that such collaboration ever took place, and the simplest explanation would be that the essential foundation already existed.

At the core of Witchcraft as a religion, there exists a basic structure containing elements known to exist in ancient times. These include a God and Goddess mated pair, mysterious Guardians, spirits of nature, a belief in reincarnation, the veneration of the Moon, the practice of magick, and secret ritual gatherings. The concept of a Goddess and God consort was common in the great deities of the

Aegean/Mediterranean such as Zeus and Hera of Greek religion, or Uni and Tinia of Etruscan religion. Guardians of the Underworld are common in ancient mythology as are tales of nature spirits. The belief in reincarnation was known among ancient Greeks and the Druids. References to the practice of magick and the existence of secret societies and Moon worship are far from absent in ancient literature. No basic element of modern Witchcraft lacks a correspondence with ancient European religion. Therefore, the argument becomes: did anything survive down through the ages?

Renowned mythologist Joseph Campbell, in Chapter Three of his book *Masks of God*, speaks of the remains of ancient pottery shards at excavation sites. Campbell comments on the period between 4500-3500 BCE, stating that "a multitude of female figurines" appears amongst the potsherds and are suggestive of an association between "fertile womanhood" and the "motherhood of nature." He states that this period contained no writings allowing us to discern its myths and rituals. Campbell then comments:

"It is therefore not unusual for extremely well-trained archaeologists to pretend that they cannot imagine what services the numerous female figurines might have rendered to the households for which they were designed."

The current phenomena within academia of this tunnel vision approach to discerning our past makes it quite difficult to consider the many possibilities that exist and could lead to our greater understanding of the truth.

Campbell presents an interesting theory that myths arise from the patterns of our own biological experience of the world around us. This is what Campbell calls the "firm syndrome" of human experience. With the rising of the Sun, our primitive ancestors awoke from the night and the realm of dreams. The night was a time of danger, and dreams often produced fearful situations. Therefore, the association of light with dispelling not only darkness itself but also the dreamworld/night fears, elevated light to the status of a rescuer and a protector. Human experience became patterned with biological responses to environment, which then became the format and structure for the expression of our myths and the themes they contain.

Campbell states that this reflects the unity of "the race of man" not only in its biology but also in its "spiritual history," which manifests as a "single symphony" expressed in the myths of all cultures.

Anthropologist Hartley Burr Alexander, in his book *The World's Rim*, argues for the idea that ceremony and imagery are part of the "human commonality" expressed in rituals and myths throughout the world. Alexander's position is that a comparison of these cultural elements from distant parts of the world reveals identical patterns combined with different expressions of one single insight. The commonality of the human experience, and of human expression, cannot be denied as key ingredients in the development and structure of cultural myths and rituals. In this sense, the "Old Religion" has been with us since the formation of humans into tribes and clans, and in this lies the unbroken chain of transmission. For, at its core, the Old Religion is not a mere collection of rituals and myths. The Old Religion is about the human experience of the soul both in the physical and metaphysical realms. It is about the understanding of the "inner mechanism" of nature, which reflects the divine process operating behind it.

Our ancestors clearly encountered the "imprints of experience" that manifested as the three distinct periods of human growth and susceptibility: childhood, maturity, and old age. No doubt these had a significant impact on the consciousness of our ancestors. The creation of the three Fates who weave the lives of humankind must surely be rooted in an ancestral acknowledgment of the three distinct stages of life. In ancient iconography, the Fates are always pictured together and appear as a young woman, a mature woman, and an old woman. It seems unlikely that the basic concept of the "Maiden, Mother, and Crone" images reflected in the symbolism of the three Fates governing the three stages of life is nothing but coincidence. The ancient Greek writer Hesiod wrote that the three great Mysteries are birth, life, and death. Today, we might phrase this as where did we come from, what are we doing here, and where do we go when we leave here?

Birth, life, and death are powerful imprints of experience in the human psyche. Among these three, death appears to capture the most attention. Campbell states that the "earliest unmistakable evidence" of ritual and mythos associated with burial dates from between

200,000-75,000 BCE in the graves of *Homo neanderthalensis*, a remote predecessor of our own species. Excavation shows these individuals buried in a fetal position with an east-west axis alignment matching the course of the Sun. Next to the body, various supplies were placed along with a food-source animal, such as a bison or goat.

Campbell also mentions a gravesite dating between 4500-3000 BCE, found in a site that contained twenty statuettes of female figures, which Campbell calls goddesses. The grave contained the remains of a little girl buried with ornamentation depicting a bird, fish, serpent, and spiral. These exact symbols appear much later in the cult of Ishtar/Aphrodite, but with the spiral symbol replaced by the labyrinth. The bird, fish, and serpent symbols also appear on one of the oldest known Witch charms, the *cimaruta*.

The Mysteries of death and of life are linked together, and at the center lies the woman as Goddess. She is the gateway through which life passes from the Otherworld into this world through the womb of a woman. Such an imprint of experience was clear and significant to our ancestors. The Mother was the creator and deliverer of life itself. Therefore, she must have power over both worlds—and so the passage of life into this world must go out through her as well. Campbell states that in Paleolithic and Neolithic art, the woman appears nude while the man is costumed in some fashion. From this, Campbell concludes that the body of the woman was the important signifier, while for the man, the importance was portrayed through the symbolic garb he wore.

The ancient Greeks perceived of the Earth as the body of a goddess called Gaea, who was one of a race known as the "elder gods" that appear in literature as the Titans. Gaea was the source for all life upon the Earth and for all the gods and mythical creatures that predate the twelve gods of Mt. Olympus. This concept comes from an archaic period predating the myths of the Olympian gods. The important factor here is the concept of a Great Mother Goddess figure from a forgotten time, which is something many modern scholars deny as ever having existed. The ancient Greek writer Hesiod was among the first to place the bardic tales of the Aegean/Mediterranean into writing. Hesiod's work is titled the *Theogony* and was composed sometime around 800 BCE. Therefore, we have references to an older theology, one that was considered even older than the Olympic god mythos at the time of Hesiod.

References to Gaea in Greek mythology appear focused upon openings in the earth itself and are intimately associated with water. Caves have been described as the womb of the Great Goddess, symbolism that spread to the cauldron and the well. Human birth begins with the loss of water from the womb, and the water that once sustained life now threatens to destroy it if the fetus is not soon born into the awaiting world outside. Campbell states that in mythology, water is intimately associated with themes of life and death. He goes on to suggest that water Guardians such as mermaids, Witches, sirens, "Lady of the Lake" figures, and goddesses may represent the personifications of the dual nature of water. In this lies the Inner Mystery teaching of why the Witch has long been associated with the cauldron, a theme we'll explore further in this chapter and throughout the book.

In ancient myths and legends, the cauldron often appears in the Underworld. Sometimes the cauldron lies within a cave or is hidden in a secret room within a castle. Cauldrons are often credited with magickal powers and magickal potions. Some famous cauldrons produced ever-renewing food, and others brewed potions that bestowed enlightenment or restored the dead to life again. All of these elements are associated with archaic beliefs related to Underworld themes.

The idea of burial, in a religious or magickal sense, is connected to the concept of rebirth or renewal. To plant a seed in the soil and cover it with earth resulted in a new plant. Perhaps doing the same with a tribal member was to ensure rebirth. From the perspective of our ancient ancestors, surely the earth itself generated life. To primitive minds viewing the emergence of animals from their burrows in the earth, and insects from their underground colonies, it must have seemed that something beneath the earth generated these creatures. Plant life, insect life, and a great variety of living creatures issued forth from another world beneath the world of humankind. What was this secret other world?

The Underworld is an ancient concept that features prominently in ancient literature. In the myth of Persephone, Campbell states that it was Gaea that opened the earth in order for Hades to draw Persephone down into the Underworld. Hecate, another Titan goddess, heard the cries of Persephone and assisted her mother (Demeter) in eventually recovering Persephone from the Underworld. Hecate becomes an important deity in understanding the antiquity of Witchcraft as a religion. This is explored in more detail in other chapters of this book.

The association of Witches and Hecate spans a literary period of over 2,700 years. Hecate is a goddess that survived from the prehistoric period of Greek religion. In one of the earliest recorded appearances (Hesiod's *Theogony*), Hecate is a goddess honored above all others by Zeus. To honor Hecate, Zeus granted her a share of the earth, sea, and starry heaven. Hesiod says of Hecate that she grants victory to warriors and athletes. And to fishers and herders, Hecate grants abundance. It is also noted that Hecate is "child nurse" to all living beings. As a granter of abundance and a nurse figure, Hecate appears intimately linked with fertility and motherhood. Scholar Robert Von Rudloff, in his book *Hekate in Ancient Greek Religion*, notes that in the earliest writings mentioning Hecate, she is associated with Demeter and Persephone. Von Rudloff also states that literary records indicate Hecate associated with "the Great Mother" on Samothrace.

Modern scholars associate Hecate with the Underworld and depict her as a dark and fearsome goddess. This depiction of Hecate does not appear in ancient literature until the second half of the fifth century BCE. Hesiod, who wrote about three hundred years earlier, makes no reference to Hecate being associated with the Underworld or as a figure to be feared. This suggests a transformation of some type that occurred at a later period. Von Rudloff comments that it was common in Greek and Roman literature to negatively portray goddesses honoring or empowering independent women that live outside of society in both the literal and figurative sense. The followers of such goddesses were equally portrayed in a negative light, as we see in the case of Witches and the goddess Hecate.

Von Rudloff notes that Hippokrates and Plutarch demonstrate an attitude of "skeptical rationalists" as they ridicule the superstitions of their "less educated compatriots." Von Rudloff then asks the question; were the academics of antiquity prompted to comment on attitudes in ancient times that they felt were foolish, for the same reasons that modern academics are motivated to counter the so-called "irrational" but popular ideas of our own time? It is indeed interesting to note that the disbelief of scholars is as ancient as the very things they disbelieve in.

HECATE, THE UNDERWORLD AND THE CROSSROADS

Homer, the ancient Greek composer, includes Hecate in his *Hymn to Demeter*. Here, he depicts Hecate as dwelling in a cave. In Aegean/Mediterranean mythology, caves are entrances to the Underworld, which strongly suggests that Hecate served as a guide or escort for the dead. Von Rudloff states that some scholars believe Hecate served as a guide for people in transition of any type. Her primary role was to help individuals crossing difficult boundaries in general, particularly those in which the "crossing" itself was significant or involved a risk. Von Rudloff refers to Hecate in the Ancient Mystery Traditions and suggests that Hecate may well have served as a guide for initiates.

The theme of approaching initiation itself can be thought of as coming to a crossroads. In ancient times, a crossroad was the point at which three roads met to form a "Y" figure. The earliest form of Hecate was a pole (placed at a crossroads) upon which hung three masks, with one mask facing each road. These poles were called *hekat-aion*. In connection with this, Hecate was called *Trivia*, which means "where three roads meet." In ancient Aegean/Mediterranean culture, the crossroads were a place of spirits, which included Underworld spirits and spirits of Fate. The latter made the crossroads a place for meditation upon choices a person needed to make in their life. In this way, the person communicated with the Fates.

In the book *Hekate Soteira*, by Sarah Iles Johnston, the author notes that while historians of religion regard Hecate as *"the horrific patroness of witches,"* there were Greek and Roman philosophers from the Hellenistic age onwards that envisioned Hecate as the "connective boundary" between the divine and human worlds. Johnston also notes that Hecate was regarded as a facilitator of communication between the gods and humankind. Additionally, the author notes that Hecate gave messages through the Chaldean Oracles and was considered the "Cosmic Soul." Homer's depiction of Hecate living in a cave demonstrates that she lives "between the worlds," standing above the Underworld and beneath the sky, the realm of the gods. When one considers the fact that the ancient Witch Medea was a priestess of Hecate, the role of Witches can be seen in a different light other than the customary one offered by scholars and commentators.

The ancient writers Horace, Ovid, and Lucan were among the first to connect Hecate to the Moon in Witchcraft, and to speak of the power of Witches to call the Moon down from the sky. Later in the writings of Plutarch, we see Hecate and the Moon viewed in partnership as the "intermediary principle." The role of Hecate and the Moon in guiding souls across the boundary between the Earth and the Celestial Realm was further developed in the first century CE. In all of this, we see Hecate reaching her own "fork in the road" or personal crossroad in which the negative and positive elements divide entirely into two separate directions or schools of thought.

In classical times, Hecate was portrayed as the queen or mistress of phantoms and other night spirits. Plutarch, in the first century CE, coined the phrase *daemones* when referring to such creatures. From this word came the Christian concept of demons, despite the fact the Greek word *daemon* (in Neoplatonist philosophy) simply designated a spirit being that was greater than a man but less than a god. In other words, a daemon was not the ghost of a person nor was it a god. It could behave in a benevolent or malevolent manner, just as could any man or any god. With the rise to power of Christianity, Hecate and the Witch, along with the daemon, became purely evil creatures.

Hecate was often depicted in iconography holding a key. As a keeper of the key, Hecate could both open and close the doors to the Underworld. Plutarch wrote that souls are "resolved back into the Moon" just as bodies are resolved back into the Earth. It was his belief that the Sun impregnated the Moon and the Moon then sowed new souls in the Earth, which furnished the soul with a physical body. Plutarch noted that the Moon was the "gulf of Hecate" and played an essential role in the fate of disembodied souls.

WATCHERS AT THE CROSSROADS

In Western literature, the crossroads were favorite gathering sites for Witches' rituals. In the book *Archaic Roman Religion* by Georges Dumezil, the author writes of small towers built at the crossroads with an altar set before them. Upon the altar, offerings were given to certain guardian spirits known as *Lare*, which were associated with seasonal themes related to agriculture and with demarcation in general. Ovid, in his work titled *Fausti*, refers to these same spirits as the "night watchmen." It is interesting to note the concept of towers and watchers also appears as a theme in modern Witchcraft/Wicca. Later in Roman religion, these *Lare* spirits would evolve into protectors of hearth and home.

The concept of guardians or gatekeepers such as Hecate or the *Lare* associated with crossroads is a theme intimately associated with the Otherworld. The ancients believed that souls dwelling in the Otherworld possessed direct knowledge of what lies in store for the living. Therefore, communicating with the souls of the dead, and the very act of divination itself, was best achieved when performed at the crossroads. The ancient belief that the Moon played a vital role in the fate of the soul was no doubt influential in the gathering of Witches at the crossroads during the three dark days of the Moon, as well as when the Moon was full. When considering Campbell's concept of "light" as a savior or protector from night terrors, it is no surprise to find the Full Moon as an important time for Witches to gather. Not only do we have the symbolism of light as a protector, but it also comes in this case as the presence of the Goddess of Witches herself.

CREATURES OF THE NIGHT

An interesting element of Witchcraft is its association with various creatures featured in Paleolithic and Neolithic art and iconography, which suggests the survival of specific concepts and connections down through the ages. Many of these creatures appear associated with lunar symbolism or have a connection to Goddess symbolism.

The most common creatures associated with Witchcraft are the frog, owl, serpent, pig, stag, goat, wolf, and horse. These are all creatures that appear in various writings about Witches from the classical period through modern times. By the medieval period, the bat, mouse, and cat also appear in the literature on Witchcraft. The tenacity of this constant theme continuing down through the ages seems to support a living tradition of some type. Additionally, there is a continuity of identification regarding specific animals associated with Witchcraft that are also connected to pre-Christian European Mystery Schools. They appear to possess a similar or identical relationship, which suggests a longstanding occult tradition of some type.

Since ancient times, the belief held that Witches possessed the power to transform into animal form. Every animal associated with Witchcraft during the classical period is also linked to the ancient chthonic cults of Old Europe rooted in Underworld mythology themes. This is likewise true of the earliest forms of deities associated with Witchcraft, such as Hecate, Diana, and Proserpina. During the Middle Ages, Witches were believed to employ animal products to accomplish physical transformation as well as power over nature. An example is the folklore belief that smearing a bat's blood on a broomstick allowed the Witch to fly at night.

One of the earliest references to Witches and animals comes from the ancient Greek writings of Homer (circa 850 BCE) in which he speaks of the Witch Circe who transformed humans into swine. Of all the animals that Circe could have selected, why did she choose pigs? In the ancient Mystery Religions, pigs were sacred to the goddess Demeter and to the deities of the Underworld. Pigs were sacrificed by throwing them down into deep caverns as an offering. The appearance of swine in Homer's tale of Circe, although distorted for the sake of storytelling, suggests the underlying reality of an authentic sect connecting Witches to known historical Pagan practices. In Homer's tale, it is now recalled in vague memories of connections that the author reduces to sensationalism. Often, the various references to animals, settings, and practices in tales of Witchcraft are also the very things known to have comprised specific aspects of the Ancient Mystery Traditions, themselves secret societies that equally confound historians.

THE GATHERING OF WITCHES

Tales of the Witches' sabbat are common in the accounts of Witch-craft following the rise of Christianity. Manuscripts from old Witch trials in Italy mention a walnut tree in the city of Benevento as the favored site for the Witches' gathering. Legend claimed the ancient tree had always been there and was in leaf all year long. In the year 662 CE, Saint Barbato converted the Duke of Benevento (a Pagan) to Christianity and had the tree cut down.

According to legend, the Witches planted another walnut tree from the seed of the original tree. References in Italian Witch trial transcripts as late as the seventeenth century continue to refer to the walnut tree as the setting for the Witches' sabbat. One of the latest accounts dates from a Witch trial in 1647 where references are made to a woman named Violanta who confessed to worshipping the goddess Diana at the site of an old walnut tree.

One of the earliest accounts of Witches gathered together (as opposed to the solitary Witch) is found in the ancient Greek figure of the *Graeae*. The name *Graeae* means "gray ones" and in mythology, these three sisters are gray-haired from birth. Hesiod, in his *Theogony*, describes them:

> "...with fair faces and gray from birth, and these the gods who are immortal and men who walk on the earth call Graiai, the gray sisters, Pemphredo robed in beauty and Enyo robed in saffron."

According to legend, the *Graeae* possessed great wisdom from birth and grow wiser as the ages pass. Although not originally referred to as Witches, such identification became the standard as their tales were retold in the future. In the retelling, the fair-faced *Graeae* of Hesiod's time become the ugly hags of a later period. The three Witches that appear in Shakespeare's *Macbeth* are clearly based upon this distorted image of the *Graeae* of Greek mythology. As we have seen in the prototypes of Medea, the priestess of Hecate, and the beautiful sorceress Circe, the origins of the Witch figure are not rooted in ugliness but rather in beauty.

It is not a natural evolution of legendary figures to completely change and reverse their general depiction or nature. If it were, then the heroes of myth and legend would eventually become the villains. However, such is not the case regarding the ancient heroes of Greek and Roman mythology whose tales have remained essentially the same for well over 2,500 years. I believe it is safe to say that a reversal in the depiction of an established character is a conscious and willful change. The reasons for why this happened to the Witch figure are explored in the next chapter, which discusses the history of the Witch.

CHAPTER 2

𝕿HE 𝖂ITCHES' 𝕳ISTORY

As discussed in the introduction to this book, the Witch and the scholar often have opposing views regarding the history of Witchcraft as a religion. I personally feel that as a modern community of Witches, we must begin to deal more effectively with this issue. What I'm addressing here is our history and our lineage, our links to the past. I say this not because we *need* an ancient lineage, which we do not, but because we have one that is too often denied to us.

In this chapter, we will examine the obscured roots of Witchcraft from ancient to modern times. Let us begin by saying that modern Witchcraft is different from ancient Witchcraft, just as modern Catholicism is different from the way it was practiced in the early Christian communities almost two thousand years ago. Religions naturally evolve over time in one way or another. This does not invalidate the religion; it simply demonstrates that it is a living, growing, and adapting entity. The religion of Witchcraft is no exception.

It is trendy these days to dismiss the existing traditions of Witchcraft as being simply modern creations that emerged in the early to middle period of the twentieth century. Some scholars claim that the concepts and tenets of this alleged twentieth-century brew were themselves based upon the writings and artistic expressions of the Romantic era of the nineteenth century. Modern scholars dismiss the idea that Witchcraft (as a religion) pre-existed this period, surviving in one form or another into contemporary times.

It is interesting to note that the ancient Greeks classified Witches among those who practiced "illicit religions." Historian Richard Gordon, in his essay "Imagining Greek and Roman Magic" (found in Ankarloo and Clark's *Witchcraft and Magic in Europe: Ancient Greece and Rome*), also states that in ancient Aegean/Mediterranean culture "illegitimate religious knowledge" was assigned to women, and since Witches were always portrayed as women in classical times, we can see why Witchcraft was never recognized as a "legitimate" religion. However, according to historian Georg Luck, in his essay, "Witches and Sorcerors in Classical Literature" (also in *Witchcraft and Magic in Europe: Ancient Greece and Rome*), we must also understand that in ancient Greek culture, a "recognized" sect was required to have an established temple. Magicians, diviners, Witches, and other subculture figures were comprised typically of the poor segment and had no funds to build and maintain temples. This is one of the chief reasons why Witches were not portrayed in ancient times as people of a religious nature, but rather as magick users or fortune tellers. This view persisted despite ancient writings that presented stories of the Witch Medea who prayed to Hecate, and the Witch Canidia who prayed to Hecate, Diana, and Proserpina. Praying is most often associated with religion and there is no unbiased reason to negate this regarding Medea and Canidia.

Much like the ancient Greek writers, modern historians dismiss the idea that Witchcraft ever constituted an authentic religion in the past. This is an inherited bias from ancient times that has colored the views of scholars down through the centuries. Modern scholars tend to view contemporary Witchcraft as something entirely new. One of the allegations made by scholars against modern Witchcraft is that there can be no connection between ancient and modern Witches because modern Witches portray themselves as "good," and Witches have always historically been portrayed as evil. This view has always struck me as similar to saying that modern humans can have no connection to "cavemen" because contemporary humans are civilized by comparison. Scholars point to modern Witchcraft as something altogether different from ancient Witchcraft. This is indeed true, and it's called evolution, which is quite different from fabrication.

In this chapter, we will explore references to Witchcraft that indicate the presence of elements commonly associated with religion, traceable back to almost three thousand years in Western literature. In our quest, we will see the Witch as an herbalist that over time became a practitioner of folk magic, and eventually took on the role of a priestess in a religion that preserved various aspects of pre-Christian European Paganism. With the rise of Christianity and the onset of the Dark Ages, the Witch figure was erroneously employed to explain the ills that befell farming communities and society in general. The Witch figure was to bear the blame while at the same time serving to divert responsibility away from those who were in charge of the well-being of villages and towns. Additionally, this chapter will explore the influence of Freemasonry, various Western occult or secret societies, folklorists' research on Italian Witchcraft, and the writings of Gerald Gardner as part of the ongoing evolution of Witchcraft in modern times. To begin our exploration, we will start with the oldest references to Witches in Western literature, which appear around 700 BCE.

The ancient Greek writings of Hesiod and Homer contain the first descriptive accounts of Witches and Witchcraft. In such tales, we find the characters known as Circe and Medea, both sharing a connection to the goddess Hecate. The earliest word used by the Greeks to indicate a Witch was *pharmakis*, from which is derived the modern word "pharmacist." Richard Gordon ("Imagining Greek and Roman Magic") states that *pharmakis "became one of the standard words for 'wisewoman/witch,' used as a substantive."* He goes on to mention during this same period the word also expressed an association with "drugs and incantations." Later, the word *pharmakis* would translate as *venefica* in Latin, which is addressed later in this chapter.

The modern English word "Witch" is not derived from Latin, even though Latin terms were used in many of the Witch trials in northern Europe and the British Isles. Instead, the word "Witch" derives from the Old English word *wicca* (pronounced "witcha") and was used to indicate a male Witch. The feminine form of the word is *wice* (pronounced "witcheh") indicating a female Witch. The word *wiccian* was a verb meaning to cast a spell. The earliest appearance of the word "wicca" is found in a manuscript of the ninth century where it is used to indicate a sorcerer. In other words, "wicca" meant an individual that used magick.

According to historian Jeffrey B. Russell in his book *A History of Witchcraft*, the word "Witch" is *"ultimately derived from the Indo-European* root weik, *which has to do with religion and magic.*" Russell states that this word produced a derivative, *wih-l,* from which originated the Old English words *wigle* (sorcery) and *wiglera* (sorcerer). This old connection between the word *weik* and "religion and magick" in connection to the word "Witch" is ignored by modern scholars, thereby helping to support their position that Witchcraft was never a religion prior to modern times. However, there is a long history of Witches connected to goddesses in Western literature, which itself would suggest a religious link of some type. This relationship appears in a wide range of literature from the writings of Hesiod and Homer (circa 700 BCE) to the Epodes of Horace (30 BCE) and to contemporary writers of the latter period such as Lucan and Ovid.

In the tales of these writers, we find the Witch Canidia calling upon Hecate, Diana, and Proserpina. We find also Circe and Medea who pray to the goddess Hecate. The list of sources linking Witches with goddesses also later includes the Diocesan Council of Conserans (1280) which associated the "Witch cult" with the worship of a Pagan Goddess and the Council of Trier (1310) which associated Witches with the goddess Diana. Even later, the list includes the works of Girolamo Tartarotti (1749) who identified the Dianic cult with Witchcraft, and the works of folklorist Charles Leland (1892) whose field studies revealed a practicing sect of Witches worshipping the Roman deities Diana and Lucifer, the herald of the dawn. But the oldest goddess connected to Witchcraft in Western literature is Hecate, who in Greek mythology was one of the Titans that helped the gods of Olympus defeat her own race.

The oldest known statuary of Hecate dates to around 430 BCE and is described by the ancient Greek historian Pausanias (second century CE) as "three figures facing one another." Later, Hecate is depicted as three female figures standing with their backs against a column, which they encircle. Hecate was identified in ancient times with the goddess Artemis, as noted by Aeschylus (fifth century BCE) who refers to her as "Artemis-Hekate" in his work titled *Hiket.* Artemis (Diana to the Romans) and Hecate were associated with crossroads, as noted by the Roman scholar Varro (first century BCE) who wrote of Hecate: *"The Trivian Titaness is Diana, called Trivia from the fact that her image is set up quite generally in Greek towns where three roads meet."*

The ancient Greek writer Hesiod makes the earliest mention of
the goddess Hecate. Hesiod tells the tale of how Hecate aided the
Olympic gods in their battle against the Titans. Because of this, Hecate enjoyed an elevated status among the Olympic gods even though
she was never formally a member. In his work (*Theogony*), Hesiod
speaks of Hecate as a goddess of fertility and abundance, associating
her with herding and fishing. With the passage of time, Hecate would
be viewed as a dark goddess of the Underworld and would become a
dreaded presence. The same vilification would befall the Witches over
the passing centuries. As we shall see, it was the agenda of Roman
officials and lawmakers to purposely malign Witches and convince
people they were dangerous company. However, the essential character of the Witch developed much earlier than this and we must look
further into the past.

The traditional village Witch figure most likely evolved from the
primitive shaman or sorcerer/sorceress character common to tribal
communities. Such individuals possessed knowledge of the medicinal properties or effects of various plants and were believed to be
in touch with the Otherworld in a special way. As noted earlier, the
ancient Greek word for Witch is *pharmakis* from which we derive the
modern English word "pharmacist." Because of their knowledge and
position within the community, the Witch figure was also most likely
the keeper and transmitter of myth and lore (since they were believed
to possess first-hand knowledge of the Otherworld).

In Latin, the word used for Witch was originally *saga*, which
indicates a fortune teller. This was later changed to *venefica*, misunderstood today to mean one who uses poisons, but as will shortly
become clear, *venefica* actually indicated one who prepares love
potions. The earliest laws against Witchcraft dealt with the use of
herbal potions employed in love spells, and the drafters felt that love
spells "poisoned" free will. However, the root word for *venefica* is
the same as that for the word *venereal*, derived from the Latin *vene*,
indicating a relationship to Venus. Another example of the benign
vene root connection is the word *venerate*, which means "to regard
with *heartfelt* deference." In the book *Phases in the Religion of Ancient
Rome* (University of California Press) by Cyril Bailey, the scholar
mentions that Venus was originally a deity of gardens and vines, the
cultivator. Putting this together, we have Venus as a goddess of plants

and the Latin word *venefica* (replacing the Greek *pharmakis* used to indicate one knowledgeable in plants) which all suggest that early Witches were in some fashion associated with the goddess Venus, if only in their dealings with love potions. There may well be more to this, however, for indeed, many centuries later (1375 CE), a woman named Gabrina Albetti is convicted of practicing Witchcraft after confessing to going out at night, removing her clothing, and worshipping the brightest star in the sky (which would actually have been the planet Venus).

The word *venefica* later evolved to indicate simply one who possessed knowledge of poisonous plants, and over the course of time, this became its singular and specific meaning. The Roman historian Livy (first century CE) mentions the first trial for practicing *veneficium* having taken place in the early days of Rome, and modern scholars assign the year 331 BCE to this trial. Reportedly, many mysterious deaths had occurred in the community and no doubt the officials were being hard-pressed by the citizens to explain what was going on. Several women were then rounded up and accused of mixing poisons, but the women claimed their potions were designed to heal. The officials produced a potion they claimed was made by the women and challenged them to drink it. The women agreed, but upon drinking the potion they immediately died. The citizens were content that the problem was resolved. Whether the potions were actually made by the women or conveniently substituted with something lethal by the worried officials is another matter. Eventually, almost all Latin words for poison (venom) were based upon *vene* as a root word for "poison," particularly when referring to Witches and Witchcraft. No doubt the Witch figure commanded respect but was also viewed with a healthy fear of their power and knowledge.

One of the most powerful figures in ancient times to be associated with Witchcraft was Circe. Circe appears in the tale of Ulysses who lands on Circe's island during his travel back to Greece. According to the story, Circe turns Ulysses' men into swine and he is enchanted by one of her herbal love potions. He stays on the island for a year and is then freed by the intervention of the god Hermes, who gives Ulysses an herbal antidote. An alternative interpretation of this scenario is that this tale was designed to excuse the gluttony and drunkenness of Ulysses' men and to pardon his acts of adultery with Circe while living on the island. In the tale of Medea, she kills her children after her husband leaves her for another woman. Is this the act of a Witch, or is it the act of a lover scorned? Such things happen even in modern society all too frequently and have nothing to do with the religion of the people involved. For example, we don't read in the news that "Mary Smith, a Baptist, killed her three children today" but we would definitely read "Mary Smith, a Witch, killed her three children today" if Mary practiced Witchcraft. The popular term given by defense attorneys for such crimes of violence is "temporary insanity" and is not in turn typically attributed to religious zeal.

With the rise of civilization and the establishment of governments, the Witch became vilified as an evil and destructive character. Laws against Witchcraft and magick appear long before the rise of Christianity in many ancient cultures such as Rome. Independent, freethinking, and self-empowered people have always been viewed as a threat by governments. The rulers of Rome feared assassination by poison (as did later the kings of Europe) and thus, anyone with an advanced knowledge of herbalism was a potential enemy. Additionally, ancient Witchcraft was believed to be a secret society, which also contributed to suspicion concerning its practices.

The ancient Roman poet Horace was among the earliest to portray Witches as ugly old hags, in contrast to the earlier theme of the Witch as a beautiful seductress, reflected in the writings of Hesiod and Homer. The Romans saw little if any value in old women and the association of old age with Witches was perhaps designed to rob them of power and vitality in the public mind. Horace writes in his *Epodes* that Witches worship Proserpina and Diana. Both deities were viewed in a negative light by the followers of the Roman state religion who favored the so-called "high gods." Diana and Proserpina were the deities of rural Pagans and magicians, both classes that were looked down upon by the sophisticated city dwellers.

In the first century BCE, Ovid wrote that a belief in Witches (*Striges*) was a superstitious peasant belief having nothing to do with state religion. Therefore, the Witch was an easy and popular figure to belittle, ridicule, and malign. Aristophanes (423 BCE) makes perhaps the clearest first connection between the Moon with the practice of Witchcraft, a theme that still appears in Western literature even much later in the works of Horace, circa 30 BCE. Lucan and Ovid were others that wrote of Witchcraft and the Moon. Ancient Greek/Roman literature also depicts the Witch as a person involved with human and animal sacrifice, practices that were actually common in the vast majority of ancient cultures including archaic Aegean/Mediterranean and Celtic cultures. However, as religions evolved over the centuries, the Witch was never portrayed as having moved beyond such practices. The view we are left to believe or accept is that the entire world moved away from human and animal sacrifice as religions evolved, but the Witch alone continued such practices throughout history. Such a view seems quite unlikely to be based in reality.

To discourage people from having personal dealings with Witches, the Witch was associated with many perversions and evil deeds. Roman officials fostered the image of the Witch as a grave robber, a very horrid thing in Roman culture because Roman religion honored the dead as well as the ancestral spirit. Lucan's depiction of the Witch Erictho is a primary example of this vilification of the Witch figure. All of these factors created and maintained an unwelcome environment for Witches, keeping them out of public favor. The fact that Witches were forced into social isolation made people feel less threatened since it became increasingly difficult for their enemies to locate Witches and obtain herbal potions, or to gain the service of a Witch for whatever purpose. The Witch was now fully established as an undesirable in society. Depicting her as old and ugly took away the physical vitality of the Witch figure and made them appear less dynamic. In ancient Aegean/Mediterranean culture, youth was celebrated and old age was dreaded. Like the Greeks before them, the Romans held to the philosophy that "good" is beautiful and "evil" is ugly. Thus, the Witch was purposely depicted as an evil old ugly hag.

With the establishment of Christianity as the official religion of Rome circa 325 CE, the Witch was already viewed as a doer of evil deeds and the Church quickly assigned her to the company of demons and devils. Following the collapse of the Roman Empire, the power of Rome was replaced by the Roman Catholic Church, which sent monks and bishops into various regions of Europe to establish churches. St. Augustine, the most influential Christian theologian, taught that Pagan religion and magick were invented by the Devil. He lived during the early fifth century CE and was the first person to associate Witches with the Devil. Thus, the attitudes of earlier Rome towards Witches, now assimilated and redesigned by the Roman Catholic Church, were carried to northern Europe and the British Isles by monks and bishops. Within a few centuries, the stereotype of the Witch as an evil servant of Satan was established throughout Europe.

St. Jerome was the first to equate the names Lucifer and Satan, which occurred due to a misunderstanding of the text used in Isaiah 14:12. Here, Isaiah refers to the Babylonian king Helal, son of Shahar, by using the phrase *heleyl, ben shachar* (literally: "shining one, son of the dawn") which was also a term for the planet Venus, often called the morning star. The planet Venus was also known in ancient times as the "herald of the Sun" because it appeared on the horizon at dawn, just before sunrise. St. Jerome, translating the Hebrew text *heleyl, ben shachar* into Latin, used the Latin *lucem ferre*, which means bringer, or bearer, of light. By the period of Late Latin, *lucem ferre* had been replaced by the word "Lucifer." Much earlier, in the Septuagint (a third-century BCE translation of the Hebrew scriptures into Greek) the Hebrew phrase *heleyl, ben shachar* was translated as *heosphoros* which also refers to Venus as a morning star. Ironically, in the Book of Revelation, Jesus himself is identified as the morning star (Revelation 22:16).

Ongoing misunderstandings of biblical text and poor translations contributed greatly to the "Witch hysteria" that resulted in the torture and death of over 100,000 people accused of practicing Witchcraft throughout Europe. In the King James version of the Bible, the verse Exodus 22:18 reads *"Thou shalt not suffer a witch to live."* However, in the original language of the text, the word for Witch appears as *kashaph*, meaning a poisoner, or more specifically one who assassinates by using poison. Therefore, *kashaph* did not literally mean a "Witch" as indicated in the King James text. Whether the mistranslation was intentional or simply misguided, the King James translation provided support to those who took the lives of many people charged with practicing Witchcraft.

Another biblical verse used to support the death sentence for those convicted of Witchcraft was Leviticus 20:27, which dealt with fortune tellers. Although this verse does not contain the word "Witch" (mistranslated or otherwise), it and other related biblical

verses were used by the Church and secular courts to indicate Witches and Witchcraft as inclusive in the meaning of the text. What this
demonstrates is that the ancient Latin concepts of *saga* and *venefica*
were still the things indicating a person that practiced Witchcraft,
well past even the Middle Ages. The only thing new was the Christian view of Witchcraft as being Satanic in nature.

The linking of Witches and Witchcraft to Satan first appears
around 400 CE due largely, as already noted, to the undertakings of
St. Augustine of Hippo. St. Augustine taught that anything Pagan was
evil and must therefore come from the works of the Devil. The Church,
convinced that anything contrary to the beliefs of Christianity must
indeed be evil, declared everything associated with pre-Christian religion as evil. Therefore, Witches were then assigned by the Church as
servants of the Judeo-Christian Satan figure, even though the Witches
themselves did not subscribe to the concept of the Devil. The Devil, or
Satan, is a Judaic concept modified by ancient Persian and Egyptian
influences. The Devil is a personification of evil, and although the
ancients certainly debated the nature of evil, the actual personification of evil as a conscious being is almost unique to Judaic theology.
Christianity, its foundation rooted in Judaic religion, inherited the
concept of the Devil or Satan from the Jewish religion. Witchcraft
was already long-established centuries before the Western/European
world knew of this Judeo-Christian concept. The Church, eager to
discredit Paganism, grafted the Devil onto pre-Christian religion. It
even went so far as to use art to portray Satan (who is never physically
described in the Bible) with horns and hooves, in the precise image of
the Pagan horned gods of antiquity.

Extreme physical and psychological torture was used to extract
"confessions" from those accused of practicing Witchcraft. The
torture continued until the person admitted to the charges against
them or until they died from the trauma. Questions regarding
devil worship were put to the accused that had no basis in any
past historical practice or in practices actually documented by any
research during the period of the trials. The Church, together with
the Inquisition, essentially created the concept of devil worship by
Witches along with the details of its beliefs and practices. People
were then forced to confess to membership in the Witches' sect by
means of horrible pain and suffering.

Despite the insistence of the Church that Witches worshipped Satan, references to the worship of the goddess Diana by Witches persist through the Renaissance era in Witchcraft trials, and are noted as late as the end of the nineteenth century by such folk-lorists as Charles Leland. Even as early as 900 CE, the Church addressed the worship of Diana by the "Society of Diana" in the *Canon Episcopi*. This document stated that the followers of Diana were deceived by Satan regarding her worship and that everything they professed to experience was a mental delusion. Historian Julio Baroja, in his book *The World of Witches*, tells us that there appears to have been a flourishing cult of Diana among the European country folk in southern Europe during the fifth and sixth centuries. Baroja notes that the sect also worshipped a male deity called *Dianum*, and comments that much of this was documented by St. Martin of Braga during his travels. Since Witches were associated in Western literature with the worship of the goddess Diana as early as the writings of Horace in 30 BCE, there seems little reason to exclude them from an association with, or membership within, the sect described by St. Martin.

THE MIDDLE AGES AND RENAISSANCE PERIOD (THE GREATER DISTORTION)

The continued vilification of the Witch figure gained a great deal of momentum during the Middle Ages and paved the way for the Witch trials that followed in the Renaissance period. During the Middle Ages, Paganism was still an obstacle to the conversion efforts of the Christian Church. Life was oppressive, disease swept towns and villages, food was not in abundance, and crop failure was not uncommon. The Witch figure became an easy target for blame and served to take pressure off the officials as they struggled to deal with the social order of the times. By the latter half of the Middle Ages, the word most commonly used to indicate a Witch was *malefica*. This is derived from the Latin word *maleficium*, which means: evil deed, crime, harm, injury, wrong, or mischief. The verb form of the word is *maleficus*, which means: wicked, vicious, criminal, or mischief-maker. An alternative word for "Witch" during the Middle Ages was the word *Striga*, derived from a legendary creature in ancient Rome that was closer to a vampire than it was to the stereotype Witch figure. The Striga evolved from an earlier legendary creature known as a "Strix." The Strix was a supernatural owl that preyed on children, eating their flesh, and the Strix later evolved into an evil woman capable of transforming herself into an owl. This theme of the cannibalistic Witch figure continued in popular belief well into the eighth century, and the Strix/Striga concept is the source of medieval tales that Witches eat children cooked in their cauldrons.

The ninth century was marked by accounts of demonic pacts, relationships with an incubus spirit, the power of Witches to shapeshift, night flights to the sabbat, and sexual debauchery. The Judeo-Christian imagination, under the weight of repressive social and moral codes rooted in the doctrines and dogma of the Church, began to mutate into something very dark and disturbing. Although Witchcraft during the Middle Ages was a secular crime assigned to acts of social disobedience, the Synod of Paris (June 6, 829) brought scripture to bear on the matter of Witchcraft, citing Leviticus 20:6 and Exodus 22:18, which dealt with the admonishment that sorcery was a crime against God and therefore worthy of the death sentence.

Historian Jeffrey B. Russell (*Witchcraft in the Middle Ages*) notes that the origin of reveling and dancing in medieval Witchcraft lies in the old Pagan festivals. A popular document of the Middle Ages known as the *Canon Episcopi* addressed this theme. It was originally designed as a warning to bishops and other Church officials of the existence of women that worship the goddess Diana, a sect that was reportedly drawing many people to itself. In one of the earliest Witch trials, a woman named Sibillia confessed to going to the "games of Diana" where she gave homage to the goddess Diana. This case was tried by the secular court of Milan on May 26, 1390. On July 21, 1390, a woman named Pierina de' Bugatis was tried for Witchcraft and gave much the same account as found in the trial of Sibillia. Pierina, a woman in her early thirties, claimed to have participated in the revels of the "Society of Diana" since she was sixteen years old.

Later in 1457, three women tried in Bessanone confessed that they belonged to the "Society of Diana." In 1576, Bartolo Spina wrote in his

Quaestrico de Strigibus of confessions drawn from Witchcraft trials that Witches gathered at night to worship Diana and to have dealings with night spirits. Modern scholars dismiss these documented accounts as being of any evidence that Witches worshipped a Goddess, or of the existence of a Witches' sect of any kind.

The next century introduced a heated frenzy that has come to be called the "Witchcraze." From this century forward, those accused of practicing Witchcraft faced horrible torture and death. Some modern scholars such as Jeffrey Russell have theorized that because the Renaissance period saw the revival of the classics and the introduction of Neo-Platonism (along with the translations of ancient hermetic texts) that the belief in magick itself was accepted and embraced among the intellectual class. Such a belief in the reality of magick held among the "upper class" made Witches even more dangerous to society in general, for if even the educated people believed then it "must be true." With the rise in popularity of "high magick" in the fifteenth century came an increase in the frequency of Witchcraft trials and the severity of punishment by the ecclesiastical authorities of those convicted as Witches.

The fifteenth century saw the publication and distribution of the texts like the *Malleus Maleficarum* (1486) and various discourses on Witchcraft. This led to the accumulation of fragmented beliefs and superstitions concerning Witches and Witchcraft that were then pieced into one cohesive view. However, many of these collected concepts bore no true relationship to one another. They were instead an agglomeration of isolated folk beliefs drawn from various regions in Europe along with various modifications and interpretations by the Christian perspective (not to mention flights-of-fancy in general). Despite this, such resulting texts as the *Malleus Maleficarum* became the definitive and authoritative work on European Witchcraft. This false composite image of the Witch became the standard and remained largely unchallenged up until relatively modern times.

The Inquisition, having the support of the Church and the papacy, dominated the Witchcraft trials of the fifteenth century and highly influenced and pressured the secular courts. Witchcraft moved firmly from being a crime against society, dealt with by the secular courts, to being an official heresy. This moved Witchcraft over almost fully

into the hands of the Inquisition and accelerated the Witchcraze
mania. One of the real tragedies of this era is that the majority of
people convicted of Witchcraft were not Witches by any definition.
Modern scholars rely heavily on Witchcraft trial transcripts, and on
the writings of those who held erroneous views about Witches, in
their discernment of the history of Witchcraft. Ironically, this material has extremely little to do with the Witches' sect. However, on a
few rare occasions, it seems clear that the accused did indeed possess
some knowledge of the Witches' sect. This is explored further in the
following chapter, *The Witches' Religion*.

The eighteenth century saw the beginning of the decline of
Witchcraft persecution. It came both in the modification of laws and
in the attitudes of judicial authorities who grew inclined not to take
the charges of Witchcraft seriously. France was among the first to
modify its laws dealing with Witchcraft, taking place in 1682. The
next to follow suit was Prussia in 1714. Great Britain modified its
Witchcraft laws in 1736 followed by Russia in 1770, Poland in 1776,
and Sweden in 1779.

In essence, the judicial system began to view the practice of
Witchcraft as a pretense to possessing power, an act of fraud.
People who performed divination, magick, or any type of enchant-
ment risked a year in prison. England repealed this act in 1951.
Following the repeal of the Witchcraft Act in 1951, the writings
of Gerald Gardner introduced the world to his view of the religion
he called *Wicca*. Gardner portrayed Witches as a secret society
driven underground by Christianity and surviving as a subculture
for many centuries. Gardner's Witches were healers and magicians
who worshipped a God and Goddess figure. They were neither
the Greco-Roman image of beautiful dangerous Witches nor the
medieval stereotype of ugly, evil Witches.

From ancient times, and even as late as the nineteenth century,
the Witch has been recognized as one who possesses the knowledge
of how to heal and harm through the use of herbs. Despite this,
the main focus of writers has always been on the misuse of herbal
potions by the Witch, almost completely ignoring the healing
practices. Even in cases where healing by a Witch appears in trial
transcripts, this act is always attributed to deception through the

power of Satan to lead the "faithful" astray. Francesco Guazzo wrote (*Compendium Maleficarum*, 1608) on the theme of the Witches' ability to heal and harm, citing incidents of both occasions. Every act of healing he attributes to the power of Satan, who, according to Guazzo, allows the healing to take place in order to confuse Christians about the "true" nature of Witches. All acts of harming, Guazzo attributes to the power and knowledge possessed directly by the Witch. This is the essential bias that ensured the reported evil character of the Witch throughout the centuries.

I believe that the reported history of the Witch is one of purposeful malignment by those who feared their power or influence. The peak of this assault is marked by the Inquisition. During this period, the killing of people found "guilty" of practicing the Christian perception of Witchcraft was sanctioned by the Church. The Inquisitors employed pain and fear of death to extract "confessions" that ultimately resulted in compliance with what the torturer wanted to hear.

There are those who still foster the false image of the Witch as a servant of the Judeo-Christian being known as Satan. The persecution of Witches has by no means come to an end in modern times. The Inquisitors are still among us today in many forms. Among them are some politicians, scholars, media personnel, and of course, various Christian evangelists and assorted fundamentalist Christians. Unlike the Inquisitors of the past, such individuals simply wish to make Witches look foolish and uneducated, often portraying modern Witches as individuals clinging to "discredited" beliefs. Others among them want to portray Witches as misfits or souls lost to the Devil's guile. But the agenda of the modern Inquisitor is the same as it was in days of old; to silence the Witch and to foster a false public image of Witches, keeping them outside of public favor.

A handful of modern scholars have published various new works over the last few years designed to undermine and derail the modern Witchcraft movement. Another target for many scholars is the Goddess movement whose adherents believe in an ancient matriarchal or matrifocal society that collapsed under the expansion of Indo-European culture. The modern Inquisitors do this all reportedly in the noble pursuit of truth, just as the Inquisitors claimed to be doing during the era of Witchcraft trials and other heresies.

To many scholars, a lack of evidence equates to nonexistence, and many use this to maintain what at best might be described as their personal doubts. Critics might do well to consider the words of historian Peter Kingsley who wrote:

> "Academically, doubt is a virtue. It is wise to be cautious, virtuous to allow for different points of view. The problem arises when this attitude hardens: then doubting becomes a certainty in itself, and we forget the importance of doubting our doubt."

THE MASONS AND MODERN WITCHCRAFT (THE COMMONALITY)

In many modern Witchcraft and Wiccan traditions, there appear various aspects that parallel those found in Freemasonry. Many scholars claim that these elements were lifted by modern Witches from the rites of the Masons. Some modern Witches claim that Witches joined Masonic orders as a means of protection and that some sharing took place, resulting in a merging of concepts and ritual expressions. Others claim that Gerald Gardner worked Masonic elements into modern Wicca. My own personal theory is that the parallels originate from a common and ancient source, and did not reside uniquely within either the Witches' sect or in Freemasonry. Some sharing between the two seems likely at some point, perhaps towards the end of the nineteenth century, and Masonic elements may have helped to embellish the rituals of certain Witchcraft systems as in the case of Gerald Gardner.

Doreen Valiente, in the introduction to her book *Witchcraft for Tomorrow*, states that two Masons (Hargrave Jennings and W. J. Hughan) set out in the mid-nineteenth century looking for *"personal verification that the Masonic Crafters and Rosicrucian Crafters were siblings of the Old Religion."* Valiente states that as a result, these Masons formed a close relationship with George Pickingill (the Witch of Canewdon) from the 1850s onward. She notes that Pickingill, a non-Mason, amazed Hargave and Hughan by *"expounding the inner secrets of Masonry."* This led the team to concede that Witchcraft may have possessed some secret arcane knowledge akin to Freemasonry.

In order to understand the parallels that do exist between Freemasonry and modern Witchcraft, we must turn to both the historical and mythical history of Freemasonry. Albert Mackey (1807-1881) was a Mason that served as grand high priest of the Grand Chapter, grand master of the Grand Council, and general grand high priest of the General Grand Chapter of the United States. In the last decade of his life, Mackey served as secretary general of the Supreme Council of the 33rd Degree. During his lifetime, he authored thirteen books on Freemasonry. In his last work, titled *The History of Freemasonry*, Mackey explores many of the various and differing legends concerning the origins of Freemasonry. His chapter titled "Freemasonry and the Ancient Mysteries" is of particular interest when comparing elements of Freemasonry with modern Witchcraft.

Mackey examines the theory (one of many) that the origins of Freemasonry as a secret society are rooted in an ancient Pagan Mystery Cult Tradition. He states that the foundation of this theory *"derives from the most important part of its ritual and the legend of its Third Degree from the initiation practiced in these religious organizations..."* The parallels drawn by Mackey are:

1. *The Preparation* of the initiate by a washing or cleansing that was both physical and symbolic.

2. *The Initiation*, which passes the initiate through the Lesser and Greater Mysteries. Mackey likens this to that which occurs in Freemasonry concerning the Fellow's Craft and the Master's Degree.

3. *The Perfection*, which transmitted the "true dogma" or the "great secret" symbolized by the initiation rite itself. Mackey states that this is identical in Freemasonry.

4. The secret nature of both Freemasonry and the Pagan Mystery Tradition.

5. The use of symbols.

6. The dramatic form of the initiation.

7. The division of both systems into degrees or steps.

8. The adoption by both of secret methods of recognition.

Mackey asks a very interesting question in his chapter:

"Is modern Freemasonry a lineal and uninterrupted successor of the ancient mysteries, the succession being transmitted through the Mithraic initiations which existed in the 5th and 6th centuries; or is the fact of the analogies between the two systems to be attributed to the coincidence of a natural process of human thought, common to all minds and showing its development in symbolic forms?"

The commonality of the human experience and the resulting human expression itself is an important element to consider when comparing belief systems. Mackey himself notes that the only "important difference" between the various Mystery Cults created by humankind was in the particular/peculiar gods and hero figures, but that *"the material points of the plot and the religious design of the sacred drama were identical."* Mackey goes on to state that the forms and representations of the allegory employed by the various Mystery schools of Greece, Samothrace, Egypt, and Persia were *"everywhere preserved."*

Mackey notes that the Mysteries were divided into two classes called the Greater and Lesser Mysteries. He comments on a preparatory stage in the Ancient Mystery Tradition and concludes:

"So that there was in the process of reception a system of three steps, which those who are fond of tracing analogies between the ancient and the modern initiations are prone to call degrees."

It is interesting to note here the reference to the antiquity of the concept of "three levels/degrees." This is something common to most current Witchcraft/Wiccan traditions. In the closing of his chapter, Mackey states that the "form and character" of certain Masonic rituals such as the third-degree rite were derived from the "funeral legend" of the ancient initiations. In Freemasonry, this theme is stylized to incorporate a mythical history related to Hiram Abiff, the head of the workmen that constructed the ancient temple of King Solomon. This sleight-of-hand move served to align Freemasonry with Judaic roots in order to pacify Christian concerns about Paganism. However, in essence, the "funeral legend" is the classic theme of descent into the Underworld and the retrieval therefrom. It is a foundational theme residing in such Mystery Traditions as the Eleusinian Mystery Cult of ancient Greece, which focused on the Goddess in the Underworld and Her return from the Realm of the Dead. In many Witchcraft/ Wiccan traditions, the same essential mythos can be found within ritual text. Again, we are looking at a common source pre-dating the meeting of the Witches' sect with Freemasonry.

Is there any support for the Aegean/Mediterranean influence in Freemasonry that may have carried a Pagan theme? In 1723, and again in 1738, Dr. Anderson published a work titled the *Book of Constitutions*. His account of the history of Freemasonry was long accepted as the "true history" of the ancient origins. In part, Anderson's account has Freemasonry coming to the Romans from the Greeks, who themselves were influenced by Eastern cults. The Greeks then brought this to the Romans, who in turn carried it into northern Europe and the British Isles. He states that almost every Roman garrison had a "Lodge" erected within its structure. Today, Anderson's material is assigned to the "legendary" or "mythical" history of the Masons by most scholars.

In 1910, a Mason named W. Ravenscroft published a book titled *The Comacines*. This book dealt with the view that the origins of Freemasonry lie in the ancient Roman College of Artificers, whose existence is confirmed in a letter referring to "a college of workmen" written by Pliny to Emperor Trajan at the end of the first century. Ravenscroft says this is supported by Professor Baldwin Brown in *From Schola to Cathedral* (Douglas, Edinburgh, 1886). According to Ravenscroft, each Roman legion had with it a company of engineers (who would have been responsible for constructing everything from bridges to siege equipment, to housing for the troops in conquered territory). Ravenscroft writes:

"...there is conclusive evidence of their survival till the time of the decline and fall of Rome, each legion having a college attached to it, which accompanied it in its various campaigns. Thus they came to Britain, and we are told that in the early 4th century there were no less that [sic] fifty-three important cities, each with its Collegium Fabrorum, in England. Some think they became the progenitors of the English Medieval Guild of Artificers..."

Ravenscroft states that the "Architectural Collegium of the Romans" enjoyed the privilege of a constitution of their own and was recognized by the state as a legal body. Following the overthrow of the Republic, when all other organizations lost their privileges, the Roman Collegia was confirmed in nearly all their former rights and privileges. A minimum of three members was required to form a college, and no one was allowed to be a member of several colleges at the same time. According to Ravenscroft, the organization met in secluded rooms or buildings exclusively appropriated for their meetings, and had *"their own peculiar religious ceremonies and priests... an archive, and their own seals."*

It is worth noting that Ravenscroft speaks of the Roman artificers in a religious sense and mentions a priesthood. This serves as one element of the formal foundation of Romanized Pagan religion that was carried into Celtic lands. There is also an interesting connection between the cult of Mithras, Roman soldiers, the "mythical" history of Freemasonry, and a secret society in England known as the "Oddfellows," as will soon be demonstrated in this section. Ravenscroft also notes that the writings of Roman authors and inscriptions found on monuments furnish "undeniable proof" that the association of artificers continued amongst the Romans for a considerable period and existed in Gaul, Brittany, and what is now England.

Following the withdrawal of Roman troops from the British Isles, Ravenscroft states that the Guild of Artificers left and settled in the district of Como, establishing their center on the island of Comacina. This is why Ravenscroft names the organization *The Comacine*. He claims that remnant factions of the Roman artificers remaining in the British Isles merged into the great Masonic Guilds of the Middle Ages, and *"that as these guilds died out, their forms and ceremonies were preserved to a great extent in our Masonic lodges..."* Ravenscroft writes of the medieval guilds:

> *"Through those guilds, however, and especially that of the Comacines, modern freemasonry may claim a grand heredity, and perhaps it may yet be found that some of the legends which have been handed down to us are not so mythical as many are disposed to think."*

Now we must turn to the cult of Mithras in further search of evidence of the Aegean/Mediterranean connection to Freemasonry. On the topic of the origins of Freemasonry, Ravenscroft writes:

> *"Some associated it with the teaching of Euclid...some with the cult of Mithras as practised in Rome, and so back into the sunworship of hoary Persian antiquity. Others say it was the outcome of the Greek mysteries; others, still, that it was taught by the Essenes...and that they descended from the architects of the Temple of Jerusalem; others, again that it was brought to England by the Culdees...and were associated with the Roman College..."*

It is known that Roman soldiers in the latter half of the Empire belonged to the cult of Mithras. One example is the *Second Adiutrix* legion (circa 69 CE) which served in Britain and Aquincum on the Danube. There is also some speculation that the *First Italica* and the legions may have spread elements of Mithraism throughout the Danubian provinces. Therefore, it is relatively safe to conjecture that elements of Mithraic philosophy were introduced into the conquered lands held by the legions of Rome. The veneration and sacrifice of the bull is at the center of the cult of Mithras, which was essentially a solar-oriented religion. In both regards, there is a strong connection here with the beliefs and practices of the Druids in the British Isles. Despite the hatred of the Romans by the Druids, various elements of the cult of Mithras were most likely too compelling for the Druids to ignore. In the following chapter, we will explore the connection between the bull and the Horned God of Witchcraft.

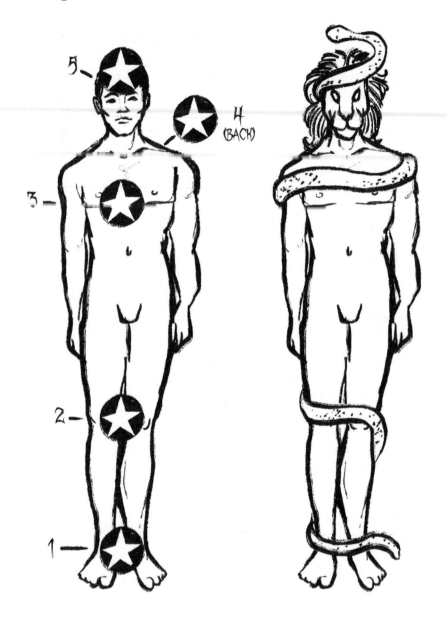

Freemasonry's "five points of fellowship" (above left): feet (1), knees (2), breast (3), back (4), and head (5).

These correlate to the divisions of rulership by the deity, as marked off by the serpent of the mithraic cult (above, right).

Within the cult of Mithras, there existed what is referred to as the *investiture scenes*, which depict ritual images associated with cult symbolism that bear a striking similarity regarding ritual elements within Freemasonry. In the book *The Origins of the Mithraic Mysteries*, by David Ulansey, the illustrations containing images, symbols, and tools within the cult of Mithras are similar in style to those of Freemasonry as they appear in the book *Duncan's Ritual of Freemasonry*. It is also interesting to compare the "five points of fellowship" in Freemasonry (feet, knees, breast, back, head) to an Orphic statue of Mithras in which the deity is divided into five segments by a serpent coiled around his feet, knees, chest, back and head. Ulansey comments that the symbolism employed in the Mithraic cult indicates the power of Mithras to end one cosmic cycle and begin a new one, for he has control over the fundamental structure of the universe. Is this image not the master builder himself, the grandest of Freemasons?

As noted in *The Cults of the Roman Empire* by Robert Turcan, the symbolic tools of Mithraism were the *wand of command*, the *libation cup*, and the *crescent-shaped knife*. The pentacle does not appear to be present as such, although there is extensive use of an undescribed "platter." Another tool mentioned for ritual use is the sword and the Sun's whip. The main rituals of Mithraism were centered around a sacramental meal. Turcan notes that the solstices and equinoxes held great importance within the cult of Mithras. The Moon is also featured in Mithraism and is associated with honey, the bull, and blood. This ritual use of the wand, cup, blade, and platter pre-date Freemasonry and Gardnerian Wicca. What we are looking at here is the commonality of the human experience.

In the British Isles, the organization known as the Oddfellows claimed to be descended from a sect formed by the Roman soldiers that once occupied old Britain. It is interesting to note that a secret organization in Italy known as the Carbonari, which eventually set up a lodge in Scotland and whose membership later included Masons, claimed to have originated from the cult of Mithras as well. It is not important whether these are historical or mythical accounts. It is important only that these accounts existed in the first place and were circulated among the members of secret organizations. We are looking simply for the appearance of views and their chronological order as we examine and compare the parallels found in Freemasonry and modern Witchcraft. At the core, we will eventually discover that the common factor, which is always present, continues to be the Aegean/ Mediterranean influences and the concepts and structure found in Italian Witchcraft or some other secret society in Italy.

The secret society of the Carbonari first appears in public records during the early eighteenth century. The organization was very powerful and influenced the politics of its era, particularly in the kingdom of Naples. The Carbonari were divided into two classes: apprentices and masters. The members made themselves known to one another by secret signs in shaking hands, and the order possessed three degrees of initiation marked by colored cords or ribbons: blue, red, and black. A triangle marked the first-degree level. The members were bound by a serious oath to observe absolute silence concerning their organization.

The similarity between the secret society of the Carbonari and Freemasonry is evident, and eventually, Freemasons were allowed to enter the Carbonari as full-fledged "masters" immediately upon acceptance. It must not be overlooked that within the Italian Carbonari structure, we find three degrees of initiation, and colored cords associated with each, plus the triangle signifying the first degree, all of which pre-dates any connection with the Masonic orders of northern Europe. Such elements appear in modern Witchcraft as well, and it would be incorrect to look to Freemasonry as the source of all things. Ultimately, we will discover that various elements of Italian Witchcraft were more influential on modern Witchcraft than was anything of Masonic origin. This is discussed further both in the section here on Gerald Gardner and in the following chapter on the Witches' religion.

As early as the first years of the nineteenth century, the Carbonari were widespread in Neapolitan territory, especially in Abruzzi and Calabria. Not only men of low birth but also government officials of high rank, officers, and even members of the clergy belonged to it. The Carbonari went on to establish a lodge in Scotland circa 1820. As a result, many elements of ancient Aegean/Mediterranean, the Mithraic cult, Hellenistic, and hermetic concepts took root in various secret societies within the British Isles such as the Oddfellows (founded between 1838-1843) and the Fellowship of Crotona, which influenced Gerald Gardner and the tradition he and others later enriched and modified. This is examined in the section on Gerald Gardner in the current chapter. However, we must now move on to examine the next chronological influence before we look at Gardnerian Wicca.

THE ROMANTIC ERA (ENTER THE MUSE)

To understand the emergence of modern Witchcraft and its roots, we must turn to religion and spirituality. These are the forces that brought Witchcraft back into the light of day beginning in the early half of the nineteenth century. To modern Witches, the Moon and the Earth are conscious beings, beautiful ancient goddesses. They communicate with those who embrace the Earth religions in a way that may never be understood by the academic community. This type of communication is known as "interfacing" and is the method used by spirits and deities to interact with humankind. Ritual is one of the ways in which altered states of consciousness can be induced that make interfacing more effective.

The ancient relationship between the Muses and humankind is one example of successful interfacing. In Greek mythology, the Muses were patrons of all intellectual activities. They freed humans from the physical burdens of the material world, inspired them in the arts and sciences, and allowed them to access the "eternal truths." The ancient Greeks understood that inspiration is rooted in the divine spark within us. The primary definition of the word *inspire* is: "to affect, guide, or arouse by divine influence." The Muses are, in effect, the spiritual or supernatural mechanism that operates between the world of humans and the gods, establishing and maintaining communication. As mythological beings, they are essentially personifications of the divine process.

The mother of the Muses was known as *Mnemosyne* (memory or remembrance) and their father was Zeus. The Muses had as a half-brother and half-sister (from Zeus) the deities Artemis and Apollo, as well as the gods Hermes and Dionysus. All of these relationships are important to understanding the resurgence of Pagan elements during the nineteenth century. Mnemosyne, the goddess of memory and remembrance (joined with her daughters who reveal eternal truths to humankind), is key to understanding the emergence of the Witches' religion into the public arena.

Unfortunately, when we speak of the actions of deities or spirits and their influence on the human mind and emotions, we lose the scholar whose methodology is unable to reveal or comprehend that which is of the gods. The scholar cannot admit to the existence of supernatural forces and at the same time write "proper" history. Historian Diane Purkiss, in her book *The Witch in History*, addresses this problem, where she writes:

> *"It follows that in order to exist according to its own self-definition, history must repress any hint of the supernatural as real or as capable of causing events… This results in a hollowness at the center of historical discourse on the supernatural, which displaces the very subject it promises to address. The supernatural must be transformed into something else so that it can be discussed…history can say nothing about angels or demons or witches until they are psychoanalytic symptoms, chemicals, illnesses, political tools, or social categories."*

Let us now consider the Muse and their mother, who is memory or remembrance. The Witchcraft trials ended in the eighteenth century (the last formal execution was in 1793) which was also the beginning of the Industrial Revolution, and a new smoke was now in the air. The nineteenth century saw people working long hours in the factories. Social and economic changes highlighted this era in which life as people once knew it had changed forever. Fewer people worked the farmlands and the focus of life turned to materialism. The old traditions that had once empowered and vitalized communities began to wither into quaint customs associated with the less sophisticated individuals of society. Humankind had parted ways with the Earth and embraced mechanization. What better setting for the Muses to appear once again to humankind, and what greater need had there been?

This, of course, begs the question: are goddesses real? Historians and other scholars cannot answer that question, but Witches can. Yes, our deities are real and they do communicate with us. However, it must be stated that there are those in the Pagan and Witchcraft community who share the views of modern scholars. Paracelsus, the famous sixteenth-century alchemist, once said:

"Magic has power to experience and fathom things which are inaccessible to human reason. For magic is a great secret wisdom, just as reason is a great public folly."

Therefore, it is not too surprising to discover individuals that find it difficult to believe in the power of magick, and in the reality that the gods manifest their will in the material world according to their own designs. Like the scholars, we will now lose these individuals as well, as we turn to the discussion of how Mnemosyne and her Muses interfaced with humankind in the nineteenth century and began the process of bringing Witchcraft, the Old Religion, into public view.

Ronald Hutton, in his book *The Triumph of the Moon*, mentions the appearance and popularity of specific deities in the nineteenth century. Hutton tells us that Venus/Aphrodite, Diana/Artemis, Proserpine, and Ceres/Demeter were featured in the poetry of this era, figuring prominently in the works of such poets as Byron, Keats, and Shelley. Hutton expresses his belief that the origins of various concepts found in modern Witchcraft lie largely in the poems about Pagan deities and the works of art that depicted them in this century. Hutton feels these were later used as a source for the construction of what became modern Witchcraft. My view as a Witch is that it is the poet and the artist who is most receptive to hearing the voice of the Muses. They speak to everyone, of course, but only those who actually listen ever hear the whispers. This is, in part, what Witches call the *voice of the wind.*

The gods listed by Hutton are Jupiter (Zeus), Hermes, Apollo, and Pan. What is striking about this is that these deities are intimately linked with the Muses, with the exception of Pan, unless we identify him with Bacchus or Dionysus, which others have done in the past. As already noted in this chapter, Hermes and Apollo are half-brothers to the Muses, and Diana is their half-sister. Venus, as we saw earlier in this chapter, is connected to Witches through the word *venefica* and Proserpine is identified by Horace as one of the goddesses invoked by the Witch Canidia. Ceres is the goddess of the Mysteries themselves. It is no coincidence that these goddesses appear together in this age

(Venus the garden and Ceres the harvest, a completed cycle). It is instead a process taking place within the Otherworld, which then begins to manifest in this world. In the Romantic period, we find emphasis on the deities associated with the planets, and in early times, the Pythagoreans placed the Muses in the planetary spheres with Venus, Mars, Mercury, Saturn, etc. Their reunion in the nineteenth century is also no coincidence.

It is worthy of note that the earliest poems of the nineteenth century mourn the absence of the Old Gods and the old spirits. Byron speaks of the Old Gods having fallen silent in his *Aristomenes: Canto First*, appearing in 1823. Johann von Schiller lamented the lost spirits of the fairy realm, as did Holderlin for the Old Gods when he spoke of the departure of the old religion. Keats mourned the loss of Pagan reverence that was once lavished upon nature in his early works. This is the first stirring of the remembrance of the Old Ways, and of course "remembrance" is the mother of the Muses.

Before we explore this further, it is essential to understand that the Pagan gods never completely disappeared under Christian domination. When humankind moved on to embrace the "one true God," the Old Gods went to sleep in the statues and stone images, awaiting the awakening to come many centuries later. The Old Gods were featured prominently in art and literature up through the Renaissance period and even appear in the Tarocchi of Mantegna, a deck of cards dating to around 1465. In the book *The Survival of the Pagan Gods: The Mythological Tradition and its Place in Renaissance Humanism and Art* by Jean Seznec, the author discusses how the gods lost their classical form during the Middle Ages, and how this was all restored in the second half of the fifteenth century. Fortunately, the Middle Ages had produced Boccaccio's work *Genealogy of the Gods*, which preserved the earlier mythological traditions.

Seznec notes that in the revival that took place around 1420, the goddess Venus is the first and most popular figure in the literary works and artistic expression of this era. As we saw earlier, Hutton says the same of the Romantic period. Is this a coincidence or is it the intervention of the Muses? Seznec also points out the rise of "Apollo and his Muses" in literature and art, and the migration of this theme to northern Europe by 1490. According to Seznec, it was not until the middle of the sixteenth century that the renewal of the "authentic mythographical tradition" was established during the Italian Renaissance.

Returning to the nineteenth century, we last noted that poets of this period first lamented the loss of Pagan veneration for nature and the Old Gods. For consoling, the poets and artists did what is human nature to do: they turned to the Mother, which in this case was a Pagan Goddess. The nineteenth-century writings related to the Goddess were more sophisticated than the ancient texts and provided new labels and phrases that encapsulated the old original Goddess and God forms and concepts. One example is Jane Ellen Harrison who saw in the three Fates of ancient Greco-Roman mythology the images of a "Maiden" and a "Mother."

Robert Graves later wrote of the Moon Goddess as being of three aspects related to the lunar phases of waxing, full, and waning. Historian Ronald Hutton claims that Graves invented the concept of Maiden, Mother, and Crone, and calls this Graves's *"great gift to modern Pagan witchcraft, the fully formed image of the Triple Moon Goddess."* However, the Roman poet Catullus, in the first century BCE, wrote of the goddess Diana as a "threefold" goddess who protects virgins, aids birthing mothers, fills barns with produce, and is "Queen of the Underworld." It is not difficult to see the pre-existing concepts here related to Maiden, Mother, and Crone. In addition, Lucan (first century BCE) wrote of Witches worshipping a Goddess of three aspects (see Chapter Two). Hutton states that for Graves, an important function of the Goddess was that she *"operated through myths and dreams, in contrast with rational modes of thought."* In this regard, we can consider Robert Graves to be one of the most important instruments of the Goddess in bringing Witchcraft to the surface in modern times.

A somewhat significant player in the work of the Muses is found in the personage of Jules Michelet. Michelet was a French historian who produced a work in 1862 titled *La Sorciere*. In essence, the book depicted Witchcraft as a surviving Pagan religion that struggled to maintain its existence during the Middle Ages. Hutton states Michelet's work proclaimed that the surfacing of *"the wisdom preserved by the witches"* (related to nature and the indwelling life forces) brought about the Renaissance period.

Hutton goes on to say, in essence, that Michelet's work viewed women as particularly suited to esoteric knowledge, and they, therefore, served as priestesses of the Witches' religion. *La Sorciere* depicts the Witches' festivals held amidst the old Celtic dolmens or in a forest clearing near the edge of the woods. The Witch is portrayed as a woman sharing a kindred spirit with the wilderness and communes equally with creatures and trees alike. As Michelet himself writes:

> *"They awake in her things that her mother told her, her grand-mother—old, old things that for century after century have been handed on from woman to woman."*

In what may be regarded as an attempt to discredit Michelet, Hutton points out that Michelet had no particular love of nature himself since he primarily lived in the city of Paris, and that Michelet did not really think very highly of women. In reality, if Michelet wrote contrary to his own personal feelings, this is actually more of an indication that the Muses wrote through him. If his feelings did not come from his own mind and heart, then from where did they spring? In any case, as Hutton points out, *La Sorciere* was essentially ignored by the literary community of its era.

W.B. Yeats is another figure with whom the Muses clearly inter-faced. Yeats is best remembered as a poet of the Romantic period, but he was also very involved in magick and fascinated by the Ancient Mystery Traditions (although he was essentially a mystic Christian at heart and remained so until his end). Theosophy was among his earliest influences, and at one stage of his life, he was also a member of the Golden Dawn. Hutton indicates that Yeats possessed a *"strong inclination to believe in the existence of a spirit world, and of deities, and to work with them."*

In 1885, Yeats became one of the founders of a Hermetic society, and sometime around 1888, he produced a collection of Irish peasant lore associated with the old race of fairies. Yeats demonstrated an interest in the ancient Druids and within a few years, he began to speak of the dawning of a new cult, which he actually worked on plans for, between the period of 1895-1902. However, he insisted that at the core of this new cult, there be a Christian focus and that the Pagan elements should be simply blended with this.

Together with his friend of many years, George Russell, the two men envisioned a return to the veneration of Irish Pagan deities. This never came in their time but eventually manifested in a less grand way with the modern Wicca movement generated by the writings of Gerald Gardner almost a century later. Eventually, Yeats became disillusioned with the revival of Druidism and, unable to free himself fully from his Christian center, could not maintain the interface with the Muses, and lost connection.

Perhaps one of the most key individuals essential to the work of the Muses was a man named James George Frazer. Frazer was a Social Anthropologist who was born in Glasgow, Scotland. He attended the Universities of Glasgow and Cambridge and was elected as a Fellow of Trinity College in 1879. Frazer became a Professor of Social Anthropology at the University of Liverpool in 1907 and continued teaching until 1922.

Frazer had a fascination with the study of myth and religion and became the first to suggest a relation between myths and rituals. The fields of myth and religion became his areas of expertise and he brought a wide array of anthropological research to bear upon them. Frazer completed a monumental work known as *The Golden Bough*, which had a tremendous impact on the scholars of his era and influenced thought well into the early twentieth century. *The Golden Bough* was published in 1890 as a study of ancient cults, rites, myths, and their parallels with early Christianity. Modern scholars tend to disagree with some of his definitions and associations and have therefore elected to reject the majority of his work. This is the classic "throwing the baby out with the bath water" approach to discovering truth.

At the core of Frazer's work, we find a focus on the ancient cult of Diana and Dianus at Lake Nemi, Italy. Frazer also brought to public attention the figure known as *Rex Nemorensis*, the "King of the Woods" who was the guardian of Diana's sacred grove. *The Golden Bough* conveyed the idea of magick and the relevance of myth and legend to the public mind. It also revived an interest in pre-Christian European Paganism and demonstrated the survival of Pagan themes that endured even down through the Christian era. Frazer was not, however, able to see the Witch figure in any way other than through the common stereotype of the Middle Ages and Renaissance periods.

But with the arrival of Frazer, the near-final stage was set upon which the Muses were to bring Witchcraft full circle back to the association of Diana and her Witches. The only missing piece remaining now was for the public to become aware that Witches still existed and continued to worship the Old Gods in modern times. For this feat, the Muses spoke to another figure of the nineteenth century, a man named Charles Godfrey Leland, who was to play a major part in the magick of the Muses in revealing the Witches' religion.

Charles Godfrey Leland is best remembered for his book titled *Aradia, Gospel of the Witches*, which was published in 1899. However, his most important work was a book originally titled *Etruscan Roman Remains*, written about seven years earlier.

The latter revealed a Witches' sect in the late nineteenth century that worshipped the goddess Diana. In several of his books, and in personal letters, Leland mentions four "Witches" who gathered research material for him. One was called Maddalena and another was named Marietta. Leland also mentions two men (one of whom may have been named Peppino) whom Leland says came from a Witch blood family. These individuals were employed by Leland to collect folklore information from traders coming down from the mountain regions in northern Italy.

During this same period in Italy, other folklorists were also investigating Witchcraft. J.B. Andrews, Lady Vere, and Roma Lister each performed field studies in three different areas of Italy: Rome, Florence, and Naples. Despite the regional differences in customs and dialects encountered by these folklorists, they each independently uncovered an almost identical Witches' sect to that described by Charles Leland in his pre-*Aradia* material. The common elements reported by these folklorists indicated that the knowledge of the Witches was passed down from generation to generation, that the sect was organized, had structure and laws, and involved magick. Modern scholars dismiss or ignore these field studies and the resulting conclusions, most often labeling them as anomalies. The classification of "anomaly" allows scholars to conveniently dismiss contrary evidence, as in the case of the Italian material, which meets accepted scholarly methodology but is contrary to the current scholarly view.

In 1886, Leland approached Maddalena (his "Witch informant") telling her he was aware of the existence of a manuscript containing the doctrines of Italian Witchcraft. He then asked Maddalena to obtain it for him, if possible, during her travels in Tuscany. On January 1, 1897, after a decade of searching, Maddalena delivered the manuscript to Leland. This manuscript was to later become Leland's book titled *Aradia: Gospel of the Witches.*

The *Aradia* manuscript portrayed Witches as the followers of the ancient Roman deities known as Diana and Lucifer. According to the text, these Witches gathered nude at the time of the Full Moon for a ritual celebration. During this ritual, the participants worshipped Diana, performed magick, and consumed cakes and wine in her honor. Unlike Leland's field studies on Italian Witchcraft, the *Aradia* material depicted Witches cursing Diana with threats if their wishes were not granted. The book also spoke of Witches using poison to kill their enemies. Such Witches were definitely not the *"good witches of Benevento"* of whom Leland wrote in his earlier works on the Italian Craft.

In the past, Maddalena had readily supplied Leland with material and information on Witchcraft, and yet it took her ten years to deliver the *Aradia* material to Leland. This strongly suggests that Maddalena was unfamiliar with the specific tradition from which it was derived. The earlier material supplied directly by Maddalena to Leland generally depicted Witches as a society of "good Witches" devoted to Diana. Therefore, the *Aradia* material indicates that whatever Witchcraft tradition it represented was not the one Maddalena herself practiced. She was apparently simply providing Leland with the manuscript he had ten years earlier asked her to find.

Despite the negative image of Witchcraft portrayed in Leland's *Aradia* material, the book became one of the most influential works on modern Witchcraft. The late Doreen Valiente stated that the writings of Leland on Italian Witchcraft first drew her to the practice of Witchcraft even before she met Gerald Gardner (see appendix). This influence is evident in the material she composed for the Gardnerian *Book of Shadows* such as the opening portion of the *Charge of the Goddess*, which is based almost word-for-word upon the sabbat described by Leland in the closing section of the first chapter of *Aradia.* The fundamental elements of what Gardner portrayed as Wicca can be found in Leland's material written over half a century earlier than the writings of Gerald Gardner. These include skyclad rituals, the worship of a Goddess and God couple, the casting of spells, and the use of ritual cakes and wine (covered in more detail in the next section). Despite this fact, modern scholars view these elements in modern Witchcraft as being the creation of Gerald Gardner and those who later added to the Gardnerian Wiccan material.

GERALD GARDNER AND MODERN WICCA (THE DETOUR)

In this section, we begin what many modern scholars view as the "mythical" history of contemporary Witchcraft and its modern construction. The basis of this view is linked to the writings of Gerald Gardner, the tradition of Wicca he presented to the world and the views of many people influenced by the position Gardner took on pre-Christian European religion. While Gardner, and those influenced by his work, really had little to do with the much larger picture of Witchcraft, "Gardnerian Wicca" became the focus for many individuals both in Europe and the United States that were interested in the study and practice of Witchcraft.

Gerald Gardner, and all that can be traced back to him, has misdirected and sidetracked historians and assorted scholars concerning the history of modern Witchcraft ever since. In reality, Gardner was simply one man, in a small region of the world, in an isolated period of time, who wrote of others he met that claimed to be Witches. His accounts related almost entirely to matters in Britain only and are not reflective of the Witches' religion as a whole in other regions of Europe. Reportedly, hereditary Witches in Britain state that Gardner's version of the Craft is actually not even reflective of old Witchcraft in the British Isles. Despite all of this, modern scholars have elected to regard Gardner's Wicca as the ultimate source for all Witchcraft traditions that exist today.

Gerald Gardner was the first to introduce the public to a religion he called "Wicca" in his book *Witchcraft Today*, published in 1954. Gardner claimed Wicca was an ancient fertility cult and that he was initiated into a surviving sect of Witches practicing this religion. He claimed to have made contact with a coven of New Forest Witches through the

Rosicrucian Theater at Christ Church in Hampshire, which he joined
in August 1938. The organization behind the theater group was known
as the *Rosicrucian Order Crotona Fellowship*, named after the town in
southern Italy where a band of mystical Pythagoreans was centered.
As noted earlier in this chapter, the Pythagoreans and the Muses have
an association, and so the work of the Muses continues with Gardner.
It was through the Fellowship of Crotona organization that Gardner
further claimed to meet the leader of this sect, a woman whom he
called "Old Dorothy." She reportedly allowed Gardner to be initiated
into the Witches' religion at her home in September 1939, suggestive
of the Witches' "year and a day" waiting period for initiation. Some
people believe that Dorothy initiated Gardner and others think it was
Edith Rose Woodford-Grimes, also known as "Dafo."

One of the members of the Fellowship of Crotona was a woman
named Susie Mason. Author Philip Heselton, in his book *Wiccan Roots*,
states a belief that the Mason family may well have been hereditary
Witches. Heselton presents a fair amount of reasonable speculation
regarding the existence of the New Forest coven. Many people have
commented that a coven practiced in the New Forest area, including
individuals not directly associated with Gardner or the Fellowship
of Crotona. One such person was Sybil Leek, who claimed to have
been a high priestess of a hereditary coven of New Forest Witches
known as the Horsa coven. Leek claimed that the coven lineage dated
back approximately seven hundred years. Another person to mention
the New Forest Witches was Louis Wilkinson, who told the tale of
a group of Witches in the early 1930s or 1940s that operated in the
New Forest. An English Witch named Patricia Crowthers claimed she
had reason to believe that Wilkinson was a member of a New Forest
coven himself, although it is something he himself denied. Another
"pre-Gardnerian" claim regarding the existence of New Forest Witches
comes from W.E. Liddell who told of nine covens, founded by George
Pickingill in the early nineteenth century, that were located in various
parts of England including New Forest.

Modern scholars dismiss these stories and several other accounts
as not being evidence that covens existed prior to Gardner's own
group. However, it should be noted that when a scholar states
"there is no evidence to support" this or that, it does not mean no
one has ever provided an account of one type or another, nor that

there are no references or claims anywhere regarding it. Instead, it simply means that whatever material does exist is not approved by the scholars themselves as being "acceptable" evidence according to their own standards.

When considering the discernment of scholars, it should be noted that they decide what constitutes evidence and what does not. The scholars then pass judgment on the matter at hand. This is not unlike the process used by attorneys who argue that various pieces of evidence are inadmissible because of the way the evidence was gathered, or that due to the character of the person the evidence itself is not reliable. Here we find that the truth is a secondary issue to legal procedure if it becomes an issue at all. Likewise, for the modern scholar, there is a real danger that protocol and methodology can override the attainment of the complete truth. Everything that does not qualify in the view of scholars as being "evidence" is relegated to the pile of non-evidence, which to many scholars then equates to non-existence, and thereby serves to maintain and support the scholar's disbelief. Second- or third-hand testimony that supports a contrary view to that held by the scholar is regarded and dismissed as "hearsay" while second- or third-hand statements made in agreement with the position of the scholar are viewed and accepted as corroborative testimony.

In the case of Gerald Gardner, the primary scholarly view is that he is the father of modern Wicca/Witchcraft. The conviction held by the scholarly community is that everything practiced and believed by modern Witches/Wiccans is traceable to Gerald Gardner in one way or another or originates from something that sprang from the influence of Gardner's writings on other people. Curiously, however, in *Triumph of the Moon*, Hutton writes that even if Gardner had created a compilation of rituals himself and established the first modern coven, it would not be entirely just to say that Gardner "invented" modern Witchcraft. Hutton clarifies this by adding that from a religious perspective, it might be possible that Gardner communed with a divine force of some type operating over the last two centuries. Hutton concludes that such a case would be highly remarkable.

Many scholars believe that Gardner did create the religion of Wicca in its entirety and that he based much of it on the writings of Margaret Murray. Murray was a British anthropologist and archaeologist that wrote about medieval Witchcraft as the survival of an organized Pagan fertility religion dating back to Paleolithic times. Her first book on the subject was titled *The Witch Cult in Western Europe* and was published in 1921. Some scholars suggest that Murray elaborated on Frazer's *Golden Bough* material to which she added her own theories.

It was Murray's contention that Witchcraft, as a religion, was based upon the worship of the goddess Diana. Murray also wrote of the Witches' God, a horned deity mistaken for the Devil. In her third book, titled *The Divine King in England*, Murray tried to make a case that all the English kings dating from the eleventh century were secretly Witches of the Old Religion. This pushed things too far for the scholars of her time, and in retaliation, they rejected this and all of her previous work as well. Most modern scholars still wave the anti-Murray banner, and those that do not, live in fear of being regarded as a "Murrayite" by the academic community should they support *any* of her findings. This is something that the respected historian Carlo Ginzburg discovered when he commented in his book *The Night Battles* that Murray's thesis contained "a core of truth." Ginzburg later commented, in his book *Ecstasies*, that his remark earned him *"ex-offico enrollment in the phantom, but discredited sect of Murrayists."*

It is likely that Gardner was inspired to some degree by the works of Margaret Murray. At the very least, he would have been excited to find that an anthropologist/archaeologist wrote in support of what he claimed to have discovered in Britain. Another text of the same period as Murray, and likely to have been influential, was Ian Ferguson's book titled *The Philosophy of Witchcraft*, published in 1924. Ferguson writes of the Witch in his preface:

> *"She was in the beginning the counsellor and consoler of man, the genius of the domestic arts, the treasury of knowledge, and the inspiration of belief. She was the prophet, priest, and king of Paganism, and her territory was the world...(in the Middle Ages) her philosophy was welcomed as a defiance of social and religious tyrannies, and even formed its tenets into a political factor of revolution...the oldest antagonism of man—the conflict between the things of earth and of heaven—now found in the witch an actual physical victim, and the long degradation of the spiritual actually*

gave to those concerned in her oppression a sense of crusade and moral victory."

Throughout the book, Ferguson's Witches are much closer to Gardner's than are Murray's.

Was there ever really an "Old Religion" of the Witches? As we noted earlier, folklorist Charles Leland and several others writing on Italian Witchcraft believed this to be the case. In a letter written to me from Doreen Valiente, dated May 26, 1999, Doreen states that Gerald Gardner had given her a *cimaruta* charm, which is the symbol of Italian Witchcraft. Gardner's *cimaruta* appears in Valiente's book *An ABC of Witchcraft Past and Present* published in 1973. Valiente states in her letter that she recently bought one for herself in "a Brighton junk shop" and had never before seen one for sale in England. Where then did Gardner get the *cimaruta* charm that he later gifted to Valiente, and is there a connection to Italy and Gerald Gardner? We know that Gardner visited the ruins at Pompeii in Italy sometime prior to 1954, as he remarks on the Mystery mural paintings in his book *Witchcraft Today*. He comments on later showing pictures of the murals to an English Witch who remarked *"So, they knew the Mysteries in those days."* We have no available proof that Gardner personally knew any Italian Witches, but we do know that he was a Mason and that when traveling in foreign lands, it was not uncommon for Masons to call upon one another. The question then becomes, "Were there any Masons living near Pompeii in Italy who also had connections to Italian Witchcraft?"

The one person that comes readily to mind is Giovanni Rescigno, who, prior to World War II, worked for the government-owned railroad system as a stationmaster in Naples. He was a Freemason and had family connections to the unadulterated Italian Witchcraft tradition of Aradia, which pre-dated Leland's Christianized rendering. Rescigno was a member of the Order of the Pentagram founded in Naples circa 1930. The Order blended together mystical elements of Roman Paganism and Eastern mysticism with material based upon the teachings of a mystical order of Pythagoreans that once thrived in ancient Crotona, Italy. The Order of the Pentagram had close ties with an occult society known as the UR Group in Rome, and the Myrian School of Esoteric Initiation. The Myrian School was originally founded in Naples by Giuliano Kremmerz in 1896. The UR Group was originally founded in Rome by Arturo Reghini, Julius Evola, and Giovanni Colazza circa 1927.

Rescigno was frequently visited by an unrelated Strega woman who often performed healings with olive oil and rue. According to his daughter, when the fascists came to power in Italy, Rescigno burned many of his books, buried others, and removed any traces from his home that would readily associate him with any secret societies. He could not afford such a discovery since he worked for the government, which by then was in the hands of the fascists who were openly hostile to secret societies. It must be noted here, however, that there is nothing currently available to directly link Rescigno and Gardner together in order to demonstrate that they knew one another in any way. If such evidence could be brought out into the light, it would do much to explain the commonality between elements of Gardnerian Wicca and Stregheria, such as the *Charge of the Goddess* and other ritual components.

Some scholars point to an organization known as the *Order of Woodcraft Chivalry* as the source of Gardner's version of Wicca. This organization was founded in 1916 by Ernest Westlake and his son, in Fordingbridge, on the edge of New Forest. The Order was based, in part, on a form of woodcraft reported to be associated with Native American practices. The elements it shared in common with Gardner's Wicca were the preparation of a ceremonial circle, invoking spirits from the four quarter directions, calling upon deity, dancing around the circle, holding a feast, thanking and dismissing the spirits, and opening the ritual circle. As author Heselton remarks, this is a very common format for a variety of earth-based religions in general. Hutton provides some information indicating that Gardner was associated with this Order or a branch of this Order, sometime between 1936 and 1949. However, Heselton states that the Pagan and ritual elements of the Order had been "changed out of all recognition" by even 1936, and therefore, a direct "borrowing" by Gardner seems highly unlikely.

In order to understand the foundation of Gardner's version of Wicca, one needs only look at the essential concepts to note the Aegean/Mediterranean roots. In a letter written to me (see appendix) by Doreen Valiente, dated June 10, 1997, she states: *"I would certainly agree that 'Gardnerian Wicca' is a blend of Mediterranean/Aegean concepts with Celtic traditions."* Coming from the person that wrote much of the Gardnerian verses herself, and helped Gardner embellish his *Book of Shadows,* such a statement seems significant.

A brief comparison of some basic tenets appearing in Leland's work and Gardner's writings may help us understand the chronology. Bear in mind that Leland's writings appear over half a century earlier. Gardner used the term "The Old Religion" when referring to Witchcraft. In the introduction to Leland's *Etruscan Roman Remains* the author writes:

"Among these people, stregeria, or witchcraft or, as I have heard it called, 'la vecchia religione' (or 'the old religion') exists to a degree which would even astonish many Italians."

In the appendix of *Aradia: Gospel of the Witches,* Leland says:

"The result of it all was a vast development of rebels, outcasts, and all the discontented, who adopted witchcraft or sorcery for a religion..."

Gardner wrote that Witches gathered beneath the Full Moon and worshipped a Goddess. Leland recorded in *Aradia* a section regarding the Witches' gathering in which the following words appear as part of a ritual:

"When I shall have departed from this world,
Whenever ye have need of anything,
Once in the month, and when the Moon is full,
Ye shall assemble in some desert place,
Or in a forest all together join
To adore the potent spirit of your queen,
My mother, great Diana. She who fain
Would learn all sorcery yet has not won
Its deepest secrets, then my mother will
Teach her, in truth all things as yet unknown."

Leland goes on to describe a ritual meal of cakes and wine, which was a theme Gardner wrote of as well. These words appear in Leland's *Aradia*:

"You shall make cakes of meal, wine, salt, and honey in the shape of a (crescent or horned) Moon, and then put them to bake..."

In another section, Leland records these words:

"O Diana! In honor of thee I will hold this feast,
Feast and drain the goblet deep, we will dance and wildly leap..."

Many people believe that Gardner introduced the theme of Witches gathering for rituals in the nude. However, earlier, Leland wrote in *Aradia*:

"And so ye shall be free in everything;
And as the sign that ye are truly free,
Ye shall be naked in your rites, both men
And women also..."

"And thus shall it be done: all shall sit down to the supper all naked, men and women, and the feast over, they shall dance, sing, make music..."

These are only a few pre-existing basic concepts that one can find in Leland's books on the Old Religion of Witchcraft that later appear in Gardner's books on Wicca. For more of these "parallels," I direct the reader to Chapter Ten where older elements of Witchcraft appearing in the modern Craft are discussed in more detail. But before we get ahead of ourselves, let us turn to the next chapter and examine the evidence for the antiquity of various themes and concepts in Witchcraft, which scholars claim are entirely modern but which clearly appear in much older literary works.

ᴛHE ᴡITCHES' RELIGION

THE RELIGION OF WITCHES IS ANCIENT IN ITS ESSENCE. It is rooted in primitive concepts suggestive of those associated with the Neolithic people of Old Europe as depicted in symbols, rock paintings, and general iconography. The religion of Witchcraft also shares a commonality with the archaic beliefs and practices of many ancient cultures throughout continental Europe and the British Isles. This is because various elements of "classical Witchcraft" spread from the Aegean/Mediterranean regions up into northern Europe and Britain, and were modified by the indigenous beliefs and practices of the various cultures that assimilated them. Bishops and monks were sent from Rome into the British Isles (and elsewhere) taking with them the indigenous views of Witchcraft in southern Europe. They naturally applied this filter to what they observed relating to the Pagan and magickal practices in various regions of Europe. Therefore, to the bishops and monks, these practitioners were identified as "Witches" since they essentially fit the pattern. This identification established a model that eventually unified various facets of the Witchcraft persecution throughout all of Europe.

Witchcraft, as it evolved over the centuries, absorbed and integrated various elements of regional Paganism, folklore, and folk magick. In its modern practice and expression, Witchcraft is a blend of old and new, demonstrating its adaptivity through countless centuries. However, there are still traditions of Witchcraft that continue to practice the Old Ways with relatively few additional modifications. There are also traditions that practice primarily modern elements. The latter have been the primary focus of modern scholars.

The old traditions of Witchcraft vary from region to region due to the differences in cultural influences. Such influences introduce variants in folklore and folk magick concepts that impact peasant systems, as the earlier sects of Witchcraft were.

However, there are key essentials that appear in the Witches' religion regardless of the region in which it appears. This strongly suggests either a common origin or a widespread organization that kept in contact with the various sects of Witches throughout Europe. The latter seems unlikely in ancient times, and the former is the subject of this chapter.

In this chapter, we will examine the various concepts and beliefs found within modern Witchcraft, and look for the historical and literary references related to Witchcraft that indicate the existence of these concepts prior to both the nineteenth century and the time of Gerald Gardner. To accomplish this, we must look at the earliest references in Western literature that involve Witches and Witchcraft. As noted in the previous chapter, such writings originate from the Aegean/Mediterranean region. We will also look at the literature on Witches that appears in other regions of Europe, although they appear at a much later period.

Regarding this later period, I prefer to use as little of the Witchcraft trial material as possible because much of the "evidence" there is considered unreliable. Most of it was compiled from the accounts of individuals that were horribly tortured into providing the details of these accounts, and the components of the "testimony" were largely guided and directed by the torturer. However, I do give credence to statements made that do not conform to what the Inquisitors wanted to hear, such as the worship of a Goddess instead of the Devil. The insistence upon providing such non-conforming accounts despite the application of torture seems compelling as to its integrity.

I've found that when studying the writings that appear in secondary such works as the *Compendium Maleficarum* or the *Malleus Maleficarum*, we can discover many of the folk beliefs about Witches that were common to the era. By comparing some of these beliefs with what we know of ancient Paganism, we can discover traces of surviving themes. Once we isolate the surviving themes, we can then look for evidence of those individuals that actively kept alive and preserved such elements down through the centuries. I believe that there is a difference between how folklore and folk magick evolved among the common people compared to groups or families of Witches. The average person does not consciously set out to maintain folk traditions. They simply participate in them, enjoy them, and may even pass them on to others by example or oral instruction. But the average individual is not typically concerned with any modifications that might be made and do not guard against them. Therefore, the custom or practice can easily change over time. The Witch, by contrast, is typically devoted to retaining traditions intact.

The Witch is well aware that they are an outcast of society and were never assimilated into the culture in which they reside, not by personal desire nor by the desires of their neighbors. Instead, the Witch finds their identity in the things that separate them from the people and the culture that rejects the Witch. Therefore, the preservation of customs and practices (even those incongruent with popular culture) is essential to the Witch because it is the only safe and reliable world they know. In the meantime, the culture and the society in which they live proceed on without the Witch in tow. Leland noted in *Etruscan Roman Remains* (1892) that the Witches of Italy keep *"an immense number of legends of their own, which have nothing in common with the nursery or popular tales such as are collected and published."*

What we discover in the literature on Witchcraft from the late Middle Ages through to the late Renaissance period are accounts of the basic components and structures residing within modern Witchcraft. These references include such things as the ritual circle, elemental spirits, ritual nudity, ritual meals, magickal acts, and the presence of a male and a female entity worshipped or venerated by Witches. These components are not isolated to any one region of Europe. For example, according to Professor Eva Pocs (*Between the Living and the Dead*), there are thirty-six documented cases in which a "fate goddess" appears in Hungarian Witchcraft spanning three centuries of Witch trials. We find that in Italy, the worship of the goddess Diana periodically appears in trial transcripts dating from 1390-1647. According to historian Carlo Ginzburg (*Ecstasies*), in Germany, the goddess Diana appears in Witch trials and is called *Unholde*, or *"die selige Frawn [sic]"* (the beautiful woman). Other female deities show up in German Witch trials transcripts as well, such as *"Fraw Berthe [sic]"* and *"Fraw Helt [sic]."* From an Italian source, Ginzburg also supplies a drawing that appeared on a proclamation from the Inquisitor Camillo Campeggi (1564) which depicts the "goddess of night" approaching a Witch. Modern scholars dismiss the mention of goddesses in Witchcraft trial transcripts and Witchcraft literature as not being proof that Witches worshipped a goddess or that Witchcraft was ever a religion.

Pierre de Lancre, a French Witchfinder, wrote a description of the Basque Witches' sabbat in his *Tableau de l'inconstance des mauvais anges et démons*, published in 1612. Lancre states that a goat figure is seated on a chair; seated to his right is "the Queen of the Sabbat" and Witches come forward, kneeling, to present children before them. This is clearly an act of reverence towards the couple. The Witches then feast and dance in celebration before the seated couple, who do not participate in the celebrations themselves. This description excludes the figures from being viewed as "High Priest" and "High Priestess" images but is highly suggestive of the concept of a venerated God and Goddess in Witchcraft. A similar account appears in the Basque Witch trial of Maria Miguel, in 1595, who confessed to attending a sabbat where two figures sat on chairs. One figure was a man with a goat's head and the other was a female figure, which Maria commented was his spouse.

As we continue, we will explore the concepts of modern Witchcraft that scholars claim were invented or compiled during the nineteenth and twentieth centuries to form modern Witchcraft. Here, we will discover that each of these concepts pre-existed these periods and were written about in connection with Witches and Witchcraft many centuries earlier. Some of the material comes from Witch hunter writings and trial transcripts, some from ancient historians and poets, and others from various folklorists and commentators.

What is important is simply that these concepts existed long before the period modern scholars attribute to the appearance of such elements in association with Witches and Witchcraft. Therefore, the claim by modern scholars that Gerald Gardner and others created these concepts and formed them into what now constitutes modern Witchcraft is not supported by the earlier accounts.

In *Triumph of the Moon*, Hutton states that other than the writings of Apuleius, there is nothing to indicate that in ancient times there was a unified image of a major goddess associated with the Moon and with nature. Hutton essentially claims that what he calls the "atypical" image of Apuleius' Goddess became the template for modern Witchcraft's Goddess figure. However, even a brief examination of ancient literature reveals otherwise. One example appears in the writings of Catullus, who, in his *Hymn to Diana* (first century BCE), equates the goddess Diana with the primary Roman goddess Juno and mentions an association with the bounty of Nature: *"Diana whose name is Juno-Lucina...filling the farmer's rough-walled barn with fruit and produce, vegetables and grain."* Here we have an identification of Diana with an aspect of Juno (the Great Goddess), a connection to nature, and an association with the Moon through Diana. This theme is explored further in the following sections addressing the Moon Goddess, the Great Mother, and the Triple Goddess. Here, we will discover the deeper connection between Diana, Juno, and the chthonic Goddess.

Another example of a major goddess associated with the Moon and with nature is Hecate. In Hesiod's *Theogony*, Hecate is described as being the most honored by Zeus, who granted to her a portion of the earth, sea, and the starry heavens. Hesiod also states that Hecate grants abundance to fishermen, herdsmen, and farmers, which associates her with nature. The association of Hecate with the Moon and with Witchcraft is a long-standing tradition from classical times.

Let us now look at each of the so-called modern concepts appearing in the Craft today, and examine each topic separately in order to discover the earlier pre-existing accounts and references. Each section contains information supportive of the others, and I encourage the reader not to skim or skip around. The chronological order here is important in order to demonstrate the connective associations.

The Triple Goddess
and the Moon Goddess

In modern Witchcraft, the figure of the Triple Goddess is one of the most fundamental tenets. The Triple Goddess is viewed as one of the primary elements of the divine feminine principle and is divided into the personifications of Maiden, MOTHER, and Crone. Viewed in this way, the Goddess reflects the life-passages of women. The Triple Goddess is also associated with the Moon, reflecting the waxing, full, and waning portions.

Modern scholars point to the idea that Witches ever worshiped a triple-aspect Goddess as being a totally modern concept and invention. However, Jacob Rabinowitz, in his book *The Rotting Goddess*, recounts Lucan's ancient tale of a group of Witches, written in the first century BCE. In Lucan's work (Lucan, B.C. 6: 700-01), the Witches make the following comment: *"Persephone, who is the third and lowest aspect of our goddess Hecate…"* This, of course, portrays the concept of Witches having a triformis or three-fold goddess, and the notion appears almost two thousand years prior to Gerald Gardner's time. In Ovid's tale (Met. 7: 94-95) Jason swears an oath to the Witch Medea, saying he would *"be true by the sacred rites of the three-fold goddess."* Such writings clearly demonstrate that, contrary to scholarly opinion, the basic concept of a triformis goddess venerated in Witchcraft is not a modern construction, and pre-exists the Romantic era and the work of Gerald Gardner and his cohorts. Horace writes of Diana as a goddess upon whom Witches call, and Catullus wrote of the goddess Diana as a "threefold" goddess. Diana is identified with Hecate by a number of ancient sources.

Diana is one of the oldest goddesses associated with Witches in ancient literature. One example of this reference in ancient times appears in the first-century BCE writings known as the *Epodes* of Horace. In modern times, Diana is quite misunderstood and misassociated. Many people today isolate Diana and think of her strictly in terms of Dianic Wicca/Witchcraft, which is a singular tradition in the Craft today. However, the worship and the very nature of Diana extends well beyond this isolated view and we need only look into the past to view Diana from the understanding of those that worshiped her or wrote about her in ancient times.

The name *Diana* is derived from the Latin adjective *dius* ("luminous") and the neuter *dium*, which designates the "luminous sky." Cicero, in his *De Natura Deorum*, wrote that Diana was so named *"because at night she makes the day."* This links Diana to the light of the Moon. Catullus in his *Hymn to Diana* (first century BCE) wrote of Diana as:

> *"Diana whose name is Lucina, lightbringer, who every month restores the vanished Moon...threefold Diana, huntress, birth-helper, and Luna shining with borrowed light. Diana, in your monthly circle measuring out the turning year..."*

At some stage of their religious development, the Romans identified Diana with the Greek deity known as Artemis, which is where the image of Diana as the virgin huntress emerges. However, as early as the sixth century BCE, the worship of Diana at Lake Nemi in Italy included offerings to her to grant an easy childbirth. Artifacts discovered at the Nemi site include a large number of replicas of the phallus and the vulva. These are not the typical things we would expect to find in association with a goddess of virginity. The lake at Nemi was known as "Diana's mirror" because the Full Moon could be seen reflected upon the surface when viewed from the temple of Diana. This is another indication of Diana as a Moon goddess.

The Roman poet Horace mentions Diana in connection with Witchcraft in his first-century BCE writings. Horace lists Diana as one of three goddesses that Witches call upon in the night, and the other two goddesses are Hecate and Proserpina. As historian Jeffrey Russell (*A History of Witchcraft*) points out, Diana was also identified with the goddess Hecate, who was originally one of the Titans. The ancient writings of Varro bear this out, as he states that Diana is the "Trivian Titan" and is also called Trivia, of the three crossroads. Aeschylus equates Hecate with Artemis and associates her with watching over the childbed, which is reflective of the Roman beliefs connected to the cult of Diana at Nemi.

Sarah I. Johnson (*Hekate Soteira*) remarks that Hecate became linked to the Moon in the late classical and Hellenistic times. Virgil (first century BCE) in the *Aeneid*, equates Diana and Hecate: *"...triple Hekate, the three faces of the maiden Diana."* In the book *The Rotting Goddess*, by Jacob Rabinowitz, we find an excerpt from the ancient *Papyri Graecae Magicae,* which equates Hecate with Artemis, Persephone, and Selene. This incantation to Hecate reads, in part:

"Dart-shooter, Artemis, Persephone, Shooter of deer, night-shining/ triple-sounding, triple-voiced, triple-headed, Selene, triple-pointed, triple-faced, triple necked, and goddess of the triple ways…and you who oft frequent the triple way and rule the triple decades with three forms…"

Here we have Hecate identified with Selene the Moon goddess, Artemis a woodland goddess, and Persephone an Underworld goddess. This triple image suggests one goddess associated with the sky, earth, and the Underworld.

According to scholar Miranda Green (*Dictionary of Celtic Myth and Legend*), there is very little evidence for the veneration of the Moon among the Celts, whereas the cults of Sun and sky are well attested. However, there do exist several identifications of Celtic goddesses with Diana. Green lists Abnoba and Arduinna as two examples, and points to Flidais as another possibility. Green also notes that a "Celtic version of Diana" accompanies an image of the "Gaulish Hammer-god" at Mainz. Other examples of identification cited are the appearance of an image of Diana with the Celtic hunter Apollo-Cunomaglus at Nettleton Shrub and an image of Diana with a statue of a Celtic triple-horned bull. According to Green, some Celtic coins depicted images of bulls with "Moon-signs" between their horns.

Green notes that the iconographic evidence for "the Mothers cult" in Britain is scattered, sparse, and relatively poorly preserved, with the majority of evidence existing in those regions of Britain where the Romans held a strong military presence. An image of a triple Mother Goddess was discovered on a relief at Cirencester, and near London, Mother images with grapes and bread were uncovered. The largest finds of triple goddesses in Britain originate from the Dobunni tribe, which also produced Mother Goddess images. These included the image of dogs, which have long been associated with the Moon and the Underworld. Also featured among British goddesses was a vessel of regeneration and replenishment, which eventually took the form of a cauldron or bucket. The connection between the Moon and the Goddess in Celtic religion is explored further in the section on the Great Goddess.

THE GREAT GODDESS

In modern Witchcraft, there is a focus on the concept of a Great Mother Goddess. She is viewed as the giver and receiver of life, the spirit of the Earth itself. All goddesses issue forth from Her and are contained within Her. As a concept, the Great Mother is viewed by many modern Witches as being reflected in both Paleolithic and Neolithic art and iconography.

Most modern scholars reject the notion of a pre-historic Great Goddess/Great Mother figure that was worshipped by early humans. A few modern scholars, such as Marija Gimbutas, support the idea of a pre-historic Great Goddess cult. Wherever the truth may lie, we do know that at some point in history, humans acknowledged deities that are known as a Great Mother or Great Goddess figure. Such images must have at least evolved from a common root source, a central concept of what was important to our ancestors. It is unlikely that the idea of a Great Goddess or Great Mother was simply invented one day in a moment of inspiration within a world that had held no previous beliefs/associations regarding such an entity/concept.

One of the clearest and oldest indications of a historical "Great Goddess" figure in ancient times is the Etruscan goddess known as "Uni," whose name means *The One*. To the Etruscans, Uni was a Mother Goddess and consort of their primary god Tinia. In the book *Etruscan Civilization*, by Sybille Haynes (a specialist in Etruscology) we read of archaeological evidence from the Bronze Age concerning a sacred spot that later became Tarquinia. Haynes comments on proof of a "great female divinity" known as Uni, and associates her as a "Nature goddess" and "Mistress of the Animals." Her primitive worship appears to have focused on a natural cavity located in a rock that sat in the center of the early community. Haynes also notes that Uni was identified with Eileithyia, the goddess of birth, and with Juno. The identification of Uni with Juno is important to our understanding of the Witches' Goddess. This will become apparent as we examine the connection of an ancient concept known as *iunones* in this chapter section.

In the book *Phases in the Religion of Ancient Rome*, historian Cyril Bailey notes that the day of the New Moon was sacred to Juno, and he states there was clearly an association of the Moon with Juno, who in her connection with Jupiter had certain functions as a sky goddess.

Juno was also known *Juno Lucina,* the goddess of light and childbirth. In this aspect, she was said to bring the newborn baby into the light, a type of escort of the soul. It is no coincidence that women made offerings to the goddess Diana for easy childbirth.

Miranda Green states that a clay figurine discovered around Cologne depicts a Celtic Mother Goddess wearing a lunar amulet. Green also comments on an image of three Mothers wearing a crescent-shaped amulet, discovered in a shrine at Gripswald. The significance of this lunar connection to a Mother Goddess lies in the Roman concept of the *iunones,* which depicted three mothers sitting together caring for a baby. The concept of *iunones* evolved into its personification as *Iuno,* which is where the goddess name *Juno* derives. In *Symbol & Image in Celtic Religious Art* (Chapter Six), Green notes that the imagery of the Celtic concept of the Divine Mothers itself owes a great deal to Roman influence and that the "triple Mothers" originate from the *iunones* concept. As Green remarks, the triadic goddesses were widely worshipped in the Romano-Celtic world. An important connection is found in the cult of Dionysus, where an image of three nurses tend to the infant Dionysus. This is explored further in the section on the Horned God.

The *iunones* become the bridge that joins the Celtic and Aegean/Mediterranean triple goddesses together. Juno becomes the personification of the *iunones* concept into a "Great Goddess" and "Great Mother" that is also associated with the Moon and with nature. As we saw earlier in the section on the Moon Goddess, ancient writings link Juno with Diana, who in turn is linked to Hecate. Here again is the essential concept of Mother, Maiden, and Crone. The worship of Diana and Hecate by Witches is also noted in ancient writings. Before moving on, we must note that once Juno becomes fully established in the state religion of Rome, we lose most of her ancient lunar connections as they become altered and modified to fit the politics and agenda of the Empire. What we are concerned with in this chapter is the rural Pagan view, which retained the nature elements, and therefore our focus must remain on the more archaic forms.

Green notes that throughout Romano-Celtic Europe, the most common animal companion to the goddesses is the dog. The dog appears in such iconography in one of two major themes. The first theme is the "lap dog," in which the goddess nurses the dog. The second theme is the appearance of the dog at the side of the goddess. Green states that Mother Goddesses appear holding grain and fruit, with a dog at their feet. The Romano-Celtic association of the dog with the Underworld is also addressed by Green. The hound is associated with Diana and Hecate, and with the Celtic goddess Nehalennia.

Nehalennia is depicted in iconography with a dog and with fruit baskets, grain, and a cornucopia. She typically appears as a youthful goddess seated in a chair. Green notes that Nehalennia was a goddess of fertility concerned with the abundance of vegetation and crops. The goddess is sometimes shown with a pomegranate, which is a classic symbol of Proserpina, an Underworld goddess. Water symbolism is also associated with Nehalennia, and Green suggests a connection to sacred springs and wells. Like the goddess Proserpina (an aspect of Diana/Hecate), Nehalennia is further associated with the sea and with journeys. A statue of Nehalennia at Dormburg shows the goddess wearing a solar amulet, and another statue at Colijnsplaat depicts her with a lunar motif. Green speculates that this may be indicative of a cosmic nature attributed to Nehalennia, in which case this goddess would be a Great Goddess figure associated with both nature and the Moon as we saw earlier in her iconography.

THE HORNED GOD

In modern Witchcraft, the primary God figure is viewed as the Horned Lord of the Animals. He represents the primal fertilizing force, the energy that serves as a catalyst to the Goddess whose vessel forms and generates new life. In the evolution of the Horned God, He becomes the Harvest Lord, the seed which must fall in order for new life to be generated. Like the stag that often symbolizes Him, the Horned God is also seen as the protector of His herd.

The widespread Pagan worship of horned gods is well documented and therefore, we have little need to try and argue that Witches would have worshiped them as well. To exclude pre-Christian Witches from having embraced the basic elements of Pagan religion in European culture would be a difficult position to defend. There are several horned gods, all sharing a connection, that are associated with primary themes residing in Witchcraft. The main deities are Dionysus, Pan, and Faunus. Of these three gods, it is Dionysus that is the bridge to Witchcraft that stretches across the Aegean/Mediterranean regions and into the Celtic lands. Dionysus is the only horned god (in any European region) whose nature can be documented by historical and literary evidence that demonstrates he contains each and every facet of the concepts attributed to the Horned God in modern Witchcraft. We shall discover in this section that ancient writings reveal Dionysus is born on the winter solstice, dies in the fall season as a harvest lord figure, dwells in the Underworld, is renewed, appears in seasonal rituals, has a female goddess consort with lunar and Underworld aspects, is a Green Man figure, and is a fertility god associated with horned animals such as the bull, goat, and stag.

In understanding the Horned God, we will also explore the horned Celtic deities, which absorbed various aspects of Romanized concepts during the almost four hundred years of the Roman occupation of Celtic lands. Naturally, such a long-term cultural influence would have a tremendous impact on indigenous beliefs over the passing centuries. One example appears in the surviving inscriptions associated with various Celtic deity statues and reliefs, which bear Romanized names and titles. The blending of indigenous Celtic beliefs with Romanized concepts created a Mystery tradition whose essence is now a vital part of modern Witchcraft as it relates to the British Isles.

In *Dionysus, Myth and Cult*, scholar Walter Otto recounts the ancient references to Dionysus appearing with the horns of a bull and in the guise of a stag. According to Otto, both Plutarch and Athenaeus bore witness to the fact that Dionysus was depicted with horns. Carl Kerenyi (*Dionysos*) mentions an ancient painting of a nude Dionysus with horns but does not tell us what kind of horns they were. Rather than a bull, the horns may have been goat horns, as Dionysus was also called *Eriphos*, which means "kid" (goat). Kerenyi notes *"two objects pertaining to the historical Dionysos cult, the goat and the mask,"* as appearing on a stone seal near Phaistos.

For over ten centuries, traces of a horned entity associated with Witchcraft appears in Christian Europe. One of the earliest identifications of the Horned God with the Judeo-Christian Devil figure is found in the records of the Council of Toledo, circa 447. Here, the Devil is described as a large black monstrous apparition with horns on his head, cloven hoofs, and an immense phallus. During the sixteenth and seventeenth centuries, those accused of Witchcraft in England and Scotland "confessed" to seeing the Devil in the form of a bull. Perhaps we are seeing a surviving element of a Dionysian component here in the bull figure or even a Mithraic factor. The woodcut images that appear in connection with Witchcraft over the centuries most often portray the Devil with the horns of a goat, which would rule out Mithras but would still include an aspect of Dionysus.

Kerenyi discusses an archaic form of Ariadne, the consort of Dionysus in classical mythology, and identifies her with Erigone. Her name means "she who was born at dawn" and may refer to "the Beginning" itself. Ariadne is also identified with Hera, who was known as *Juno* among the Romans. It is interesting to note that the name "Juno" is related to the Latin form *iunix*, indicating a cow (heifer), and that Dionysus was often portrayed as a bull. In this wedded image, we find an interweaving here with those concepts we explored in the section on the Great Goddess. A compelling link then appears between the worship of Dionysus, the triple Mother (and child-nurse) images of the *iunones* concept, and the deity images of the Witches' religion. These and other patterns repeat themselves many times in the ancient concepts of Witchcraft that also appear later in the modern sect.

Kerenyi writes of Ariadne that *"she must have been an aspect of the Great Goddess of Brauron who, under the name 'Artemis' was the Moon Goddess."* In the earliest designation of Erigone in myth or legend, she appears as Aletis. Aletis is known as "she who wanders about," and in her myth, she is accompanied by a dog. The epithet of "she who wanders about" sounds very much like a metaphor for the monthly journey of the Moon, and the companion hound reminds us of the goddess Diana. In Kerenyi's depiction of Erigone, it is not difficult to find a connection between Dionysus and the basic foundation of the concept/image of the Witches' Goddess. It is worthy of notation that Ariadne herself (even though in a later form) was known as "the mistress of the labyrinth." This is suggestive of a connection with spirals, which are associated with Neolithic tombs and goddesses of death and renewal.

In his book *Dionysos*, Kerenyi portrays Ariadne as having a dark aspect and suggests parallels that identify her with the *"dark crow virgin"* goddess Koronis and with *"Persephone, the queen of the underworld.*" Kerenyi describes coins from the fifth century BCE that depict Ariadne with lunar symbolism. One coin features the face of Ariadne on one side, and on the other side appears a labyrinth with a star in its center. The labyrinth is flanked by a waxing crescent Moon and a waning crescent Moon. In one of her myths, Ariadne is pregnant at the time of her death and (as Kerenyi basically puts it) her child is therefore born in the Underworld. In another myth, Ariadne dies and is buried with her unborn child still in her womb. Kerenyi states that here Ariadne *"carried her child with her into the underworld"* and *"it may be supposed that she gave birth in the underworld."* This basic concept is one of the fundamental aspects of the mythos in modern Witchcraft but is an ancient theme and not a modern construction.

In the writings of Athenagoras, an archaic myth is told wherein Persephone is impregnated by a god in the form of a large serpent, and she later gives birth to Dionysus. In the rites of Eleusis, the birth of a mysterious child from the Queen of the Underworld was essential. Kerenyi notes that the bull later replaced the serpent in this mythology, for in ancient times, the two were said to beget one another. The serpent was often symbolized by entwined vines of ivy, and Dionysus as the bull god wore a wreath of ivy on his head. The serpent is, among other things, symbolic of the impregnating seed, and is a symbol associated with Proserpina/Persephone. The initiates of the Mystery Cult at Eleusis drank a brew of roasted barley groats mixed with water and the tender leaves of some undisclosed plant belonging to the pennyroyal species. James Frazer notes in *The Golden Bough* that in ancient times, the spirit of the harvest was said to take the form of a bull, and whoever gave the last stroke at threshing was called the "barley-cow."

In the Roman Mystery Cult of Dionysus (where he was also known as *Bacchus*), the Mysteries of the cult at Eleusis were absorbed by the Romans. The rites at Eleusis were constructed around the descent and ascent of the Goddess, the solstice and equinox seasons, and the god Dionysus. Manly Hall, in his book *The Secret Teachings of All Ages*, notes that these Mysteries spread to Rome and Britain where initiations were later performed in both regions. This would help explain many of the similar components that exist in the Witchcraft traditions of northern and southern Europe. It is also interesting to note Hall's reference to the *Essay on the Mysteries of Eleusis* by M. Ouvaroff, in which we find passages from the ancient philosopher Porphyry, who reveals that the symbols of the Greek and Roman Eleusinian Mysteries included the circle, triangle, and cone which all appear in modern Witchcraft as well.

In modern Witchcraft, the Celtic god Cernunnos often appears as the god of the Witches. In the book *Witches*, by T.C. Lethbridge, the author identifies Cernunnos with the horned consort of the goddess Diana. Lethbridge suggests that the torcs held by Cernunnos in Celtic iconography are signs of his lunar connection to the Goddess of the Moon. Scholars point to the earliest depiction of Cernunnos appearing in a fourth-century BCE cave drawing at Camonica Valley in northern Italy. Here again, we have the southern and northern European connection. In my book *Wiccan Mysteries*, the Italic origins and their influence upon Celtic religion are explored further.

Cernunnos most frequently appears as a stag-horned god but is also often shown with a bull. Some examples include the images discovered at Nuits-Saint-Georges in Burgundy, Reims, and Saintes. The triple-horned bull image appears in Gaul and Britain and was associated with shrines. Dionysus was associated with a triplism and appears in the Orphic Hymn Book under the name *Trigonos*. The festival cycles in the Cult of Dionysus were known as the *trieteris*, two main annual festivals highlighted by the cyclical introduction of a third festival.

The ancient historian Strabo mentions the veneration of Dionysus among the Celts and describes a specific sect of Celtic women that live on an island. The description of their cult is very similar to that of the Maenads who were female followers of Dionysus in ancient Greece legends.

In *The Witches' God*, the Farrars suggest that Cernunnos survived in British folklore under the name Herne. The Herne figure is associated with Windsor Great Park and is said to appear in times of national crisis. Herne is associated with the Wild Hunt, a popular theme in Celtic and Germanic lore, and one that appears in Witchcraft trial transcripts. If Herne and Cernunnos are one and the same, then a case can be made linking Witches with Cernunnos. The Wild Hunt was essentially a procession of spirits or ghosts that roamed the

countryside and is mentioned by Regino of Prum in regard to the
night revels of the fellowship of Diana (*Canon Episcopi*). Historian
Jeffrey Russell mentions Herne in connection with the Wild Hunt
and states that his name links him to *"brightness and the cult of the
Moon."* The earliest reference to the Wild Hunt in a Witchcraft trial
appears in the transcripts concerning a woman named Sibillia. She
was tried in 1384 by the secular court in Milan.

The association of the Horned God with plant life appears in
abundant images throughout all of Europe. In the imagery of Old
Europe, it is perhaps best reflected in the various depictions of
Dionysus. He appears as a bearded man with a crown of ivy or an
effeminate youth wearing a fawn skin and crowned with a wreath
of laurel and ivy. Dionysus is also sometimes depicted with panther
skin or a black robe. In later periods, Dionysus is portrayed with
long curly hair, crowned with vine leaves and grapes. He holds a
thyrsus (a thick fennel staff mounted with a pinecone) in one hand
and a chalice cup in the other.

The thyrsus wand is a composite symbol of plant and seed representing the union of his forest nature (pinecone) merged with his
agricultural nature (fennel). The chalice held by Dionysus represents
the womb of the Great Mother from which he issued forth (for he
is the Divine Child of European mythology, also known as the *Child
of Promise*). The extended chalice is also symbolic of the offering up
of his own divine nature, for it contains his liquid essence, which is
sacrificed. Therefore, Dionysus stands bearing the symbolism of the
ancient Lord of the Harvest, the Slain God.

It is interesting to note that the earliest known Celtic image of
the Green Man comes from the fifth century BCE and is pictured in
the book *The Green Man: The Archetype of our Oneness with the Earth*
by William Anderson. This image, now called the St. Goar pillar, is a
blend of the earlier Etruscan art style with that of the Celtic La Tène
culture, as noted by the author. In his book, Anderson attempts to
link Cernunnos to the Green Man image and seems to believe that
Dionysus and Cernunnos are "cousins" derived from an earlier deity
who was the son/lover of the Goddess.

The Green Man image as envisioned within an Agricultural Mystery tradition is always associated with the essence of intoxication

(whether spiritual or physical). Sometimes it is in the use of hallucinogenic plants such as mushrooms, believed by many to have
been employed by early shamans and also by the European Witch
Cult. More commonly, the intoxication lies in the use of grapes
and grains for the production of wine and beer. The intoxicating
essence is symbolic of the transforming nature of the quintessence
that resides in the indwelling spirit or "god-nature" of the plant. To
consume the nature of the Harvest Lord is to become one with his
spirit. This is the basis of the Rite of Communion found in many
religions, old and new.

In addition to the Agricultural Mystery teaching of the indwelling essence, we find the teaching of transformation itself. The
earliest God forms are associated with the rising and dying of vegetation. All of the tenets of belief connected with reincarnation and
transmigration are to be found in the cycles of the plant kingdom.
The seasons of the earth, ever returning in the Wheel of the Year,
are but amplifiers and signalers of the mystical powers of nature at
work in the fields and forests. To link oneself to the mythos of the
dying and returning god is to assure oneself of "salvation" from the
forces of death and annihilation. This was the essential premise of
the Dionysian cult, the Eleusinian Mysteries, and even Christianity.
Plutarch consoled his wife in a letter written in response to the
death of their daughter, assuring her of the immortality to be found
in the Dionysian Mysteries.

The transformation Mysteries of agrarian culture also appear in the
Celtic tale of Taliesin, circa 500 CE. In this tale, the character known
as Gwion accidentally receives enlightenment from three drops of
magickal elixir brewed in a cauldron by the goddess Cerridwen.
Gwion flees in fear of reprisal and is pursued by Cerridwen. During
the chase, Gwion is magickally transformed into various creatures in
order to aid his escape. Cerridwen responds each time and changes
herself into that which preys upon each form taken on by Gwion.
Finally, Gwion becomes a grain and is swallowed by Cerridwen in the
form of a bird. This grain impregnates her and she later gives birth to
the bard Taliesin.

The mystical theme of transformation associated with agriculture
is found in many European folktales. Gimbutas tells us that the

essential mythos of the Harvest Lord is preserved in texts dating from the era of Homer and Hesiod up into the periods that generated modern folklore. The mystical agricultural theme is well-reflected in the story of the passion of the flax and the dying God. In ancient Greece, he was *Linos*, in Lithuania, he was *Vaizgantas*, and in Scotland, he was known as *Barleycorn*. It is noteworthy that the common word for *flax* in European languages unites Old Europe with Celtic Europe. In Greek, it is *linon*, in Latin *linum*, and the Old Irish is *lin*, which is also true of Old German.

Tales that contain the Mystery teaching address the planting of the seed and its struggle to sprout from the earth. This is followed by the plant having to endure the elements. Then in its prime, the plant is pulled out of the ground and its parts are subjected to thrashing, soaking, and roasting. Eventually, it is combed with hackle combs and thorns, spun into thread, and woven into linen. Finally, it is cut and pierced with needles, and sewn into a shirt. Here indeed we find the sacrifice of the Harvest Lord for the welfare of his people.

In the classical Greek myth of Dionysus, he is first slain and then dismembered. Next, Dionysus is boiled, roasted, and then devoured. The Orphic myth of Dionysus includes the same sequence but adds the recomposition and resurrection of the bones. The ancient Greek philosopher Heraclitus (fifth century BCE) states that Dionysus and Hades are one and the same. Here, we find an association of Dionysus with the Underworld (a classic mythos in modern Witchcraft related to the Lord of the Shadows). Further evidence of this connection is provided in a tale about the labyrinth of the Minotaur (and Dionysus and Ariadne) from the book *Ecstasies: Deciphering the Witches' Sabbath*, by Carlo Ginzburg:

"...*That the Labyrinth symbolized the realm of the dead and that Ariadne, mistress of the Labyrinth, was a funerary goddess, are more than probable conjectures. In Athens the marriage of Dionysus and Ariadne was celebrated every year on the second day of the Anthesteria: an ancient springtime festival that coincided with the periodic return to the earth of the souls of the dead, ambiguous harbingers of well-being and harmful influences, who were placated with offerings of water and boiled cereals.*"

THE SABBAT

In modern Witchcraft, there exists a set of ritual celebrations or feast days. This is often imagined as the Wheel of the Year, a design of eight festivals depicted as the eight spokes of a wheel. The festivals mark the time of the solstices and equinoxes and the periods that fall directly between each one. In addition to the Full Moon and New Moon celebrations, the sabbats are times when Witches gather to venerate the forces of nature.

Tales of the Witches' grand gatherings are centuries old and appear in many different regions throughout Europe, where they have remained firmly rooted in the local folklore beliefs of countless generations. However, most scholars reject the notion that the Witches' sabbat ever took place in any form prior to modern times, believing instead that the tales were either contrived by the Inquisitors or originated from some form of psychological hysteria. Historian Carlo Ginzburg (*Ecstasies*) suggests that the wild accounts of the Witches' sabbats may be due to hallucinations produced by the ingesting of the fungus known as *Claviceps purpurea*. This fungus was known to have grown on rye and survived the process of making flour, where it produced ergot poisoning. Ginzburg points out that certain species of *Claviceps purpurea* contain an alkaloid (ergonovine) from which the drug LSD (lysergic acid diethylamide) was synthesized in 1943. He also notes the ancient use of a mushroom called *Amanita muscaria* that was employed to attain an ecstatic condition, as well as another substance called *bufotenine*. Bufotenine is a psychotropic substance found in the skin secretions of toads, a creature long associated with Witches and Witchcraft.

Historian Jeffrey Russell states that the ancient festivals of Dionysus became a blueprint for the rites allegedly practiced by medieval Witches. As noted earlier, Witch trial transcripts from the sixteenth and seventeenth centuries contain accounts of the "Devil" in the form of a bull. Doreen Valiente (*An ABC of Witchcraft*) wrote that the origin of the word *sabbat* originated from the shout *"sabazius"* which was a featured element in the ancient rites of Dionysus. In the *Orphic Hymn Book*, the god Sabazios is identified with Dionysus, and in the fifth century BCE, the cult of Sabazios was accepted in the city of Athens. Here we are told expressly that the Mysteries of

Sabazios were the same as the Mysteries of Dionysus. In the cult of Dionysus, the festival known as the *Lenaia* was held every year to honor the birth of Dionysus. The women belonging to the cult of Dionysus were called *Lenai* and were believed to take part in lustful rites. It is interesting to note that among the Greeks and Romans, the sex worker Witch was known as a *lena*, the Witch bawd ("Imagining Greek and Roman Magic").

The earliest formal reference to the Witches' sabbat appears in the trial records from Toulouse and Carassone, circa 1335. One example is the trial of Anne Marie de Georgel, who "confessed" to having attended the sabbat and having sexual intercourse with a figure that appeared as a black goat. As noted earlier, the black goat appears as the Witches' God figure in the 1612 account by Pierre de Lancre, the French Witchfinder, and in the Basque Witch trial of Maria Miguel in 1595. In the book *The Witches' God*, by Janet and Stewart Farrar, we read that the goat god Akerbeltz was invoked by Basque Witches during their sabbats, which were called *Akelarre/Aquelarre* (field of the he-goat). In 1608, Francesco Guazzo wrote, in his *Compendium Maleficarum*, of an Italian Witch who led a woman into a field on the night of St. John the Baptist, and *"traced a circle on the ground with a beech twig, muttering some words from a black book."* Next, there appeared two women with a black goat and a man vested as a priest. Between the horns of the goat burned a black candle.

Ginzburg (*Ecstasies*) suggested that the sabbat elements appearing in various texts and transcripts were reflective of a distinct set of archaic folk beliefs, covered over with an "Inquisitorial veneer." Ginzburg's theory recognizes the "Otherworld" themes related to traveling in spirit form, the land of the dead, and other pre-Christian European beliefs as being the foundation for the commonality of various aspects of Witchcraft as they appear in trial material. Naturally, it would only make sense that if an ancient Witches' religion survived into the Christian era, it would reflect the earlier influence of common European Pagan themes.

The depiction of the classical Witches' sabbat does indeed contain several key elements of European Pagan concepts. It is an evolutionary blend of the sophisticated elements of the cult of Dionysus with archaic forms of European Paganism mixed with the primitive aspects of peasant folk practices. It is rooted in ancestor worship, fairy lore, and "otherworld" exploration, much of which is connected to Neolithic concepts. Central to the theme is communication with the spirit world, the presence of a Queen of the Dead, the feast of the dead, the courting of goodwill from the ancestral spirits, and some form of transformation. The practice of offering food to the spirits of the dead appears in the late October and early November festivals of various regions of Europe. The custom of Halloween in America is a related celebration, although it has been reduced to a fun folk practice lacking the religious elements of its roots. Feasting with the spirits of the dead is an ancient practice, noted in such traditions as Samhain, and is reflected in woodcut images of Witches feasting with supernatural beings. The Inquisitors altered the spirits of the dead, transforming them into devils (a replacement image of the Otherworld or supernatural figure) as reflected in the early woodcut images of the Witches' sabbat. Eva Pocs (*Between the Living and the Dead*) points out that the night goddess of the dead appears as Diana and Hecate, the Germanic Holda and Perchta, the Celtic Matre and Matronae, and so forth.

CAKES AND WINE

The ritual use of cakes and wine appears in many modern Craft traditions as a sacred ritual meal, and both are featured in the ancient rites of Dionysus. The inclusion of a sacred meal within a ritual is an extremely ancient theme. From days of antiquity, cake and bread were baked in various shapes for ritual purposes. The most common shapes included flowers, snakes, birds, and the typical loaf we know today. The bread oven featured prominently in Old European shrines. Bread ovens made in the likeness of a pregnant belly have been found as early as 5000 BCE. Some anthropologists, such as Marija Gimbutas, point to the bread oven itself as a prehistoric symbol for the incarnation of the Grain Mother.

Ritual feasts during the Witches' sabbat are a theme found in the records of the Inquisition and also appear in many old woodcut illustrations. According to scholar Robin Briggs (*Witches & Neighbors*), a woman named Jeanne Le Schrempt (accused of Witchcraft in 1613) reported that during the sabbat, some Witches drank from silver cups. The inclusion of a silver cup or chalice also appears in modern Witchcraft. In 1899, folklorist Charles Leland wrote of the "Witches' supper" held during the sabbat in his book *Aradia: Gospel of the Witches*. Leland's material depicted Witches making cakes of meal, wine, salt, and honey, which they formed into the shape of a crescent Moon. The cakes were then blessed in the name of the goddess Diana.

The consuming of cakes and wine in a religious context is often associated with a ceremony intended to create a union between worshipper and deity. The cake represents the body of any given deity and the wine symbolizes the blood. To consume the body and blood is to become one with the essence of the divine. In many traditions of Wicca/Witchcraft, this ceremony incorporates the mythos of the Slain God or Harvest Lord.

According to Kerenyi, the opening of the vessel of wine at the winter solstice signified the birth of Dionysus. In the ancient mind, intoxication was caused by the actions of a spirit that dwelled in plants, herbs, grapes, etc. Ingesting a plant or plant product allowed the spirit to directly enter a person. Therefore, the opening of the vessel containing wine released the spirit of the grapevine back into the world. Drinking the wine connected the spirit of the deity to the spirit of the person celebrating the ritual.

The ritual use of cake also appears in the rituals of Dionysus. Like the wine, the cake also possessed the indwelling spirit of the grain. Kerenyi suggests that the poppies may have been one of the ingredients. He describes a certain ancient Goddess statue depicting her wearing a headdress of poppies. The poppies show clear indications of incisions. Kerenyi states that in order to obtain opium from poppies, such exact incisions must be made. Kerenyi also comments on the decline of opium use in the Mystery Cults due to diminished cultivation, and we might look to Ginzburg's theory of ergot mold as a viable alternative.

In any case, what is essential is the ancient concept that it was the indwelling spirit that intoxicated an individual, and not the substance itself. Fermentation was the Child of Promise awaiting birth.

THE CHILD OF PROMISE

In modern Witchcraft, the figure of the Child of Promise is born at the winter solstice and is equated with the rebirth of the Sun God. He is also known as the Divine Child, the newborn Sun God of the new year. Rituals in honor of the Divine Child are well attested as early as the ancient Greek period of Crete. A bronze shield from this period, carried in cult dances honoring the Divine Child, bears the image of the "lord of the wild beasts."

In his book, *Dionysos*, Kerenyi presents the image of a "bull child" names Zagreus, born from the womb of Persephone, who was known in the Roman Mysteries as Proserpina. In Crete, Dionysus was known as both Zagreus and Chthonios. In ancient Greek, the word *zagreus* meant "catcher of the game" and indicated one who caught animals alive, as in a pit (*zagre*). Kerenyi states that *zagreus* has as its root the word <u>zoe</u>, which means "life." The word *chthonios* means "subterranean," and is associated with death.

As the "Great Hunter," Zagreus is the God figure of the hunter society. Historically, members of hunter groups typically identify themselves on certain occasions with the beasts of prey. Kerenyi states that their feast days must be regarded as realizations of the hunter's "aggressive" and "murderous" life. The covenant between the hunter and the hunted appears in all primitive hunter societies. This includes the eating of the raw heart (or some other organ) taken directly from the freshly slain animal. However, the essence of the pact is the promise of renewed life. The hunter eats the heart of the animal and wears its pelt and horns in annual ceremonies. Thus, does the animal live on forever.

Kerenyi states that a transformation took place in which the god of the hunt was recognized in the prey. In this is an archaic form of a later mystical theme wherein "God becomes man/flesh." The body and blood of the animal evolve into the body and blood of the God. With the rise of agrarian societies, the animal spirit was transferred into the crops. In turn, the body became the grain and the blood became wine. The gods of the forest then became the gods of the furrow.

In the myth of Zagreus, Demeter gives herself to Zagreus on a "thrice-plowed field." In an epic poem from the sixth century BCE (Alkmeonis), the writer speaks of the union of Gaea and Zagreus:

"Mistress earth and Zagreus who art above all other gods." Kerenyi remarks that the writer must have regarded Zagreus *"as the supreme god of heaven, the counterpart of Mother Earth."*

Robert Graves, in his book *The White Goddess,* wrote of the consort of the Goddess and Her son. Graves portrayed the son as a twin figure, the God of the Waxing Year and the God of the Waning Year. There is a relationship here between the Divine Child of Old Europe and the Divine Child of the Eleusinian Mysteries, which is the root source of the Child of Promise in modern Witchcraft. The mythos of the Divine Child is, of course, rooted in archaic beliefs associated with Dionysus, and according to Gimbutas, can be traced back to Neolithic times.

In *The Goddesses and Gods of Old Europe,* Gimbutas states that the "Year-God" cycle begins with the birth of the Divine Child. The child is nursed by a masked goddess in the form of a bear, snake, or bird. Gimbutas says that the Divine Child represents the awakening or rebirth of the spirit of vegetation. Gimbutas also notes that in mythology, the Divine Child is reared by Artemis, Demeter, or Athena. This, in turn, brings us back to Dionysus.

According to Gimbutas, Dionysus is a pre-Indo-European god of great antiquity, his archaic origins reflected in the bull iconography of Neolithic times. Gimbutas equates Dionysus with the "Year God" who is concerned with the renewal of winter and spring. The agricultural themes, cult fertility symbols, and the marriage of the Horned God to a "queen" figure associated with the worship of Dionysus is also explored by Gimbutas in her book *The Goddesses and Gods of Old Europe.* Here, we find references to a man wearing horns and an animal hide who engages in sexual intercourse with a woman to complete the wedding ceremony. This is suggestive of the "Great Rite" that appears in the older systems of modern Witchcraft/Wicca.

The Year God represents the male-stimulating principle in nature that is the catalyst to growth. His primary symbol is the phallus. Gimbutas describes "wine cups" with phallus stems found by the "hundreds" in the settlements of Danilo, Butmir, and Vinca, which date from the sixth century BCE. Here, we are reminded of the birth of Dionysus being symbolized by the opening of a wine vessel at the winter solstice.

DRAWING DOWN THE MOON

The rite known as "Drawing Down the Moon" is referred to in ancient times and also appears in modern Witchcraft. One of the earliest references comes from the Greek writer Aristophanes (circa 423 BCE) who speaks of Witches that can *"Draw Down the Moon."* The use of a mirror in ancient magick to direct moonlight into a wooden box is a fairly well-known concept dating back to ancient Greece. The Roman poet Horace (30 BCE) writes of Witches that use a "book of incantations" (*Libros carminum*) through which the Moon may be *"called down"* from the sky. Here we see the survival of this theme spanning over 400 years in the Aegean/Mediterranean literature.

A reference to the belief that Witches can Draw Down the Moon also appears much later in a book titled *The Discoverie of Witchcraft* (1584) by Reginald Scot. In Chapter Nine of Book Five, Scot writes of a belief that local English Witches are said to have the power to *"pull down the Moon out of heaven."* In the book *Spellcasters*, by Pauline Bartel, there appears an interesting illustration dating from 1693, which shows a Witches' sabbat being held beneath a Full Moon flanked by a waxing crescent on one side and a waning crescent on the other. This specific image of Moon worship or symbolism also appears in modern Witchcraft.

The writings of the ancient Roman poet Horace give us perhaps the earliest accounts of Italian Witches and their connection to a lunar cult. In the *Epodes* of Horace, written around 30 BCE, he tells the tale of an Italian Witch named Canidia. Horace says that Proserpine and Diana grant power to Witches who worship them, and that Witches gather in secret to perform the Mysteries associated with their worship. Other ancient Roman writers, such as Lucan and Ovid, produced works that clearly support the same theme, demonstrating that such concepts were common to the era.

In Charles Leland's *Aradia: Gospel of the Witches* (1899) we also find a reference to Italian Witches gathering for lunar rites:

"Whenever ye have need of anything, once in the month and when the moon is full, ye shall assemble in some secret place, or in

a forest all together join to adore the potent spirit of your queen, my mother, great Diana. She who fain would learn all sorcery yet has not won its deepest secrets, them my mother will teach her, in truth all things as yet unknown. And ye shall be freed from slavery, and so ye shall be free in everything; and as a sign that ye are truly free, ye shall be naked in your rites, both men and women also..."

THE BOOK OF SHADOWS

In modern Witchcraft, the Book of Shadows is a personal book in which rituals, spells, symbols, special thoughts, and other things are recorded. Each Witch keeps their own personal book. Traditionally, the book has a black cover with parchment pages and is handwritten with a quill pen and dipping ink. However, many modern Witches simply use a journal book, record book, or even a special notebook and write with a ballpoint pen.

To some modern scholars, such as Ronald Hutton, the inclusion in the Gardnerian Book of Shadows of symbols, and other material, found in the earlier *Key of Solomon* is "evidence" of its contemporary nature. However, in the *Journal of Social History*, volume 28, 1995, an article by Sally Scully (Department of History at San Francisco University) seems to indicate otherwise. Scully presents trial transcripts from the case of Laura Malipero. In 1654, the Inquisitors retrieved from her home "several crudely written spell books" along with a copy of the *Key of Solomon*. The transcripts indicate that handwritten copies were being made. If we accept the inclusion of Italian Witchcraft material in Gardnerian Wicca, it is easy to clear up the issue of the appearance of the Key of Solomon material. In any case, the mention of a handwritten book kept by Witches is documented in the trial transcripts over three centuries prior to the writings of Gerald Gardner. Supportive of the Italian origins is the material found in the *Compendium Maleficarum*, a seventeenth-century Italian Witch hunter's guide written by Francesco Guazzo. Guazzo notes that *"Witches use a black book from which they read during their religious rites."*

RITUAL CIRCLE, ELEMENTALS, FOUR QUARTERS, AND THE WATCHERS

In modern Witchcraft, rituals and works of magick are performed in a large circle marked upon the ground in some fashion. The circle is set up with an alignment to the North, East, South, and West quarters. The elemental spirits of Earth, Air, Fire, and Water are evoked to bring creative energy to the ritual setting. Guardians of the four quarters are evoked to protect and observe the proceedings. The God and Goddess are also evoked and venerated through the ritual ceremony.

In the revised version of Leland's *Aradia: Gospel of the Witches* (Pazzaglini, 1998), Chas Clifton (a contributing author) remarks on a reported comment made by Aidan Kelly in his book *Crafting the Art of Magic*, which Clifton himself supports. Kelly is quoted as essentially having said that if a Witch casts a circle and invokes the four-quarter Guardians followed by an invocation of the gods, then such a Witch is basically a "Gardnerian" in the broadest sense. This view not only discounts the commonality of human expression and the human experience in general but also dismisses the pre-existing concepts that appear in earlier writings on Witchcraft.

In Book One, Chapter Eighteen of the *Compendium Maleficarum* by Francesco Guazzo (1609), we read that Witches work with spirits of certain specific natures. Guazzo lists these as *fiery, aerial, terrestrial, and water*. Here, of course, are the elemental creatures also related to modern Wiccan beliefs. A woodcut illustration in the book depicts Witches gathered in a circle drawn upon the ground. Guazzo states that Witches used beech twigs to trace their ritual circles. Empedocles (a student of the teachings of Pythagoras) was historically the first person known to have taught the concept of the four elements as a single cohesive doctrine. He lived around 475 BCE in his native homeland of Sicily where he presented the teachings concerning the four elements as the fourfold root of all things (*Ancient Philosophy, Mystery, and Magic: Empedocles and the Pythagorean Tradition* by Peter Kingsley).

Modern scholars believe that the concept of the "Lords of the Watchtowers" or "Watchers of the Four Quarters" in contemporary

Witchcraft was borrowed from the much earlier Enochian material attributed to John Dee. However, the concept of quarter Guardians and towers dates back to archaic Roman religion and may well be Etruscan in origin. In early Roman religion, the guardian spirit was known as the *Lare*. Prior to evolving into household spirits, the *Lare* protected demarcated plots of farmland, sectioned into squares. In the book *Archaic Roman Religion*, historian Georges Dumezil comments that an altar was set in front of small towers, and offerings were given to the *Lare*. Dumezil also notes that the *Lare* were originally worshipped at the crossroads. This associates them with Hecate and with classical Witchcraft.

In the book *The Lure of the Heavens*, author Donald Papon comments on a work titled *Of Things Occult and Manifest (The Book of Intelligences)* written in 1385 by Antonius de Monte Ulmi. Papon reports the text as presenting *"four chief orders of intelligences or spirits for the four points of the compass."* Papon recounts that this order operates under "celestial influences." In *The Cults of the Roman Empire*, historian Robert Turcan describes a Mithraic panel depicting the personified winds in Roman religion (Eurus, Boreas, Notus, and Zephyrus) occupying the four corners, and being encircled by the stars. In Roman religion, the four winds were associated with the North, East, South, and West.

The term "Watchers" associated with the four quarters appears in ancient writings. In the early stellar cults of Mesopotamia, there were four "royal" stars called the Watchers. Each one of these stars "ruled" over one of the four fixed points common to astrology. The star Aldebaran, when it marked the vernal equinox, held the position of Watcher of the East. Regulus, marking the summer solstice, was Watcher of the South. Antares, marking the autumn equinox, was Watcher of the West. Fomalhaut, marking the winter solstice, was Watcher of the North.

Most modern traditions regard the watchers as an elder race of some type. In Leland's *Aradia: Gospel of the Witches*, we read a reference to an elder race:

"… Then Diana went to the Fathers of the Beginning, to the Mothers, the Spirits who were before the first spirit, and lamented unto

them that she could not prevail with Dianus. And they praised her
for her courage; they told her that to rise she must fall; to become the
chief of goddesses she must become a mortal."

THE DESCENT OF THE GODDESS
TO THE UNDERWORLD

The Eleusinian Mysteries of ancient Greece involve themes of
descent and ascent, loss and regain of light and darkness, and the
cycles of life and death. In *The Secret Teachings of All Ages*, author
Manly Hall states that the rites associated with these Mysteries
were performed at midnight during the spring and autumn equinoxes. As noted earlier, Hall reports that the Eleusinian Mysteries
spread to Rome and Britain where initiations into this cult were
performed in both countries.

The Eleusinian Cult contained the Greater Mysteries and the
Lesser Mysteries. The Lesser dealt with the abduction of Persephone
by the Underworld God, a classic descent myth. The Greater Mysteries dealt with the Quest for the Return of the Goddess, and the
rites were performed in honor of Ceres (an agricultural goddess who
was patron of the Mysteries). The Celtic goddess Cerridwen shares
much symbolism in common with the Roman goddess Ceres. This is
explored in greater depth in my previous book *Wiccan Mysteries*.

In the general mythos, Persephone (known to the Romans as *Pros-*
erpina) descends into the Underworld and encounters its Lord. The life
essence of the world disappears with her, resulting in the first autumn
after which winter befalls the Earth. The Lord of the Underworld
falls in love with the goddess and desires to keep her with him in
the Underworld. Ceres intervenes on her behalf and pleads with the
Underworld Lord to release Persephone. At first, he refuses and argues
that because Persephone has eaten the seeds of the pomegranate (an
ancient symbol of the male seed), she must remain in the Underworld.
There is an interesting parallel here, for in fairy lore, if a person ate
any food while visiting the fairy realm, then they could not return to
the human world. Eventually, the Lord of the Underworld agrees to
release Persephone on the condition that she must return to his realm
for half of each year.

THE FAIRY AND THE WITCH

To our ancestors, fairies were not the pretty winged figures depicted in modern times. Fairies were considered to be a dangerous race for humans to encounter, and great care needed to be exercised. In early folklore accounts, there appears to be a strong link between fairies and Witches, as though both originated from a common non-human source. Cultural historian Owen Davies, in his book titled *Witchcraft, Magic and Culture 1736-1951*, comments on the similarities between the night gatherings of Witches and fairies. Davies quotes folklorist Elijah Cope as having said that fairy lore and Witch lore were often linked together, as indicated by Cope's research in Staffordshire. Folklorist E.S. Hartland is also quoted as having identified fairies and Witches as being of equal nature.

Sicilian folklorist Giuseppe Pitre claimed that it was impossible to distinguish between Witches and fairies in Sicily. The trial records of the Spanish Inquisition in Sicily depict an interesting view of Witches and fairies. The documented accounts of the fairy faith on the island of Sicily provide one of the purest forms of the fairy sect. These documents span a period from 1547 to 1701 and concern the indigenous practice of magick and Witchcraft are recorded in 3,188 cases preserved by the Inquisition.

The fairy sect in Sicily was known as the *donna di fuora* and its membership was said to include both fairies and humans. The fairy sect was divided into groups known as companies. Each one comprised an odd number of individuals ranging from seven to nine members, and only one man was allowed in any company. Each company was headed by a woman called Queen of the Fairies. The fairy queen also bore such titles as *La Matrona* (the Mother), *La Maestra* (the Teacher), or *Donna Zabella* (Lady Wisdom/Lady Sybil). The recorded names of these companies appear in Inquisitional records under these titles: the Company of Nobles, the Company of the Poor, the Company of Palermo, the Company of Table and Distaff, the Company of the Mother, and the Company of Ragusa.

The primary purpose of the *donna di fuora* society was to serve as healers within the community. According to historian Gustav Henningsen (*The Ladies from Outside: An Archaic Pattern of the Witches Sabbat*), they practiced an ancient form of fairy magick by which they could either harm or heal. The *donna di fuora* also served the community as mediator between humans and fairies. During this era, it was a widespread belief that serious accidents and sudden illnesses were often caused by fairies that had been angered in some way. Members of the *donna di fuora* were called upon to appease the fairies in an attempt to persuade them to heal the afflicted. Only the *donna di fuora* possessed knowledge of the required spells and offerings that could appease the fairy folk. According to the records of the Inquisition, members of the *donna di fuora* also possessed a power called *toccatura di brujus* (Witch touching) by which they could cure or harm through a laying on of the hands.

The *donna di fuora* claimed to attend ceremonies beneath the walnut tree in Benevento, a tree that features prominently in the tales of Italian Witchcraft. The membership professed to travel in a spirit body in order to fly to Benevento for their ceremonies. According to the Inquisition, the *donna di fuora* claimed to attend the "games of Diana" held at Benevento. Mainland Witches in Italy "confessed" to being members of the "Society of Diana" despite the Inquisition's attempts to make them confess to worshipping the Devil.

Even after the rise of Christianity and the decline of Paganism, Italian peasants still honored the sites once sacred to the fairy folk. In the book *Legends of Florence*, written in 1895 by Charles Leland, there are several beautiful tales of fairy encounters. In Italy, fairies are believed to inhabit fountains, bridges, wells, towers, woodlands, and beautiful gardens. In legends, they always reward humans who honor them and bring misfortune to those who insult them.

ITALIAN WITCHCRAFT

In Western literature, Italian Witchcraft is the second oldest form of Witchcraft mentioned. The first accounts in Western literature are the tales of Greek Witchcraft, appearing a few centuries earlier than Roman Witchcraft. The Old Religion of Italy contains perhaps the most specific elements of archaic European Witchcraft. With the exceptions of Sicily and Sardinia (which, as island cultures, contain largely insular forms of Witchcraft and folklore), the Old Religion of Italy is primarily rooted in ancient Etruscan religion. As noted earlier, Etruscan religion focused on a Great Goddess and consort God figure. These deities ruled over a universe divided into various realms of influence, which were individually controlled by powerful spirits. The veneration of the ancestral spirit was also important in Etruscan religion.

The roots of Italian Witchcraft extend back into the pre-history of Italy. Italy was a mosaic of cultural and social groups scattered throughout the regions of the peninsula. The main ethnic groups included the Latini, Calabri, Samniti, Sabini, and Etrusci. However, there is marked archaeological evidence between the twelfth and ninth centuries BCE (Proto-Villanovian) suggesting a unity of so-ciological structures, ideas, and customs. Examples of this appear in the form of funeral items and the similarity of charms carved from bones throughout Italy.

The Etruscans emerged as a power in Italy around 1000 BCE, and, according to the late Professor Marija Gimbutas, they were the heirs to the Mysteries of the Neolithic cult of the Great Goddess in Old Europe. As with much of Europe, ancient cave drawings and artifacts found in Italy reveal primitive ceremonial beliefs concerning hunting and the animal kingdom in general. Ancient shamanic-like beliefs evolved into tribal religion over the course of many centuries, eventually taking the form we now call *La Vecchia Religione* (The Old Religion). In this religion, we find a blend of beliefs common to both hunter-gatherer and agrarian societies.

The writers of the Hellenistic and Roman period encountered surviving elements of primitive conceptions and practices in Italy so distant from the rationality of the classical world that they sometimes provoked astonishment and incomprehension. Most striking were traces of an animistic conception of the supernatural and the omni-present importance of divine signs and divination. Some writers found what they believed were surviving elements of a former matriarchy reflected in the high social and religious status of women (in Etruria and even in early Rome). Encountered also were ancient beliefs in the material survival of the dead in their place of burial, and all the rites implied in such a belief (house-shaped urns and tombs, rich funerary apparatus, funeral games, etc.).

Historian Georg Luck ("Witches and Sorcerers in Classical Literature" in Ankarloo and Clark's *Witchcraft and Magic in Europe:*

Ancient Greece and Rome) states that the "universality of magickal beliefs" migrated from ancient Babylonian, Assyria, and Persia reaching Greece and Italy in their prehistoric periods. Primitive religion and magick provided a way for people to understand and interact with the world around them. Luck comments that in ancient times, Witchcraft was a type of "science or technology" serving to provide a way of seeing and understanding the world, as well as establishing methods of dealing with it for personal purposes.

Luck states that around the sixth century BCE, a social distinction arose between the "ignorant" and "backward" majority versus the "sophisticated" and "enlightened" minority. Luck remarks that many of the tensions between the two groups were rooted in the development of magickal beliefs and practices from prehistoric times. He adds that in time, such occult sciences as astrology and alchemy merged with ancient practices, and survived the "victory of Christianity" among the *Pagani* who lived far removed from the cultural centers.

In Italy, the Witch Cult and other Mystery traditions openly flourished up until the fourth century CE, when agents of the Church looted and destroyed Pagan temples. In this manner, the Church disrupted Pagan celebrations and prevented the ancient rites from being performed upon the traditional sites. In 324 CE, Emperor Constantine established Christianity as the official religion of the Roman Empire. The Pagan temples were destroyed or converted into Christian churches.

Gradually through the years, Pagan customs were absorbed by Christianity. The Old Religion withdrew into secrecy away from the attention of the populace. Only small groups of people continued to gather at the ancient sites and perform the old seasonal rites. The majority feared the attention of the Church. However, the village and townsfolk continued to seek out the local Witch for healing and magickal help.

Following the collapse of the Roman Empire in the fifth century CE, Europe fell into the Dark Ages. The Roman Catholic Church replaced imperial Rome as the unifying factor in Europe. Latin remained the language of learned scholars and helped to preserve much of the knowledge we now possess about ancient cultures and magick. Italy led Europe out of the Dark Ages with the Renaissance period originating in Italy during the early fourteenth century. By the fifteenth century, the Renaissance spread to France, Spain, England, and the Netherlands. Besides art, science, and literature, the Renaissance produced many books on natural magick and occult philosophy in general. Magick during this period referred to a body of concepts constituting a metaphysical science.

With the Renaissance came the resurrection of the lost Greco-Roman books of magick. In particular, the Renaissance produced the great Hermetic teachings which are the foundations for many modern magickal teachings and traditions. The Hermetic books, originally written in Greek sometime around the third century CE, appeared in a pseudo-Egyptian style or form. These texts preserved the ancient teachings of Persia, Chaldea, India, and the Greek Mystery Cults. As a body of accumulated teachings, they were heavily influenced by Neoplatonism, Gnosticism, and Neopythagoreanism. The occult manuscripts of the Renaissance period laid the foundation for magickal texts eventually appearing throughout all of Europe.

In 1460, Cosimo de Medici came into possession of many Hermetic manuscripts from Macedonia and the waning Byzantine Empire. He ordered Marsilio Ficino (an Italian philosopher and theologian) to translate these texts; through his efforts, we now possess a body of occult knowledge that is still the basis for magickal thought. In the later period of the Renaissance, these magickal texts appear in France, England, and Germany.

Neoplatonism, a philosophy based upon the teachings of Plato, greatly influenced southern European occult traditions. Plotinus, a Hellenized Egyptian, brought about its revival circa 244 CE. Plotinian Neoplatonism was itself revived in fifteenth-century Italy by Marsilio Ficino. John Colet is credited with introducing Neoplatonism into England, which paved the way for the Cambridge Platonists of the seventeenth century. The doctrines of Plotinus became the official teachings of the Platonic Academy and greatly influenced even Christian theology.

Many schools of Neoplatonism, such as the Pergamene, engaged in magickal practices. By the fifteenth century, such tenets were firmly established and influenced many friars and monks engaged in the translating of ancient texts. One such example is Tommaso Campanella, a seventeenth-century Dominican friar, charged with heresy and imprisoned by the Church for trying to reconcile science and reason with Christian revelation. The monks and friars who, during the Middle Ages, wrote down the Celtic legends we now possess, were no doubt learned in Neoplatonism as we find many Mediterranean concepts in Celtic myth and legend. It is likely that as Roman Catholicism passed into such places as Ireland, so too did the Mediterranean teachings influence Christian theology. In late antiquity and early medieval times, philosophies of various religious traditions were attracted to, and influenced by, Neoplatonic thought.

In Italy, certain regions held strong to the Old Religion despite the power of the Church. Tuscany in northern Italy was the strongest center of Paganism, followed closely by the region of Benevento in lower central Italy. However, in time, even these strongholds fell to the power of the Church. All survivals of Pagan belief, worship, and practice were condemned as demonic and were suppressed by Christian theology and law.

The Synod of Rome in 743 CE outlawed any offerings or sacrifices to Pagan gods or spirits. The Synod of Paris in 829 CE issued a decree advocating the death of Witches and sorcerers citing the Biblical passages of *Leviticus 20:6* and *Exodus 22:18*. In 1181, the Doge (Orlo Malipieri) of Venice passed laws punishing the making of potions and the performance of magick. Although Witchcraft was officially a punishable crime in Italy throughout the thirteenth century, the Witch mania of northern Europe did not sweep Italy until the early fifteenth century.

Francesco Guazzo, an Italian Ambrosian monk who grew up in the region of Tuscany, writes of the Witch Sect in his book *Compendium Maleficarum*. It was written at the request of the Archbishop of Milan (Frederico Borromeo) and published in 1608. Guazzo describes in great detail the structure of the Italian Witch sect, as well as many other European systems. In Chapters Twelve and Eighteen, Guazzo indicates that Witches gather in circles drawn upon the ground with beech twigs and work with spirits of Earth, Air, Fire, and Water, among others.

Guazzo notes in Chapter Ten that Witches adhere to certain laws within their society. In Chapter Six, Guazzo states:

"The infection of witchcraft is often spread through a sort of contagion to children by their fallen parents...and it is one among many sure

*and certain proofs against those who are charged and accused of witch-
craft, if it be found that their parents before them were guilty of this
crime. There are daily examples of this inherited taint in children…"*

Guazzo states that Witches *"read from a black book during their
religious rites"* and he notes a religious demeanor among Witches in
Chapter Eleven, where he writes: *"For witches observe various silences,
measuring, vigils, mutterings, figures and fires, as if they were some
expiatory religious rite."* Guazzo's depiction of Witchcraft seems to
indicate a rather structured and organized cult and is consistent with
accounts from Italian Witch trial transcripts dating from 1310-1647.

Folklorist Lady Vere de Vere also describes a structured Witch
cult in an article she wrote in 1894:

*"…the community of Italian witches is regulated by laws, traditions,
and customs of the most secret kind, possessing special recipes for sorcery" (La Rivista of Rome,* June 1894*).*

Folklorist J.B. Andrews later added:

*"The Neapolitans have an occult religion and government in
witchcraft, and the camorra; some apply to them to obtain what
official organizations cannot or will not do. As occasionally happens
in similar cases, the Camorra fears and yields to the witches, the
temporal to the spiritual" (Folk-Lore: Transactions of the Folk-Lore
Society,* March 1897*).*

In all of this, we see a long-standing tradition of the art of Witchcraft, surviving from ancient to modern times. Although remaining
hidden in secrecy, it surfaces on occasion as evidenced by the literature
previously in this and previous chapters. Let us now turn to the next
chapter and explore the Art of Witchcraft itself.

~ CHAPTER 4 ~

THE ART
OF WITCHCRAFT

WHAT IS THE ART OF WITCHCRAFT, and what do Witches really do? There is so much myth and legend surrounding this topic that it can be difficult to separate fact from fantasy. Having been a practitioner of the Art myself for over thirty years, I hope to shed some light on these subjects within the pages of this book. It has been a long, strange, and mystical journey for me and I hope I can now successfully communicate some of its wonders to you.

I begin with the words of one of my earliest teachers: *"A witch does not believe, a witch knows. A witch does not embrace faith, a witch embraces experience."* In other words, Witches form their religious and magickal beliefs from personal experience and not from faith. The basic teachings of the Craft are guidelines and stepping stones but the walk itself is personal. Some Witches reject doctrine and dogma of any kind, but I personally feel that specific tenets provide a healthy and necessary balance to measure one's path against. The established teachings of any religion provide the "measuring stick" for a specific view of reality. As a Witch, I am not bound to this "center stick" with a chain, but rather secured to it with a tether. With either the wisdom or folly of my own free will, I can lengthen or release the tether as I wish.

Knowing where and what the center is provides balance and keeps one grounded in the reality of one's religious or spiritual vantage point. There is a very real risk of losing the center or not having one to begin with. If you don't have a center, you can wander aimlessly for years, never knowing that you're doing so. If you don't have a home, it is difficult to realize you have lost your way. Some Witches may argue that only personal beliefs matter, stating "the self knows all" and the only true gauge is whatever "feels right" to the individual.

It is not my intent to diminish the value of personal discernment, as personal discernment is a vital spiritual tool. I simply caution against becoming so self-focused and self-absorbed that we may lose sight of the "universal truths" and those contained within the "group mind" of a people or a culture. In the old tarot decks, *The Fool* card depicts a traveler so absorbed with his own thoughts that he is about to step off a cliff. The dog of reason barks at his heels trying to alert him to the peril. But he is inattentive to outer warnings and continues on his walk, stepping off into the abyss. This teaches us that our personal walk is best taken in accord with the laws of nature and with the ways of divinity reflected in the mechanism of nature.

With the advent of certain New Age influences circa 1980, many tarot designers redefined *The Fool*. Instead of folly and self-deception, *The Fool* card came to symbolize the adventurer, trailblazer, and one's personal journey to enlightenment. In this light, New Age people saw personal intuition as superior to experienced instruction. In this mentality, the self then became both student and teacher at the same time, and personal beliefs in religion and magick were viewed as having superseded ancient knowledge and wisdom. Taking this position, some people claim that magick can only affect them if they believe it can. I don't know what kind of magick that is, but I do know that true magick is not dependent upon anyone's belief in it, nor is it diminished by the lack thereof. It works because it is real and functional energy. It is not the power of the mind, although the mind certainly plays a part in the magickal process. The inner workings of this process will become clearer as the following chapters unfold.

In the chapters ahead, I will lead you into an understanding of Old Ways magick. This is true magick, not the "weekend Witchcraft" nor "airy-fairy balls of light and fluff" variety so common in many contemporary books on the subject. The Witches of old were both revered and feared, and this in part led to the sanctioned killing of Witches during much of the Renaissance period of European history. All of this did not happen because Witches sat around meditating and sending "good vibes" to friends and neighbors. Witches were not hunted down because they simply knew the properties of herbs or read tarot cards and runes to foretell the future. They were hunted because they were self-empowered people practicing a powerful magickal and religious system, and this was perceived by the Church as a danger.

The magick of Witchcraft is like the Full Moon. It has a quiet strength as it moves through the night. The Moon is less assuming than the Sun, and its subtle light hides the truth of its powerful impact upon ocean tides, emotions, plant and animal life, menstruation, and fertility cycles themselves. The magick of Witchcraft is of the same nature; it works behind the scenes and it is like a mist that moves in unnoticed until one finds themselves suddenly within the fog.

In the following chapters, I will show you how to develop the necessary mentality to practice Witchcraft, and I will reveal the inner mechanisms that will allow you to become adept at the Art. Remember always that your magick will only be as strong as the foundation upon which you build it, and will only endure in accordance with the time and energy you've invested in study and practice. The established ways of the Old Religion are the well-worn paths to enlightenment. When we come to the end of roads already walked by those who came before us, we clear our own trail, which in turn extends the well-worn path for those who follow behind us.

There are those who lack the discipline required for true magick because they have simply borrowed the knowledge of others instead of doing the work that is required to integrate it all into one's own consciousness. What is important to understand is that the efforts themselves lead to the unfolding of personal power, just as the journey itself leads to the destination. On a mundane level, for example, one cannot become physically fit by reading books written by bodybuilders; one has to perform the exercises. So too, is it with magick. Some people will argue that, no, magick begins in the mind. My response is yes, in part, magick does begin in the mind, but so too does self-deception.

THE MENTALITY

The classic Pagan image of the Witch, as opposed to the traditional Christian image, is often a person wearing a hooded cloak. A
magickal ring is worn upon the hand, and the Witch is adorned with
a magickal talisman hung upon a necklace. Typically, a cane or staff
is carried, and the Witch may even be accompanied by a raven, cat,
or some other mystical creature. In this portrait of the Witch, we see
one who is learned in herbs, potions, and charms. We also commonly
attribute psychic vision and the command of magickal occult forces
to the Pagan image of the Witch.

That there is transformative power within imagery is unques-
tionable. One need only observe people in costumes at a party to see
how the wearing of a different persona can influence the character
of individuals. In shamanic practices, the wearing of an animal pelt
or the mimicking of some creature serves as a catalyst to altered
states of consciousness. In Witchcraft, the wearing of a hooded
robe, slipping on a magickal ring, and breathing the scent of ritual
incense or oil all serve a similar purpose. It is a stopping of the
mundane world, a time to submerge the everyday personality and to
invoke the higher nature.

Witches are nature people, and they seek alignment and harmony
with the forces of nature. This requires that they first obtain a balance
of the elemental forces comprising their own personal nature. Once
this is obtained, then the Witch can turn to embrace the elemental
forces that animate nature (and from which the Witch draws their
power). Alignment with nature provides an earthy balance to the
Witch, a quiet strength suggestive of all that the Witch can draw
upon for their magick.

Witches perceive the world differently than do most people and
traditionally have often lived outside the towns and villages. There
is a seemingly aloof quality that can be observed in one who has
practiced Witchcraft for a time. I'm not speaking of detachment or
lack of desire, but rather of seeing everything as equal in a connective
pattern of cause and effect. Therefore, nothing holds more importance
than anything else, and accordingly, there is no singularly strong
attachment to any one specific thing because everything is equal. In
this mentality, the self is not elevated but is instead acknowledged

as equal to everything surrounding it, and thus, the ego is held in balance. Knowing how to weave and unweave these patterns gives the accomplished Witch the confidence to face the negative and the positive things of life with confidence in the ordered cycles of things. Therefore, "non-attachment" to the Witch means to remove oneself from random occurrences and to embrace life as an unfolding of cycles responding to energy patterns. The Witch then becomes part of the natural cycles instead of being subject to them. In other words, they are a participant rather than a victim.

Despair gives way to patience as the Witch awaits the shift in polarity, understanding that negative is followed by positive and that every ending is a new beginning and vice versa. Just as winter turns to spring, so too decline turns to increase, loss to gain. The Witch also knows that if needs be, they can reshape prevailing patterns through magick, speeding up the natural forces at play within all things, for Witches have always been the weavers and shapers of magick. Witches can never truly fall into the victim mentality, for within them is the inner nature of bud and leaf and stem, ever renewing, ever green.

The Witch dwells at the center of a magickal universe in much the same way that a spider sits at the center of its web. The spider touches the expanding threads connecting its universe and is aware of anything coming into contact with them. It can distinguish between the ripples of a breeze disturbing the web and the touch of an insect on the web. The spider also knows when a section of its web has been damaged or changed in some way and moves to correct the situation. So too is it with the Witch, for everything is linked together by etheric ripples sensed by the aura surrounding the physical body.

The Witch is a watcher and a weaver. They walk the path of magick accompanied by various spirits and under the guardianship of the Goddess and God of the Old Religion. The portals that lie between this world and the next are gateways through which the Witch can cross back and forth. Knowledge of these gates, and the inner mechanisms of the planes that lie beyond, are all part of the Witches' Craft.

One of the keys to occult knowledge is what I refer to as "leapfrog enlightenment." Essentially, this means we first study an object, a plant for example. We look at its blossom and then move to meditation upon the energy behind the form (that which causes a blossom to appear). Next, we meditate upon the principle itself. In so doing, we move mentally from the object to the spiritual concept that empowers it (its astral substance). We next move mentally from the spiritual concept to the imagery that manifests the concept (makes it cohesive). In focusing the mind in this manner, we "leapfrog" from the physical plane back up through the planes of manifestation, following the trail backward in an attempt to encounter the source itself.

THE INNER MECHANISM

I think it is safe to say that the Witches' Craft is one of alignment with the forces of nature. Through alignment, the Witch becomes a channel through which energy can be drawn, accumulated, and directed outward. A Witch is self-empowered, and by that, I mean they do not rely upon social status, wealth, or favor for self-worth. The Witch's power comes from their alignment with natural energies flowing across the Earth at the time of the solstice, equinox, and Full Moon. This is, in part, why rituals were created at these times, so that the Witch could bathe in the natural current of energy, concentrated into a living pool of energy that we call the ritual circle.

There can be little doubt that the seasonal periods that mark growth and decline within nature itself, and the power of the Full Moon over bodies of water, are real agents of transformation. When Witches gather within a magickal ritual circle they are, in effect, bathed by a condensed wash of energy inherent in the season, time, and place at which they gather. This focused and concentrated immersion charges the body of the Witch, making their own energy field like that of nature's at the time. When one resonates with a like energy, one moves closer to being like that energy.

In occult perception, three points are necessary for a manifestation to take place: time, space, and energy. This is symbolized by the triangle that we call the *symbol of manifestation*. Time is linked to the season or lunar phase. Space is the ritual setting, and energy is the force raised or drawn within the confines of a magickal circle. Temples, churches, groves, and shrines also all reflect the principle of the triangle of manifestation.

When energy can be collected through this magickal formula, it can then be directed towards a specific goal, bound to an inanimate object, or stored for later use. The energy itself is like clay, meaning that it is shapeable and impressionable. Just as one can imprint an image upon soft clay, one can also imprint a formed thought upon the etheric/astral substance of magickal energy. The substance of concentrated magickal energy is also shapeable like clay and can be formed into a magickal vessel. Witches often refer to this as the *cone of power* which can be raised within a ritual circle.

The process of shaping energy is performed through the mind, using visual images. These visual images are impregnated with emotional energy generated by the Witch. Typically, this emotional energy rises from dance, deep breathing, sexual stimulation, or the recollection of emotional events experienced by the Witch. Once the energy is generated, the Witch links the visual image together with the emotional energy through the use of a sigil or symbol. Thus, the power of the mind is joined with the sensory properties of the body, all blended with the spirit of the Witch (the emotional charge) which is yet another reflection of the power of the three points (the triangle).

To illustrate this principle, let's look at an example. Suppose I desire to charge an object with a thought-form. To anchor or bind the thought-form to the object, I must first select or design a symbol or sigil. Just as our spirit or soul requires the life force in our body in order to stay connected with the flesh, so too does the thought-form require a connective energy of some type. The object itself will be the body for the thought-form and the symbol will be its life force.

Once I have selected a symbol or sigil, then I must begin to focus upon the image of the desired goal. In other words, I have to picture the outcome. Once accomplished, I then visualize the symbol and replace the image of the outcome with the symbol. I do this by concentrating on the symbol and affirming that it is now the essence of the desired outcome. It requires less mental focus to maintain the desired goal in my mind when it is reduced to a symbol.

The next step is to raise the energy that will empower the work at hand. For solitary practice, the Odic breath method is effective. The Odic breath works on the principle of bio-electro-magnetic energy generated by the physical body. This energy is explored in great detail in my previous book *Wiccan Magick*. Begin by simply taking three deep breaths, exhaling slowly. This will help relax you, focus your mind, and initiate the surge of blood through the lungs. The surging of blood through the lungs is the living current of energy, and just as blood cells absorb oxygen in the lungs, so too do they pick up the etheric charge of emotional energy (the formed thought).

When you are ready to begin creating the magickal charge, first place the selected symbol before you and gaze at it for a few moments. Affirm what it represents to you, and then very slowly take a very deep breath as you stare at the symbol. At the point you feel your lungs have completely filled with air, quickly take in three sips of air. Repeat the entire process three times (one deep breath and three quick sips). This technique will create an increase in your bio-energy field. As you exhale each breath, breathe out upon the object you desire to charge.

Feel your breath literally pouring out magick into the object. In your mind, picture the object glowing with energy each time you exhale upon it. Once fully charged with energy, affirm that the energy is bound to the object. If the object is not fragile, then squeeze it between your hands as though packing the energy in with your hands. Placing a symbol either physically or etherically on the object is also a good idea. If the object is fragile, then you will need to mimic the aspects I suggest without actually touching the object.

WORDS OF POWER

The most effective words of power I have encountered are those learned through the experience of a situation within a controlled setting linked to a sound. In other words, the teacher creates an atmosphere by choosing a place, the lighting, the scent, and the sounds associated with the desired state of consciousness. This is not unlike an experience common to most people in which a song or perhaps a scent instantly recalls the memory of a special place or person from our past. The same neural pathway link associated with the connection between place and event is evoked in the type of word of power I suggest.

Phobias are good examples of the power of neural pathways and the things that trigger associations. Anxiety and unreasonable fears are often evoked through flukes in the neural pathway connections of memory as well as those evoked due to the imprinting of negative experiences and their associated catalysts. In a healthier sense, we can create new pathways that will evoke pleasant or powerful states of consciousness. These can be employed to counteract negative states of consciousness that are evoked throughout worn or undesired connections.

To illustrate how words of power may be created, let's look at an example. I want to create a word of power designed to invoke a sense of the Moon's mystical power, something that will help me to feel magickal when I wish to perform a spell or other work of magick. First, I choose a scent that I wish to connect the feeling to. This is something that I will later use to anoint myself with when I use the word of power. Next, I choose a word or phrase that I want to serve as the invocation. Last, I pick out a setting where I can see the Full Moon in a rural setting, or perhaps a coastal or lake setting. To be successful in creating a word of power, one must fully emerge oneself in the emotion of the event.

On the night of the Full Moon, I sit or stand beneath the Moon and watch it for a few moments. I then begin to think that this is the same exact Moon beneath which ancient Witches once gathered. Here is the same Moon to which ancient offerings to the Moon Goddess were once placed. As I begin to feel this connection mentally and emotionally, I bring the scented oil to my nose and gently breathe in the fragrance, performing this three times. After this, I look at the Full Moon, once again breathing in the scent, as I whisper the word of power. To align the word of power to the Moon, I can also whisper the word three times (for the triformis goddess aspect) or nine times (for the power of the Moon in general).

If performed correctly, every time the word of power is whispered or spoken from that time forward, you will shift back to the consciousness of the night in which it was created. Following its creation, never speak the word of power in a mundane setting. Only use it to invoke a shift of consciousness. The same will be true for the scented oil. After you have successfully employed the word of power several times, you can then pass it on to another.

To do this, simply take the person back to the setting (or type of setting) in which you first created the word. Then have the person look at the Moon as you speak about the connections. In other words, you can say "You stand/sit now beneath the same Moon at which the Witches of Old once gathered. Here above you is the ancient Moon to which the priests and priestesses of old once placed the sacred offerings." Then pass the scented oil beneath the person's nose three times, telling them to breathe in softly. As they do so, tell them that they breathe in the essence of the ancient Moon. Once you feel that the person is at their most receptive stage, whisper the word of power into the person's ear.

THE ROLE OF THE MOON

Witchcraft has long been linked to the Moon and particularly to the Full Moon. The mystical quality of the Moon at night is unmistakable, perceived by poets, magicians, and Witches for countless centuries. In ancient times, the light of the Moon itself was believed to possess magickal properties. Ancient thought held that a woman could become pregnant by sleeping nude beneath the Full Moon and awakening covered in the morning dew. In early Christian Europe, many held that allowing the moonlight to fall upon one during sleep was to bring insanity.

To Witches, the Moon is the symbol of magick and transformation. The process of cyclical reformation can easily be seen as the Moon moves from phase to phase in an ever-repeating pattern. The Moon is the weaver of itself, the shapeshifter, and the Witch. It is only natural that the Moon became a symbol of the mystical connections and metaphors reflective of religious and magickal tenets of the Witches' Craft. In the following chapter, we will examine the connection of the ritual circle with the Full Moon.

On a physical level, the Moon itself generates energy that is a catalyst for magickal effects. The Moon influences the ebb and flow of astral forces in much the same way it influences the tides of our Earth. When the Moon is waxing from New to Full, it aids in the formation of astral images. As the Moon wanes from Full to New, it aids in dissolving poorly formed images. The energy of the waning

Moon also serves to dissolve astral forms that are no longer being empowered by thoughts or desires.

The magickal system of Witchcraft is based upon the principles and characteristics of the Moon itself. Magickal energy is drawn from the accumulation and direction of the subtle occult properties of the Moon's light. Additionally, power is tapped from the Moon's gravitational influences on energy fields surrounding the Earth. According to ancient lore, the actual essence of lunar power originates among the stars. The Sun draws and absorbs stellar radiation, channeling it into our solar system. The planets within our solar system absorb this collected energy and merge it with their own vibrations or energy patterns.

The planets emanate a composite energy as previously described throughout our solar system. Each planet's energy or vibratory pattern is unique and influences other planetary forces within its sphere of influence. The Moon absorbs, condenses, and channels all of these forces, which are then carried to the Earth within the lunar light spectrum. In other words, the Moon becomes the transmitter of this magickal composite of energy upon the Earth. Without the Moon, we cannot employ the universal forces that were first drawn into our planetary system by the Sun.

Science confirms that the Moon radiates more than just reflected light particles. Scientific instruments confirm the Moon also radiates infrared and microwave frequencies. The infrared emanations are strongest from the first quarter Moon to the Full Moon, where its levels are four times the amount of radiation compared to its lowest point. It is weakest from the third quarter phase to the first quarter. Its lowest emanation occurs at the time of the New Moon.

Microwave emanations are strongest just after the Full Moon and New Moon, reaching their highest levels three days later. Microwaves are transmitters, and therefore, magickal energy raised at the time of the Full Moon is fully released through microwave activity by the third day following the Full Moon. In occult terminology, the number three is the symbol of manifestation, and in physics, microwaves are transmission frequencies. Therefore, we can say that magickal energy is accumulated and generated by the Moon and is carried to the Earth on the occult counterparts of these lunar emanations.

It is noteworthy that heat liberates energy within a magnetic field, and that the infrared emanations (heat waves) are highest at the time of the Full Moon. The Full Moon is the time when most works of magick are performed, impregnating the magnetic mantle of the Earth with magickal thought-forms. In this formula, heat releases magickal charges held in the Moon's etheric sphere of influence and microwaves transmit the charge into the Earth's magnetic mantle.

The Moon's light is subject to polarization that varies from phase to phase. Polarization in this context is the measurement of light particle density. When the Moon is in its first and third quarters, the most concentrated levels are present, the latter being its peak level. A neutral polarity occurs when the Moon is full, increasing the electromagnetic field through which the Sun, Earth, and Moon pass. Thus, the magnetic mantle of the Earth is most stimulated at the time of the Full Moon.

DIVINATION

From the perspective of the Old Ways, divination is simply the glimpsing of astral forms appearing on the astral plane. According to metaphysical law, everything that ever manifests within the material plane first appears in the astral dimension. For example, if we consider a machine of any kind, we understand that it was first imagined and then designed in detail. This is, in effect, the stage of its astral formation. Once the material is gathered from which the machine will be constructed, we say that it is in the elemental stage. When the workers and materials come together and are fashioned according to the design, then the object is considered manifest within the physical dimension.

Using this same metaphysical formula, someone with psychic ability can discern the astral images, gaining impressions of what is forming there, or has already taken shape. This person can then project future events that will manifest in accordance with what has taken root within the astral dimension. However, the astral substance is moldable like clay, and various energies can reshape or transform it. Therefore, new patterns can emerge that may alter what had already taken shape in the astral plane, or is currently forming there. As the new shape takes form, the manifestation of the former stage is altered. Because of this principle, we say that the future is not predestined or predetermined.

In Witchcraft, the art of divination is used more or less to look into the patterns forming in our lives. Divination allows us to prepare for what is coming or to do something to change the course of events. The divinator can look at the astral forms and tell what is most likely to occur if nothing alters the astral patterns they perceive. It is then up to the individual to make a decision concerning their future in accordance with this knowledge

SIGNS AND OMENS

The ancients believed that the gods spoke to humankind through various creatures or events within nature. In the earliest of times, various phenomena within nature were viewed as divine forces. Thunder and lightning, for example, were the phenomena that later evolved into a god of thunder and lightning. Following the natural event itself, various phenomena were perceived as spirits. This later evolved into associating animals with the phenomena (frogs with rain, bats with darkness, and so forth, which then caused certain creatures to be worshipped as the source of the phenomena). In time, these creatures were depicted in human form accompanied by the former divine animal form, now seen as a cult animal. Therefore, the appearance of a specific animal was seen as a sign from the god it once was in an earlier time period.

In accordance with the environment in which any specific culture found itself, the four directions of North, East, South, and West became associated with the elemental forces of creation itself: Earth, Air, Fire, and Water. These quarters also shared a connection with the migration of birds and various herds, a factor that had earlier held great significance when the gods were in animal form. Therefore, the appearance of a creature associated with the cult of a god or goddess, in any one of the four directions, meant something specific within the cult. So too did the disappearance, the time of day or night, as well as the synchronicity of any natural phenomena timed to the action or appearance of the creature.

If, for example, prior to a battle, a bird of prey flew in the direction of the enemy, swooped down, and snatched a rabbit. This could be interpreted as a sign from the gods that victory was assured in the coming battle. Priests and priestesses were trained in the interpretation of signs and omens and were very important to ancient societies. As humankind moved into an agrarian society, the spirits within plants grew in importance with regard to divination. The remains of tea leaves in a cup, for example, were believed to be occult signs left by the plant spirit pertaining to future events.

For all of the reasons stated in this chapter, omens and signs held great importance as humankind moved away from living in harmony with nature to trying to control nature. Due to the separation of humankind from the natural aboriginal life that attunes a living thing to its environment, humans had to rely upon those creatures that still maintained the primal link; the plants and animals themselves. In other words, the flora and fauna became emissaries between the spirits of nature, the gods, and humankind.

This resulted in a list of magickal and ritual correspondences that included various plants, herbs, trees, and animals. By offering the proper items preferred by a god or spirit, people could evoke their aid and power. In reverse, a god or spirit could bring the plant or animal to the awareness of a human, thus communicating on some level in an attempt to show its goodwill, confirm its aid, and so forth. Due to such ancient mentality, we possess today a time-honored table of correspondences for herbs, minerals, animals, and natural phenomena, and all their occult connections.

TOOLS OF THE CRAFT

In the art of Witchcraft, we employ several basic tools such as the pentacle, wand, dagger, and chalice. Each of these is an extension of our own personal power, a symbolic inner connection to the divine spark within us that allows for external creation. The tools are, in part, a type of communication that we use to converse with the spirit world. Each tool is linked to a concept, which in turn is a metaphor related to an occult concept. The physical representation of the tool allows us to literally "get our hands on" the concept.

Each of the traditional tools I mentioned has a history of great antiquity. Each tool connects to an ancient belief system and therefore carries the momentum of the past with it. The wand is linked with the worship of the sacred tree. The chalice is associated with the ancient shell or gourd used by our ancestors in which to place sacred offerings. The dagger is linked to the Transformation Mysteries that arose when humankind began to forge tools from metal. The pentacle is connected to the very Earth itself, the source of life and the Mysteries of the Underworld.

Just as one creates a tool, one must also create the mental link to the concept it represents. For to brandish the tool is to wield the concept. This is one of the essential basics of the magickal art of Witchcraft. In order to accomplish this, one must create the mental pathways that make the appropriate associations. On the astral plane, we say that "thoughts are things" and by this, we mean that mental images become manifest in the etheric substance of the astral dimension when properly projected by the human mind. Therefore. it is important to form within one's mind the necessary imagery and conceptual links to the occult energy stream flowing from the ancient beliefs of the past.

In the next chapter, we will examine these concepts and the physical tools that reflect them. In so doing, we will learn the connections that lead to consistent and effective magickal workings. For the tool is simply the outward symbol of the inner realization. Without this realization, the pentacle is little more than a slice of clay or stone, the dagger a sharp piece of metal, the chalice a pretty cup, and the wand a stick of wood. So let us turn now to the next chapter and begin to open our understanding to something greater.

CHAPTER 5

THE WITCHES' TOOLS

There are many tools used in the art of Witchcraft. The most common are the ritual blade, pentacle, chalice, and wand. These items are the four classic ritual tools of Western occultism. As noted in Chapter Two, they even appear in ancient Mithraism as the wand of command, the libation cup, the crescent-shaped knife, and the platter. In Witchcraft, we also find the cauldron, broom, ring, and scourge, and other items can also be used as magickal tools. In this chapter, we will explore the use of various tools as they apply to both states of consciousness and keys to manipulating metaphysical energies. Here, we shall examine each independently to discern its use in the art of Witchcraft.

Some Witches feel that they have reached a point in their magickal development at which they no longer require physical tools. While it is true that one can eventually perform magick without the use of physical tools, it is also true that magickal tools remain as bridges to the supernatural forces to which they are linked. When we use items intimately connected with nature, and with the elemental forces these tools draw upon, we become more fully empowered. We extend beyond ourselves and the limitations of our physical existence. In other words, the self reaches beyond its personal and finite limitations and links with a higher nature or power.

In a certain sense, tools are catalysts for various states of consciousness. Once the mental pathway is connected between association and result, then the desired state of consciousness can be invoked at will. However, the use of a tool makes this process automatic once the occult principles of the tool are fully comprehended and integrated into the conscious and subconscious mind. Such occult principles are linked to archetypal patterns, a river of energy flowing from the momentum of the past. In this way, the tool serves the Witch as both a catalyst for the transformation of consciousness and a connective bridge to occult energy awaiting at the end or source of the link or extension.

When the Witch holds a magickal tool in their hand, it is a key that can unlock the portal to occult energy. It is also a link or extension into the realm from which that energy flows. In the case of the pentacle, wand, blade, and cup, we typically associate this occult energy with the elemental forces of Earth, Air, Fire, and Water respectively. From an occult perspective, *like* attracts *like*. Therefore, to possess an elemental tool is to draw the elemental counterpart. Because within the astral plane, thoughts become things, the tool is the tangible communication of the principle it represents and thereby creates a manifestation of the directed will of the Witch as they manipulate the tool in accord with functional occult principles.

All of the principles I mention here are portrayed in the symbolism of the classic *Magician* card of the tarot. In such decks as the Rider-Waite/Albano-Waite, we find *The Magician* standing before the ritual tools of Western occultism. *The Magician* holds up a rod, the connective bridge between the higher and lower dimensions. In this example, *The Magician* does not hold up both arms proclaiming the self as the bridge, but instead, the symbolism depicts the tool as the bridge. To make oneself the bridge is to enter into the realm of the Slain God/Divine King mythos, which is something quite different. Later in this chapter, we shall see the relevancy of such a connection to the tools, but for most Witches, a less sacrificial walk is preferred.

It is interesting to note the shift in tarot symbolism when viewing decks created after 1970. The earlier decks preserve traditional occult symbolism formed within the collective consciousness of our ancestors, the Group Mind. Many decks created later depict individualistic adaptations of occult themes; some even go so far as to simply employ personal artistic expression rather than time-proven occult principles. Therefore, I personally believe it is wise to study the earlier tarot decks before incorporating the relatively modern ones. In this way, one can transfer the occult concepts of the archetypal consciousness absorbed from the traditional symbolism of the older cards into the modern artistic expression of self-awareness reflected in many of the contemporary cards. Let us now explore the time-proven occult principles associated with ritual tools.

THE WAND

In ancient times, many cultures worshipped various types of trees. The oak, willow, birch, elm, rowan, and walnut are a few that figure prominently in Witchcraft. The tree was sacred, in part, because its roots went deep down into the earth. The Earth itself was mysterious, a thing from which seedling sprouts burst forth into the world of the living. The ancients believed that beneath the soil existed a mysterious realm. Seeds laying in the darkness of the Earth embraced and absorbed secret knowledge there, carrying it with them as they rose up through the soil as various plants.

A tree, the strongest of all plants, extended its roots into the Underworld, the dark realm of departed spirits and shadowy gods. Branches of the tree reached upward to the Heaven World, the realm of the divinity. Between the Underworld and the Heaven World stood the trunk of the tree, a bridge connecting both of these realms to the Earth. It was for this reason that the old Slain Gods of Europe were bound to trees so that the God himself became the bridge whereby humankind could connect directly with the Heaven World and Underworld through Him.

It became the tribal custom for a leader to carry a branch taken from the sacred tree of the clan. This branch was a sign that the leader walked as an emissary of the gods. From this practice arose the association of the staff with prophets, shamans, and wizards. Over the course of time, the custom arose of others using smaller branches of the sacred tribal tree for religious and magickal use, and from this custom, we now have the concept of the Witches' wand.

The wand was traditionally measured from the inside of the elbow to the tip of the middle finger. This represented the full extension of the arm, and thus the full extension of one's personal power into the world. The staff was traditionally the height of the individual plus the length of their wand (in a metaphysical sense, the heights to which they reached, plus the full extent of their power).

The wand, because it is a branch taken from the tree, is associated with the element of Air. As the branch grew, it stretched in the air and swayed with the wind. Therefore, the power of Air is intimately connected to the wand and is inherent in the wood itself. Because the branch is a "reacher towards the Heaven World," it is linked to spirit and divinity. Therefore, the wand is a tool used to evoke or invoke the gods and the spirits of nature. A typical Craft invocation reflective of the wand's nature is:

"I invoke thee by seed and root, and stem and bud,
And by leaf and flower and fruit do I invoke thee…"

In this invocation, we connect to the principle that in turn links us to the metaphor. To be joined with the metaphor is to unite with its source.

In this invocation, we see the reflection of the wand as the branch of the tree, budding and bearing fruit. Typically, the wand is carved into a phallic image to denote its fertile correspondences. The wand links us to the power of nature when we align our consciousness to the memory of bud, flower, and fruit within the wood itself. This in turn links us to the seed it once was, which lay beneath the earth where strange secrets dwell. When we hold the wand, we become the sacred tree rooted in the earth, and we become the trunk of the tree. From us extends the branch that is the wand, and we become the reacher towards the heavens.

THE WITCHES' TOOLS ~ 117

A wand should be selected for the type of wood and the association of that wood with occult themes, as well as the feel of the wand. The suggested reading list in this book contains some good guides to tree symbolism, and you may want to do further research on this topic. If you want to make your own wand, you can hollow out the end and fill it with magickal herbs. As noted previously, the wand should measure from the inside of your elbow to the tip of your middle finger. The hole in the wand can be sealed with wax or clay. If you purchase a wand, or one is given as a gift, you can bathe it in an herbal potion.

Prepare a purifying brew comprised of equal parts of the herbs: vervain, basil, woodruff, hyssop, and myrrh. Boil three cups of water, to which you add the herbs and a pinch of salt. Allow the herbs to steep for five minutes and then allow cooling for about ten minutes. Immediately afterward, bathe the wand in the brew (dipping it seven times) and then rinse it off with fresh water. Dry the wand and set it aside.

To charge the wand, go out on the night of the Full Moon just after sunset and prepare an altar. Upon the altar, set two white candles near the back area, separated about nine inches apart. Between the candles, place an offering of white flowers. In the center of the altar, set a bowl of fresh water, about half filled. To the right of the bowl, place some incense and a silver bell. Leave everything in place until the Moon is directly overhead, roughly about midnight.

When you return, light the incense and the candles. Then lift the flowers and state that you offer them to the goddess of the Moon. Next, take the bowl of water and sit comfortably with it in your lap. Lift the bowl and look down into it, adjusting the bowl so that the Moon is reflected on the surface of the water. Once you see the Moon clearly, close your eyes and say:

"Light of the Moon
That shines for me,
Touch within, divinity.
Out of the night
Your beam, your tower,
Pass now to me
The ancient power."

Drink some of the water, and as you do so, imagine that you are taking in the magickal essence of the Moon's light.

Set the bowl back on the altar and pick up the wand in your left hand. Then, with your right hand, cup some water and pour it out over the wand so that the water runs back into the bowl. Repeat this three times, saying each time:

"Water that shines
With the Moon's soft light,
Here in the dark pool
Of magick's night,
Carry to wood
The bright essence we share,
And empower this
Ritual tool of the Air."

Next, extend the wand upward toward the Moon and hold it there. Take three deep breaths, exhaling out upon the wand with each breath. Imagine that you are transferring the essence of the moonlight that you drank moments before. Before you draw each breath, say these words:

"Air that carries
The Moon through the night,
A whispering silence
To empower this rite.
I Draw Down the Moon
From the night and beyond,
Sealed with life's breath
In this magickal wand."

The wand is now charged and ready to be finished to your personal taste. You can paint or carve symbols along the shaft, add crystals, feathers, or anything you desire. Let your intuition guide you.

The Chalice

The chalice is a tool connected with the Goddess through womb symbolism. Originally, the chalice was a gourd, large shell, or wooden bowl used to contain the sacred liquids used in the rituals of pre-Christian European Paganism. By the Renaissance period at the very latest, we find the ritual chalice made of silver appearing in magickal systems. Silver is a metal sacred to the Moon Goddess and therefore, in modern Witchcraft, we typically employ this material for our chalices. Where once the wand was dipped into a wooden bowl or gourd within a ritual context, in modern times, we find the athame dipped into the chalice (wood to wood and metal to metal, like attracts like).

Many hereditary Witches still employ a mortar and pestle made of wood for ritual use instead of the athame and chalice. The word *pestle* is derived from the Latin *pistillum*. *Pistillum* is also the origin of the word *pistil* which indicates the ovule-bearing organ of a flower. In this, we see the connection between that which penetrates and that which is penetrated. The word *mortar* is derived from the Latin *mortarium* indicating both a bowl and a mixture. The etymology of the word *mortar* points towards a receptacle designed to be penetrated and mixed with other substances. In other words, the mortar and pestle are symbols of the procreative act of regeneration and transmutation.

In Witchcraft, the chalice is used to hold the ritual wine. In matrifocal times, this was the blood of the Goddess and the blood of the Moon contained within the original gourd or bowl. With the rise of patriarchal power and the creation of agrarian society, the blood of the Goddess symbolized by red wine became the blood of the Slain God of the harvest. The cult of Dionysus is perhaps the best-known example of such symbolism.

Within a spiritual context, the chalice is a vessel of offering and receptivity. Just as we ourselves, as worshippers of deity, are in effect vessels awaiting the pouring forth of spiritual light, so too is the chalice the vessel of containment and fulfillment. The chalice holds the intimate liquids of ritual celebration, just as we ourselves are filled with red liquid essence. In this concept, we find affinity with the chalice, and in the relationship of being filled and emptied in our own existence. The chalice is not just a tool representative of the element from which it is made. The power of the chalice lies more in potentiality, what it can contain rather than what concept its material connects it to.

THE PENTACLE

Clay and stone pentacles were the earliest Craft symbols of the earth and of material existence. The Earth is the foundation and the source of life. From the perspective of our ancient ancestors, the Earth itself produced plant life in some mysterious manner. Various animals appeared from beneath the soil and disappeared into the earth through caves, holes, and burrows. To dig into the soil was often to reveal the hidden life within, such as insects, worms, and the like. Soil itself was somehow magickal since it seemingly created life, and for this reason, the ancients used natural clay for many purposes.

The wooden pentacle is a vestige of early warfare in which the shield was used for protection. Shields of hide stretched across wood frames were some of the earliest forms, followed by wooden pieces joined together and reinforced by metal. The custom arose of painting symbols upon the shield to protect warriors in battle (often the image of an animal totem). In time, the star or pentacle arose as a shield adornment as was the case in the shield of the legendary knight Gawain.

The pentagram symbol itself represents the four elements of creation known as Earth, Air, Fire, and Water, all held in balance and overseen by a fifth element known as Spirit. In the case of Gawain, this is a symbol of the sacredness of his quest, for his shield design depicts one who is not bound by material gain but rather directed by a higher calling. The pentagram itself is a very ancient symbol and appears in Greek symbolism as early as the eighth century BCE, and on rings in southern Italy circa 500 BCE. Images of pentagrams first appear in the British Isles during the latter half of the Middle Ages and are largely found engraved on rocks.

In the Craft, the pentacle serves as the focal point of magick, for it is the material plane towards which magick is directed for manifestation. Objects are placed upon it as a focal point for magickal charges, or objects can be transported within the ritual circle using the pentacle in much the same manner as one uses a platter. The pentacle can also be placed to guard an opening in the ritual circle for people to pass through as needed. In addition, the pentacle can be carried to each elemental quarter and presented, star facing outside the circle, to invoke the Watchers and to bind the elements.

In a magickal sense, the five-pointed star etched upon the pentacle symbolizes the principle of elemental harmony bound to the physical dimension. To brandish the pentacle is to wield the power to evoke balance and harmony, to bind chaos. To astral spirits, thoughts are actual things, and therefore presenting the pentacle to them evokes the principle it represents, making it a reality to which they must comply.

THE RITUAL BLADE

The forging of metal into tools and weapons elevated human society from a primitive culture to a technological one. The metalsmith was of such importance that many cultures included a god of this art in their mythology. Some legends report that so valued was the smith that he was often made lame in an attempt to prevent his escape from the community. The blacksmith, arising from the Iron Age, reflects in many ways the Lame God of Old Europe. The Lame God is often depicted dressed in a black hooded robe, limping in the spiral dance.

In Witchcraft, we commonly find the black-handled knife known as the *athame*. It is a tool of elemental Fire because the metal itself was forged in fire and retains the memory of this transformative power. To wield the ritual blade is to brandish the force inherent within Fire. The metal, in effect, *remembers* the fire that forged it into a blade. The use of the term "remember" was once an old craftsman term to denote materials that did not lose their shape nor revert back to their former state. Fired clay is another example of a material that "remembers" its transformation through fire.

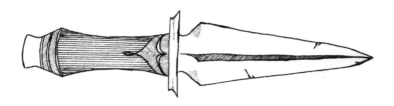

To employ the ritual dagger is to declare possession of the power to magickally transform something. The tip of the blade is a symbol of the tongue of fire and declares to any astral entities the reality of transformation grasped in the hands of the Witch. The blade communicates the message that *"I can reshape you, transform you, and carve you anew."* Where the wand is a tool of persuasion, the blade is a tool of command. To various spirits, this principle becomes a reality manifest within the dagger.

The dagger is most often employed to trace out a ritual circle. In most traditions, the physical circle is marked by rocks or rope or is etched into the soil. The dagger traces over the physical circle, usually a few feet above, and the Witch visualizes energy passing out of the blade where it leaves an energy replica of the physical circle with which it merges. At the conclusion of the ritual, the energy is released by lifting it up with the blade and directing it off into the atmosphere.

The dagger is also used to evoke the Guardians of the four quarters. Traditionally, a pentagram is traced in the air with the dagger while the Witch separately faces each quarter: North, East, South, and West. Here the dagger serves as the symbol of the forces that open the portals to the Otherworld. The blade is also used to evoke the elemental beings and does so by its affinity with the creative force of transformation, which it symbolizes. The elemental beings are attracted to the creative principle since they themselves are the active principles of creation within the physical dimension.

Traditionally, the athame is made of steel with a wood handle colored black. Ebony wood makes a very nice handle. Once you have obtained the athame, wait until the waning phase of the Moon to begin preparing it. The best time is three days following the Full Moon. Boil two cups of water and then add a teaspoon of these herbs to the water: mandrake, myrtle, and nettle. Simmer for twenty minutes, strain, and then refrigerate the water overnight. The mandrake is the key that opens the doorway between the worlds, linking humankind with the Otherworld. Myrtle is the herb of the fairy race and enlists aid in working with elemental spirits. Nettle is a protective herb, a guardian plant.

To charge the ritual dagger for use, it must first be heated over an open flame for a couple of minutes. This awakens the memory of the creative force of Fire within the blade. Once the blade is hot, say these words:

"Blade of steel, your charge shall be, to banish all I bid of Thee!"

Then immediately plunge the blade into the herbal potion (poured into a bowl) in order to seal the memory. Afterward, dry off the blade and set it aside.

To complete the process. you will need to magnetize the blade. This must be done during the waxing phase of the Moon, at least one week prior to the Full Moon. Take a medium size magnet and rub it from the hilt to the tip of the blade, firmly and moderately, nine times on each side of the blade. Then rub it again, nine times, on the first side of the blade, for a total of twenty-seven times. For an extra charge, repeat this three times, for a total of eighty-one times. Be sure to always go in the same direction with the magnet. As you stroke the magnet along the blade, periodically say these words:

"Blade of steel, your charge shall be, to attract all things I bid of Thee!"

The final process for charging the athame is to connect it with the Earth and Moon. Look at a calendar and note the night of the Full Moon. Two days prior to this, you will want to bury your athame in soil. If necessary, you can use a ceramic pot, but ideally, you should find a secluded area of ground from which you can easily see the Moon when it is full. Once you decide where you will place the athame, take it by its handle in your left hand and say these words:

"Seed to soil, death to birth, I join you now with the power of Earth."

Then, push the blade all the way down into the soil. The handle should be the only portion of the athame now above ground. Now it is time to leave the area undisturbed.

On the night of the Full Moon, you will return to the spot where you buried your athame and then perform the final step. Traditionally, you should go out beneath the Full Moon at midnight, but if this is not practical, any time after nine p.m. will do. Kneel in front of the athame and look up toward the Full Moon. Take hold of the athame handle with your right hand and hold your left hand up, palm facing toward the Full Moon. Next, close your right eye, look directly at the Moon, and say these words:

"Beneath this light,
That the ancients knew,
When time and season,
And tide were true,
I call upon the ancient boon,
And with my hand,
Draw down the Moon"

Then, quickly close your hand as though you are grasping the Moon. As your hand closes, look away so that you no longer see the Moon in the sky. Bring your left hand down and cover your right hand with it, so that both hands now hold the handle of the athame.

Remove the blade from the earth, clean off the soil, and keep the athame wrapped in a dark cloth overnight. The athame is now ready to use for your next spell or ritual.

THE WITCHES' CAULDRON

In the book *The Great Mother* by Erich Neumann, the author states:

"The vessel of Transformation—viewed as magical can only be effected by the woman because she herself, in her body that corresponds to the Great Goddess, is the cauldron of incarnation, birth, and rebirth. And that is why the magical cauldron or pot is always in the hand of the female mana figure, the priestess and later the witch."

The symbol of the womb, the generative force within nature, held great ritual and religious significance to our ancestors. Caves, shells, gourds, and other such objects were all symbols of the Great Goddess. From Her, all living things issued forth and returned, all in an endless cycle of life, death, and rebirth. Perhaps more than any other Great Goddess symbol, the cauldron has endured the passage of time.

The cauldron is intimately linked to Witchcraft as both a symbol and a tool. Stereotypes common within modern Judeo-Christian society portray the Witch stirring a cauldron of dubious brew. To Witches, however, the cauldron is the symbol of the magickal womb of the Goddess. Within it are nurtured things of a magickal nature, awaiting birth through a spell or ritual work of magick. During certain rituals, objects are placed into the cauldron for integration or transformation according to the season of the year. In this manner, we view the cauldron as a force of germination and transmutation. Every human was once within the womb of their own mother, and every ancient culture was once in the womb of the Great Goddess. Therefore, the cauldron recalls the mystical source of everything that comes into manifestation.

In ancient mythology, the cauldron often appears in the hands of a deity or some supernatural being. In many Celtic myths, the cauldron is hidden in the Underworld or some magickal castle or labyrinth. This is, in part, symbolic of its primal nature and that which is not readily accessible without a personal test or journey of some sort. In Aegean/Mediterranean myths, the cauldron is closer to attainment within the physical dimension and typically resides in an open cave protected by a goddess or a sorceress such as Hecate or Circe.

In both the Celtic and Aegean/Mediterranean cultures, the skull is associated with the cauldron. This is symbolic of the higher etheric nature reflected in the skull and the lower material nature mirrored in the cauldron. In a magickal sense, the skull represents the ability to transform concepts into material form (the creative power of the mind). Likewise, the cauldron represents the power to transform material objects into magickal forms. Thus, we sometimes see, reflected in art, images of the skull sitting in front of the cauldron or floating within the boiling brew of the cauldron. In Italian Witchcraft, the skull symbolizes the ancestral spirits. Connected to the cauldron, which is the womb figure, the skull represents the connection to ancestral spirits (or spirits of the dead in general) and the cauldron becomes the portal to the Otherworld. This is not unlike the symbolism of the sacred well in many European cultures.

THE WITCHES' BROOM

The broom, as a ritual tool, evolved into a composite of both male and female fertility. The shaft symbolized the male's phallus and the foliage symbolized the female's pubic patch. The fact that it was made from plants of the field linked it to the generative powers of nature, while its symbolism to human genitalia connected it to human consciousness, making it a tool (the magickal concept manifesting in a mundane form). During the era of the Inquisition, the ritual broom was lightly bound around the shaft making it easy to remove for ritual use as a wand. In this manner, it was safer for the Witch to possess a ritual wand since it was disguised as a common household item.

As a ritual tool of Witchcraft, the broom is used to sweep the ritual setting for purification. It is also laid across the entrance to the ritual circle as a protective barrier whenever the circle is left open for whatever reason. In symbolism, the broom represents purification, and since "thoughts are things" to an astral entity, the broom becomes a very real deterrent. On a magickal level, a Witch's broomstick is comprised of three different plant materials. The handle is made of ash, the sweep of birch twigs, and the binding lash is made of willow strips. Ash represents the Witch's power over the elements, birch symbolically protects from evil spirits, and willow declares the Witch's allegiance to the goddess Hecate Triformis.

The broomstick comprised of three materials is a triad symbol announcing to all spirits that the Witch operates from authority in the name of Hecate. Therefore, the broom can become a tool of power over spirits of night, shadow, and darkness. Banishment is performed by sweeping toward the circle's portal entrance or thrashing the air to chase off unwanted spirits. In its connection with Hecate, the broom is also a symbol of transformation, shape-shifting its form just as Hecate takes on any of the three aspects herself. Therefore, the broom is a vessel of the powers within night, shadow, and darkness.

THE RITUAL SCOURGE

The use of flagellation in a religious ritual context is of extreme antiquity. Herodotus speaks of it having originated among the Egyptians. Ancient writers such as Plutarch, Cicero, and Seneca wrote of the flagellation of young males in front of the altar of Diana at Lacedaemon in Greece. Lucian and Silenus relate how priestesses held up a small statue of the Goddess while boys were lashed by whips. Following this, priests inspected the lash marks on the flesh, using them to discern omens from the Goddess. It is interesting to note that flagellation in front of a statue of St. Mary was a common practice among certain Franciscans as noted under the Pontificate of Sixtus IV and in the work titled *Opus Mariale* by Bernardinus de Buftis.

As a ritual tool, the whip or scourge is a tool of purification and transformation. This is explored further in various chapters of this book, and you may wish to use the index to track down subsequent connections. Purification arises from a combination of mental endurance during the act itself, along with the effects of various endocrine secretions into the bloodstream as a result of the pain stimulation. Together with a rhythmic lashing, there is a measured effect upon mind and body. Flagellation can evoke the primal consciousness, especially when performed as mentioned along with the flickering of candlelight or before the flames of a fire. The combination of a metered lashing and the play of light and shadow resulting from the firelight can produce an altered state of consciousness.

The fact that enduring pain is a rite of passage is evident in the birth of a child. It is also reflected in the physical altercations between young males. In a ritual and magickal context, we find it expressed among certain tribes of Native Americans whose warriors pierced their flesh with hooks and hung themselves suspended from the ceilings of their lodges. In various indigenous cultures, the act of circumcision at the onset of puberty is viewed as a rite of passage through pain.

Flagellation appears in the initiation rituals of various Western Mystery Traditions. Egyptian tomb art depicts certain Egyptian deities carrying a flail. Some of the murals in Pompeii depict whips being used in initiation rites. The Greeks and Romans had a goddess of initiation known as *Telete* who carried a whip. In Telete, we find that suffering leads to enlightenment when willingly endured for a personal purpose.

THE WITCHES' RING

The Witches' ring is both a symbol and a tool. As a symbol, it identifies the wearer as a practitioner of the Old Ways and declares one as a user of magick. The ring connects the Witch to the metaphysical concepts whereby Witches weave their magick. The ring serves as both a reminder to the Witch of the forces at hand and acts as a conduit to and from those occult forces readily available to the Witch.

You will need an oil and an incense dedicated to the Goddess of the Moon. Most "Witch shops" or occult stores carry a version of these. You can use a mixture of camphor and jasmine if unable to find a prepared oil or incense. Use one part camphor to three parts jasmine. Before using this in a spell or ritual, place it beneath the light of the Full Moon for at least an hour.

The preparation of the Witches' ring should begin two days before the first night of the Full Moon and is completed beneath the Full Moon. Midnight is best but nine p.m. will do, if necessary. The rite calls for a ring with a stone setting. Consult the table of correspondences in Chapter Five of this book for a stone that you wish to form an occult alignment with. Once you have the ring you desire to use, then perform the following ritual:

Consecrate the ring to the four elements. This will require four small bowls set on your altar in the positions of North, East, South, and West. The North bowl will contain salt, the East bowl a smoking stick of incense, the South bowl a red votive candle, and the West bowl will contain fresh water. Beginning with the North bowl and moving clockwise, dip the ring in each bowl and state that you consecrate this ring by the powers of Earth (North), Air (East), Fire (South), and Water (West).

Now pour a small amount of your personal perfume/cologne into a metal burning bowl. Light the fluid. Hold the ring over the flame, turn it, and say:

"I dedicate and consecrate this ring with a stone of _____ and metal of _____ to be a ring of Witchery unto me with the powers of the Goddess three, the Lady of all Witchery, and as my word, so mote it be."

Censer the ring over an incense dedicated to the Moon Goddess, passing it through the smoke three times. Then, anoint the ring with an oil dedicated to the Moon Goddess. Wrap the ring in a thin red cloth and leave it for two nights in a place where the Moon will shine on it each night, at the same hour (at least one hour after sundown, on an odd-numbered hour).

On the night of the Full Moon, chant the following over the ring (still in the red wrapping):

"Any and all who perfect an image of me, with my likeness or as a crude consecrated image to be me, to do me bodily harm or to injure me spiritually and try to take my breath away, to cause me to dwindle or pine, pine away to nothing, to wish evil upon me, to

badger me with their anger or bad thoughts, by picture, image, or name, the ring of my Lady protect me, metal and stone, flesh and bone, safe forever in your powers, free from evil, fear, or despair, on the sender of the evil will rebound by the law of the Lady thrice crowned, hearken all unto me, as I speak, so mote it be."

At this point, you are done. Wear the ring whenever you are in a ritual setting or whenever you feel the need for protection. On the night of each Full Moon that follows, anoint the ring again, holding it up to the Moon. Rub a drop of oil on the stone and say something to the effect that you bless and charge this ring in the name of the Goddess.

PROTECTIVE PENTAGRAM AMULET

If you prefer to wear an amulet rather than a ring, then on the night of the New Moon, take your pentagram piece and then trace it with your finger (left hand). Once the figure is established, proceed as follows:

On the night of the Full Moon, light the burning bowl and suspend the amulet over the spirit flame, tracing the symbols with the tip of the spirit blade or finger: first the star and then the circle.

Next, hold the amulet in your left hand, and with the tip of the athame (or your finger) touch the first point and say:

"I call upon the Source of All Power to protect the wearer of this pentagram against all that is evil, negative, or unbalanced."

Touch the second point and say:

"I call upon ye spirits and Guardians of the Western powers to protect the wearer of this pentagram against all that is evil, negative, or unbalanced."

Touch the third point and say:

"I call upon ye spirits and Guardians of the Southern powers, to protect the wearer of this pentagram against all that is evil, negative, or imbalanced."

Touch the fourth point and say:

"I call upon ye spirits and Guardians of the Northern powers, to protect the wearer of this pentagram against all that is evil, negative, or imbalanced."

Touch the fifth point and say:

"I call upon ye spirits and Guardians of the Eastern powers, to protect the wearer of this pentagram against all that is evil, negative, or imbalanced."

Complete the charge by placing the tip of your athame (or right index finger) upon the center of the pentagram, and say:

"I bind here, by all of these powers and forces, this unyielding Pentagram of Protection. To thee, thy course by lot hath given charge and strict watch, that to the wearer of this pentagram, no evil thing approach or enter in."

You may wish to strengthen the spell by burning an incense of angelica, Solomon's seal, dragon's hood, dittany of Crete, and periwinkle.

Now visualize a blue flame moving up and out from the bowl, and mentally form it into a five-pointed star. Visualize it merging into the pentagram. Next, dip the amulet into the flame three times and present it to the North.

To conclude, hold the amulet in your left hand and place the tip of the spirit blade or finger against the power symbol, then say:

"Henceforth art thou a pentagram of protection and a force of awesome power! In the names of the Great Goddess and God, so be it!"

Now that we have taken a serious look at the tools of the Witches' Craft, it is necessary to understand something of the inner art of Witchcraft itself. Let us turn to the next chapter and begin to unravel the secrets of this ancient magickal tradition.

ᴛHE ᴍAGICKAL ᴀRTS

Tʜᴇ ᴄᴏɴᴄᴇᴘᴛ ᴏꜰ ᴀ ᴄᴏɴɴᴇᴄᴛɪᴏɴ between Witches and magick dates from ancient times, and indeed it would be difficult to separate one from the other. The ancient Greek myths of Medea and Circe speak of a time when Witchcraft was something of the gods, and it may well be that these figures are, in reference, the surviving remnants of a predominantly female magickal society existing long before the Indo-European invasion of Greece. As noted earlier in this book, ancient writings portray Circe and Medea with Hecate, to whom prayers are offered. This is one of the earliest portrayals of Witches in a religious context.

In the second century BCE, Witches of the Marsi (a tribe in central Italy) held a reputation in Rome as great magicians. The ancient Roman poet Horace wrote, in 30 BCE, of Witches who could "Draw Down the Moon from the sky" and who worshipped Proserpina, Diana, and Hecate. Apuleius, in the second century CE, wrote of the power of Greek Witches to transform into animal forms and to work various types of magick.

The ancient tales recounted to us by these early writers all speak of the power to attract energy, direct it, and transform the mundane world through the ability to wield occult forces. This is indeed the Craft of the Witches. In the following sections of this chapter, we will examine the ancient methods through which magickal power could be harnessed and controlled. We will also discern the ancient formulas that ensured successful works of magick.

THE MECHANISMS OF MAGICK

There are certain basic and fundamental aspects related to the art of magick. An understanding of the foundation upon which magickal concepts are based is very important and will allow you to develop your own unique applications rooted in sound magickal principles. Magick, like any art, has its essential basic method and structure, and yet, an individual can bring their own talents, intuition, and expression to it.

At the heart of magick as a system lie the four elements of creation: Earth, Air, Fire, and Water. The following are the traditional magickal correspondences of these four elements:

Earth: Stability, fertility, restoration, balance
Air: Stimulation, creativity, expansion, change
Fire: Motivation, empowerment, energizing, transformation
Water: Blending, cleansing, combining, softening

Earth: Acts through decomposition
Air: Acts through dispersion
Fire: Acts through combustion
Water: Acts through evaporation (and mixture)

Earth: Associated with the Northern quarter
Air: Associated with the Eastern quarter
Fire: Associated with the Southern quarter
Water: Associated with the Western quarter

Earth: Magickal color–yellow
Air: Magickal color–blue
Fire: Magickal color–red
Water: Magickal color–green

Earth: Cold + dry
Air: Hot + moist
Fire: Hot + dry
Water: Cold + moist

Earth tool: Pentacle
Air tool: Wand
Fire tool: Blade
Water tool: Chalice

Earth signs: Taurus, Virgo, Capricorn
Air signs: Gemini, Libra, Aquarius
Fire signs: Aries, Leo, Sagittarius
Water signs: Cancer, Scorpio, Pisces

When creating rituals and works of magick, these correspondences and others given later in this chapter serve to weave together all the necessary correlations to stimulate the astral material through which magick manifests. During a work of magick, various aspects can be combined for magickal influence. This practice of blending correspondences is one of the most personal elements of the Witches' Craft.

Because works of magick relate to specific natures, you can dispose of ritual debris in a manner connected to its elemental correspondence. The effect of this method is in the merging of the magickal energy with that of the universal elemental energy:

Fire: Burn in an open flame
Air: Toss into the wind or evaporate
Water: Drop into moving water
Earth: Bury in the soil

These are only a few of the many possible associations. If the work of magick relates to more than one element, you will want to incorporate the appropriate combination of actions. Match the aspects of what the work of magick was designed to influence with the ritual action needed when disposing of debris or employing charged objects for spell casting and the like:

Fire: Motivation, passion, vitality, virility, force, etc.
Air: Intellect, creativity, artistic, mental activity, etc.
Water: Love, fertility, emotion, mutability, etc.
Earth: Strength, endurance, fortitude, stagnation, etc.

To further explore the inner mechanisms of magick, we must look at the traditional paraphernalia of the Witches' Craft: candles, oils, herbs, condensers, charms, and incantations.

CANDLES

On a mundane level, candles provide a subtle light by which one can perform magick at night, a time-honored tradition of the Witches' Craft. On a magickal level, candles are charged to contain energy and act as small batteries to empower one's spells. The heat of the candle also serves, in the long run, to help release the magnetic energy generated during a magickal working. On the physical dimension, heating a magnet releases some of its magnetic charge, and the same is true on a metaphysical level concerning the electromagnetic energies generated by individuals within a ritual circle.

Candles can also be used in magick to represent the person or situation that the spell is designed to influence. In such cases, a symbolically colored candle would be chosen, linking it to the nature of the work at hand. If the candle represents a person, then the color of the candle would reflect something about that person. The same is true of any given situation, the color having something reflective of the nature of the magick's target.

Some Witches like to use candles made in the image of a human when performing magick related to a person. Other Witches use a standard candle, anointing it and naming it after the person for whom the magick is intended. All of this helps to focus the mind. The candle can be anointed with an oil (or cologne) symbolic of what the candle represents. Then, words may be spoken over the candle such as:

"I name you _____, you are _____."

Or for a situation you might say:

"Here is _____, this candle is now _____."

The way in which the candle is used for spell casting varies according to many factors, some simply personal preference. Typically, a candle is anointed at both ends and the oil is rubbed into the center as though you are putting the magick into the candle. The candle can then be used as is, or to add additional power it can be rolled in dried herbs of your choice. Some Witches prefer to hollow out the base of the candle and pack a pinch of symbolic herbs inside, sealing it with melted wax afterward.

Sometimes a candle is notched into sections for the purpose of burning a section at a time. Each section marks off one hour or one day of the spell casting. Such a use of the candle tends to build up energy and is particularly effective when focusing energy upon an event taking place at the time. For example, candle magick can be performed while a friend or loved one is undergoing surgery. If the surgery is to last three hours, then the candle can be notched into three sections. Another example would be if you had to wait three days for the outcome of a certain decision, then you could notch the candle into three sections, allowing the candle to burn down to one notch each day. The candle becomes, in effect, the physical link to the influence, and the point of focus for the powers of the mind. Employing this principle, you can help rid yourself of an unwanted situation by drawing seven concentric circles on a poster board. Each space between each circle must be wide enough to fit the base of the candle. In the center circle, place two candles, one to represent you and the other to represent the situation you wish to rid yourself of.

Notch only the "situation candle" into seven sections. Each day, burn the candle down to one notch, then move the candle out to the next circle, leaving the candle representing you within the center. Do not light your candle, but simply anoint it with your personal perfume or cologne. Each time you burn the candle, sit with it and concentrate on ridding yourself of the situation. See it clearly in your mind's eye. At the outer-most circle, allow the candle to burn itself out. Bury the wax debris in the earth and burn the poster board. This is one of the few exceptions to disposing of ritual debris in accordance with elemental nature, as described earlier.

INCENSE

Incense is, almost literally, the wisp of one's magick. It is the medium of the mind, the flux, and movement of thoughts, the shaping and reshaping of consciousness drifting before one's eyes. In the rising and dispersing of smoke, there is magick. Smoke provides the substance and the environment for one's thoughts to materialize. It also provides the vehicle, or propulsion, by which one can transmit into the astral dimension.

The magickal use of incense is threefold. It conditions the mind by stimulating the sense of smell (along with any physiological effects of the ingredients themselves). It draws spirits through its magickal associations and astral connections. Finally, according to ancient beliefs, it raises or lifts the energy of the spell, as well as the incantations, up into the ether.

Memory pathways are created by the scent of the incense, and the same is also true of oils. Everyone has experienced this when a certain fragrance brings back a childhood memory or a particular setting or situation from the past. The advantage of this fact for magickal purposes is that specific scents can invoke previous magickal states of consciousness. For example, if a specific scent is introduced to someone during a profound initiation experience, encountering its fragrance in the future will begin to trigger the mentality of the initiate as it was at the time when the scent was originally experienced.

For magickal effectiveness, the type of incense burned must correspond to the nature of the magickal work itself. Most spells use an incense of planetary symbolism or deity association. For example, love spells typically incorporate an incense of Venus, binding spells an incense of Saturn, and so on. Drawing upon various sources of power contributes to building up a significant energy charge without totally depleting oneself of personal power.

Incense can also be used to add power to your ritual candles by passing the candle slowly through the incense smoke, three times, in a circular clockwise manner. This helps to create the alignment within the mind of the corresponding powers upon whose aid you call. Remember, within the astral dimension, thoughts are things. Whatever you successfully impregnate the astral substance with will manifest or will cause responses to the intent of your magick as well as to the vibrations of the mechanisms you employ.

OILS

Oils are similar to incense in as much as they relate to the sense of smell. In addition to this, and more importantly, oils have the ability to hold magickal charges for longer periods. When an object is anointed with a charged oil, the object then becomes charged as well. This principle is what we call *contagion magick*. In other words, what comes into contact with something leaves its influence behind. An example of this on a mundane level is that sugar sweetens whatever it mixes with or berry juice stains cloth; something of its essence is merged with the essence of something else. It is a lesser thing but has a profound effect upon the greater thing.

As mentioned earlier, traditionally, candles are anointed with an oil which is then rubbed along the length of the candle. Concentration upon the intent of the charge is important at this point of the spell. This works on the principle of contagion magick. Not only are you passing the influence of the charged oil into the candle, but your thoughts at the time are a contagion to the energy of the act.

The purpose of oils in a work of magick is to add power. Therefore, the Witch as well as the candles should be anointed if it is appropriate to the spell. In this act, there is the joining of mind and power, act and intent. As a Witch, you will want to make a variety of oils and have them available for later use. Oils previously charged for personal power can come in very handy when you need to work magick but are physically/mentally fatigued.

Translucent-colored glass is very effective as an aid in charging oils. Translucent plastic works also, but most Witches tend to have an aversion to working with plastic in a magickal context. To charge an oil with a basic nature, select a container of symbolic color and pour the oil into it. Then place the container out in the Sun for three hours, preferably during the first three following sunrise. Later, when you add your own specific magickal charge, then set the container out beneath the Full Moon for three hours, preferably from nine p.m. to midnight. From this point on, never allow the sunlight to fall directly upon the container. Sunlight tends to dispel astral energy and can weaken magickal charges.

HERBS

Herbs are the primal link back to nature for the Witch. In effect, herbs are the stepping stones to reaching certain magickal destinations. Herbs, like oils and incense, correspond to planetary symbolism and have astral connections. Yet, herbs exercise a deeper level of influence than oils and incense. The herbal plant is a living vessel for a spirit or entity. This is similar to the relationship between our own spirits and physical bodies. When treated properly, the "consciousness" of the herb can aid our work of magick. The magickal abilities of the Witch are reflective of their own rapport with nature and the things of nature.

Herbs may also be used in a spell for their pharmaceutical properties, creating remedy potions and the like. In some cases, herbs can be used as offerings to spirits and deities because of their sacred natures. Some spells incorporate herbs as charms to be carried or buried in a particular place. This is related to the teaching that an herb contains a magickal spirit, or can evoke one's aid, and so the herb itself becomes the object of magickal influence.

The herb as something magickal in and of itself stems from the old lore of Witches related to planting, growing, and harvesting. Early Witches believed that a spirit was involved in every phase of the plant: seed, sprout, growth, bud, flower, and fruit/grain. As the plant grew, spirits would come to the fields and visit it. Here, they passed on something of their essence to the plant. Also, the plant had emerged from beneath the earth, a magickal and mysterious realm. Therefore, due to its sojourn within the earth, the plant bore the occult essence of this hidden realm.

CONDENSERS

Condensers, although similar to oils, are more diverse in influence. A condenser can be any liquid substance containing a magickal charge. The advantage of a condenser over an oil is that condensers can dry and evaporate with relative quickness. This makes condensers ideal for times when you wish no obvious trace of the material left behind as evidence of a magickal work at hand. Condensers also blend better with other liquids than oils and are readily absorbed by dry substances.

Condensers may be comprised of more symbolic ingredients than oils; therefore, they tend to be more useful in magick. Oils, on the other hand, adhere to objects better and can be easily blended with wax when making magickal candles. The practical application of condensers and oils is very similar for magickal purposes. Therefore, one would employ oils in the same manner as condensers. The only real distinction occurs when adding either one to something someone will ingest. The oil will be much more noticeable to taste than the condenser would be. Many perfumed oils tend to have a very bitter taste.

Most condensers are formulated pertaining to their elemental nature as well as to their pharmaceutical nature. Liquids from melons, for example, are generally considered to be elemental Water. The juice of a pepper is considered to be elemental Fire. Salty liquids are of the Earth element, and minty or flowery liquids are elemental Air. These examples are just a few and are general rules of thumb.

To employ a condenser, simply link the desired goal to the nature of one or more elements. Once you have the mixture, then magickally absorb the corresponding etheric elements using the elemental breathing technique described in this chapter under the subtitle "creating artificial familiars." This serves to unite the physical and astral components. An example of this is a healing condenser made from mint extracts to treat asthma. In this case, the mint is an Air condenser magickally linked to the lungs.

CHARMS

Many works of magick incorporate the use of charms. The charm can be a natural object such as a root, stone, shell, or even something handmade. In the case of a handmade object, symbols may be engraved along with runes or words of power designed to summon aid from spirits or deities. Natural objects are employed when they resemble something pertaining to the spell, such as a heart-shaped stone for a love spell.

Charms work on the "like attracts like" principle of magick. This is an aspect of mimetic magick. Mimicry has been used since ancient times for magickal purposes. Ancient hunters made drawings and icons of animals in an attempt to lure the actual creature into appearing. Shamans dressed in various animal pelts to invoke the spirit of the creatures. In this same way, charms become a focal point for the mind, drawing and joining "like to like." Such connections are basic to magickal formula. There must always be some link or connective element between what one desires and the means to manifest that desire.

INFORMING

Informing is the art of transferring mental images through the *willpower* of the mind, into target objects or substances. As human beings, we all possess the creative spark of that which created us. Therefore, on a lesser scale, we too can create by drawing upon the indwelling spiritual essence of our own being. All that is required is to bring one's will under control and to employ it to build crystal-clear images. Added to this is the energy of *burning desire* to empower the image and transfer it.

The most effective method to stimulate the breath is to employ sexual stimulation. It is through such stimulation that the power centers of the body open in response, flooding the central nervous system and stimulating the endocrine glands. The blood becomes electromagnetically charged by the metaphysical heat created by the stimulation and quickened breathing. The essence of this charge is carried in the vapor emitted from the lungs, the breath of magick. Many ancient magickal texts employ the breath in spell casting and other works of magick.

Once the blood is magickally heated, then the mind infuses it with a mental image symbolizing the desired effect. This image is essential to binding the magickal charge so that it can be transmitted upon the breath. The charge must be allowed to build within the blood until you feel a sensation of internal heat and pulsating blood. Once this point has been reached, then the breath may be directed out toward the charm or talisman that will contain it, or towards the target you wish to influence. To successfully wield energy, you must be able to concentrate and project (fix and direct) with the power of your mind/will.

As an aid to understanding the act of informing an object, picture a soft bubble about the size of a grapefruit. Imagine that you are holding it between your hands. Then concentrate on exactly what it is you want to place in this magickal bubble. Then reduce the desire down into a symbol. As an example, if you want to pass healing energy into the bubble, you might visualize a red cross or a caduceus. At this stage, you then visualize the symbol itself moving into the bubble and appearing within it. To complete the process, you then visualize the bubble merging into an object you wish to charge, or you mentally send the bubble off to a person, place, or situation.

EMPOWERING RITES AND SPELLS

There are certain factors that contribute to creating the magickal atmosphere by which one can empower a spell or ritual work. These basic elements are sigils, energy, focus, direction, release, goal, and contact. In this section, we will examine each of these magickal factors individually, and thereby come to a fuller appreciation for what they contribute to a successful spell or ritual.

A sigil is a symbol containing the essence of what it represents. To a degree, a person's signature is a sigil because it reflects something of one's own nature. The sigil serves to fix or bind the focus of one's magick. It is also the physical body for the magickal energy to attach itself to, thereby allowing it to work in the physical dimension.

Energy is the life essence of one's magickal workings. Energy gives life to the sigil just as the flow of blood gives life to the flesh body. Because we bear within our souls the creative spark of that which created us, we too can create. Occult energy is abundant within the fixed atmosphere of the Earth. We can draw upon it through the many techniques outlined in this book. Once drawn, the energy must then be focused.

To focus magickal energy, one must be able to visualize. The greater the ability to picture images in detail, the greater the power of the mind to bind energy to a sigil. Before anything can be created in physical form, it must first appear on the astral level. In other words, if one is going to make a functional material object, then one must first design it. Once the physical sigil has both form and the energy to animate that form, then it is time to direct the magickal charge.

Direction of magickal energy can be performed through many techniques. First, you should have a good idea of what compass direction the target of your magickal work lies in. If you're working in a ritual circle, then you can perform the work of magick facing the appropriate quarter related to the target. If the target is simply an amulet or talisman, then it is best to orient the work to the North quarter. In occult correspondences, the North is the realm of power and also relates to the element of Earth, which in turn relates to the physical dimension. If you do not know the direction of the target, you can simply direct the energy upward into the bound ether. Use the wand or athame as a pointing tool, directing the power as you release it.

Releasing the magickal charge is essential to any work of magick unless the magickal charge is intended to empower a physical object (in which case you would bind it to the object). One technique for releasing energy is to simply clap your hands quickly and sharply three times. Another is to slowly and purposefully exhale your breath outward while gesturing the triangle of manifestation sign (see illustration). Some Witches prefer to thrust their arms forward, palms flush, as one would who is trying to forcefully push something away. Once released, the energy must now make contact with the target in order to affect its influence.

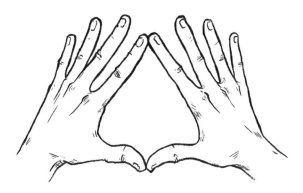

The Triangle of Manifestation is a tool for directing the magickal charge, releasing the empowering energy that will accomplish a magickal work.

To make contact, you must visualize the target as you release the magickal energy. You can even look at a symbolic picture just before releasing the spell. One important rule of making contact is to not dwell upon the outcome of the spell. Thinking about the outcome and yearning for it will only drain the energy and in many cases, can actually negate the spell by grounding it. Any emotional tie or mental reflection connected to the spell will keep a portion of its power linked back to you like a tether. You must give it full and unrestrained freedom to work if you wish the spell to be truly effective.

A MAGICKAL FORMULA

Now that we have looked at the basic elements of working magick, let us now look at the formula for creating spells and other works of magick. Apply the concepts already discussed in this chapter to the following formula.

1. The proper timing (Moon phase, season, time of day, nature of the spell, nature of the target, etc.).

2. Ingredients that correspond to the nature of the spell (colors, scents, associations, symbols, etc.).

3. A source of energy to empower the spell (a spell without something to give it power is like a flashlight without batteries).

4. A focal point or connection with the target of the spell (images, pictures, lock of hair, article of clothing, etc.).

5. The mechanism (words, gestures, manipulations, symbols, etc.).

6. Direction or channeling of energy (where is it going and how will it get there?)

7. Release (if you don't send it off, or let it go, then you've still got it with you).

8. Results (true magick will always work except for two reasons: you did not perform the spell properly according to the formula, or a greater power is resisting your spell).

PRAYER FORMULA

Prayer, like all things in a serious magickal system, has a structure and is based upon metaphysical concepts. Essentially, there are five basic stages to prayer:

1. Greet

2. Identify

3. Praise

4. Request

5. Thank

Let's take each one and examine it independently. The common courtesy of greeting by name or title is something that needs to be extended to deity as well. Witches tend to view specific deities as various aspects of the Divine Source itself. For example, the goddess Diana would be divinity expressed in a lunar nature, while Fauna would be divinity reflected within plants and animals of the woodlands. Divinity, as the Source of All Things, is unknowable to human consciousness. What it is, where it is, and how it came to be are concepts we cannot fully grasp. In order to gain some perception of it, we divide it into masculine and feminine aspects. In other words, the Divine Source is viewed as Goddess and God, separate and yet representative of the whole.

In an attempt to connect with deity as expressed in any form, we give it a name and an attribute. So, we might call upon deity saying *"Greetings, Diana."* But that is not enough in and of itself. To make the magickal connection, we also include the nature of what we call upon, and so we say *"Greetings, Diana, goddess of the Moon."* Still, this falls short of the total connection. We need to "inform" the divine consciousness we address, refining and defining the alignment we seek.

To complete the link, we say *"Greetings, Diana, goddess of the Moon, protector, provider, champion of the poor, outcast, and the oppressed."* Now we have informed the vehicle of divine consciousness, identifying it so that it recognizes itself in our description, whereby it can manifest to us in the mode we seek.

Now that we have greeted and identified deity, we turn to its praise. Praise is, in part, the emotional investment of whoever calls upon any deity. The old Craft teachings tell us that the gods need our worship even as we ourselves need food and drink. In this regard, our praise is part of the energy that nourishes our deities. On a mundane level, think about how a hug from a close friend or loved one can energize you or give you a sense of well-being. Praise is like a hug to a god or goddess. For the purposes of magickal prayer, it is most effective to list the qualities and strengths of the deity you call upon.

In our example of Diana, we might say:

"Diana, you whose beauty is like the beauty of the Full Moon amidst the stars. You bless the woodlands with your presence and all wildlife adores you. Diana, so great is your power that even the poor and lowly are rich when they speak but your name."

You can go and on about her connection with the Moon, tides, and so forth (whatever comes to mind).

Now it is time to make the request. The request should be as exact as you can make it. The gods have a most curious sense of humor, so be as precise as you can when making requests in order to avoid ending up in a comical or ironic situation. State what you don't want in the situation as well as what you do want. Many modern Witches incorporate the phrase that the request harms no one, including oneself. Strictly asking for money, for example, can result in it coming to you in ways you would not wish, such as through a will, or in some illegal or unethical manner. One of my earliest teachers said that asking for money offended the gods because it suggested that with sufficient money one would not need the aid of the gods.

Finally, give thanks for what you request. To not do so is to risk damaging the rapport you have established with your deity. Remember always, that a relationship with deity is not unlike that of a personal relationship with friends or family. Stay in contact for the sake of contact, and don't go to your deity only in times of need.

MAGICKAL DEFENSE

When a person walks the path of magick, psychic or magickal attacks can and do occur. Attacks can manifest in many ways. Mild attacks typically display themselves in a series of personal accidents generally of a minor nature, or in a run of unusually bad luck. Moderate attacks manifest in such things as nightmares, nameless fears or anxiety, sudden illness, and disruption of one's personal life. Serious attacks manifest in life-threatening accidents, profound loss of personal vitality, hallucinations, and life-threatening illness, and may even result in death.

If you suspect that you may be under psychic or magickal attack, first look at the mundane physical causes of your situation. A psychic or magickal attack upon your person should always be the last consideration. One consistent sign of an actual attack is that the worst problems occur between midnight and five a.m., and in the majority of cases, the Moon will be in its waning phase.

When you have determined that the attack is genuine, light some dragon's blood incense (made from the dragon's blood reed) and keep the area you are in well-lit. Light tends to dissolve astral energy and will help to dissipate anything attempting to form in the area. Cast a circle around you and trace large pentagrams in the air at each quarter, and then above and below you. Sit or lay down with your ankles crossed, right over left, and your fingers interlocked with palms laying on your solar plexus. This pattern weaves a shielding that blocks energy from passing into your body through the solar plexus, which is the entryway. It is wise then to pray to your deity for protection or to chant songs of power. You should also wear your pentacle and keep your ritual blade handy (remember, it is a weapon on the astral level).

Preventative magickal defenses are always a wise precaution. Crystals should be placed at all entrances to your home, including window ledges. Also, place a crystal near your bed, either on the headboard, suspended from the ceiling, or upon the nightstand. They should be informed magickally, and can later be roused by striking them together three times. Bathing in salt water should always be performed when under serious attack. The crystalline nature of the salt and the magnetic properties of the water will help break up the astral/etheric contamination of your aura.

If the occult forces at work against you are strong enough to create physical phenomena (such as noises, scents, mists, glowing spheres, moving shadows, or smoke), then dissolve some salt into vinegar and pour this into bowls set about the house or area. For serious manifestations, use nitric acid in place of vinegar, and set them as you would the crystals described earlier. Artificial familiars can also be created and informed magickally to protect you at night, especially if you must sleep during a phase of attack. Since all magickal attacks leave an energy trail back to the sender, the familiar spirit can be used to track the sender down.

CREATING ARTIFICIAL FAMILIARS

The first thing that you will need is a power stone or crystal. Next, you will need to make or obtain an image statue of your familiar. The statue must be hollowed out with a hole at the base for drainage. If you do not want to hollow out your statue, you can simply drill a hole in the base and seal it with wax or cork. This hole will be sealed until the familiar is released. A ceramic animal or any "piggy bank" style figurine can easily be used for this purpose. In the case of a bank, simply seal off the money slot with clay.

Place the power stone inside the image and fill the image with the four elemental condensers almost 2/3 full. These fluids are charged with various elemental influences and are used to add extra potency to spells and other magickal workings. Use equal measured parts of each condenser:

Fire Condenser: Chili pepper juice or "hot sauce" made from peppers (a red color is best, if possible)

Air Condenser: A mild brew of mint tea

Earth Condenser: Mineral oil

Water Condenser: Cucumber juice or watermelon juice

Once you have these substances, then you will begin to prepare them as follows. Take four small bottles and pour a different fluid into each one. Label or mark the bottles according to the corresponding element. Next, absorb and project the appropriate element into the bottle. This technique is very important to the art of magickal influence. It is through this absorption, condensation, and projection of the elements that certain metaphysical forces are drawn toward manifestation.

Techniques:

Absorbing Fire. Sit comfortably and imagine yourself in the center of a sphere of Fire (nothing exists but you and the sphere). Inhale, imagining that this Fire is drawn into your body. Draw it into your entire being. Imagine that you are hollow and are being filled with Fire. Imagine the heat, the energy, the force. Count with a beaded string or necklace as you draw each breath, keeping track of how many times you inhale until you are filled with Fire.

While you are inhaling an element, imagine the desired characteristic which corresponds to it. Mentally fix it and emotionally fix it. Once you have completed this stage, then visualize yourself (inside and out) glowing red. Now you are ready to project the element. Exhale upon the object you wish to charge, visualizing the color pouring out and the object glowing with it. Imagine the heat pouring out also. With each act of exhaling, count again with the beaded string or necklace. You must exhale exactly as many times as you have inhaled.

Absorbing Air. This is performed in the same manner as was Fire, except for the following: Imagine the sensation of growing lighter. Do not imagine any temperature changes. The color for visualization in this element is blue.

Absorbing Water. Do the same for this method as was done for the others with the following exceptions: Imagine the sensation of coldness filling you. Become heavy but fluid, and feel the weight of movement (not stability as with earth). The color associated with Water is green.

Absorbing Earth. This is performed in the same manner as the other elements with the following exceptions: Imagine the sensation of weight, feel the loose soil pouring in (like the sand in an hourglass). Do not imagine clay earth, as this has water in it. Do not imagine a temperature change. The color associated with Earth is yellow.

Having completed the absorption and projection, you will need to connect these fluids to their physical counterparts, as follows:

Fire Condenser: Pass the bottle through a flame for a couple of minutes, concentrating upon the element.

Air Condenser: Suspend the bottle from a tree (or any high place) so that it hangs in the air for a time. Concentrate upon the element.

Earth Condenser: Bury the bottle in soil for at least three hours, concentrating upon the element of Earth as you place the bottle in the ground. Afterward, you will retrieve the bottle.

Water Condenser: Place the bottle in a natural body of water (lake, ocean, stream), concentrating upon the element. Afterward, you will retrieve the bottle

Because of the magnetic properties of liquids, these bottled fluids will absorb and contain the magickal essences of the elements. It is the etheric substances that are actually condensed through this technique.

Now that the condensers have been prepared and charged, you will need to place three drops of your blood into the image chosen to house your artificial familiar. This will provide the familiar with your own vital energy, which will help it to maintain its link to the physical plane. Extra power may be added by placing fresh semen or vaginal secretions within the image. If these sexually produced fluids are used, you must remember that any mental images you formed during the sexual stimulation have left their energy imprint in the magnetic fluid. Such energies will influence the nature of the familiar to varying degrees (acting very much like subconscious thoughts for the familiar).

Now the image is prepared to receive the familiar. Make sure that the image is tightly sealed then proceed as follows: Stand before the object (having filled it with the liquids, and sealed it) and begin to raise an energy sphere between your palms. Draw this energy from your base chakra. Bring it up to your personal power center (just below the navel) and project it out into your palms.

Once formed, mentally transfer the sphere into the statue. Then, pick it up and exhale upon it three times. As you do this, state that you are giving it the breath of life. Visualize a blue light passing into the statue and mentally see the object glowing. Give the familiar a name at this point. The familiar is then ready to be instructed. Speak to it, providing it with all the necessary instruction required, including the purpose and function for which you created it. Tell it when it is to work and when it is to return to the image for rest, which it must do each day during the daylight.

It can remain on the physical plane for seven days, but no longer. After this period of time, you must dissolve it as later described in this section. When you desire to call your familiar, take up your wand or athame in your left hand. Point it at the ceramic familiar image and visualize it glowing white. Mentally or verbally speak the name of your familiar, saying "Come, _____." Then visualize the etheric image of your familiar separating from the ceramic image. See it before you in your mind's eye.

To direct the familiar at this point, simply condense it into a sphere of light. Afterward, return the familiar to the image. Do this by conscious and focused visualization. Use the familiar's name when sending and retrieving it. On a mundane level, your relationship with the familiar is like one with an obedience-trained dog. You must be in control at all times and never allow the familiar to do anything it was not directed to do. If it attempts this, then mentally direct it back into the housing image.

At the end of seven days, begin to dissolve the artificial familiar. Each day, for seven consecutive days, pour out a portion of the fluid upon the earth. Make sure that you still have some liquid to pour out on the seventh day. Do not pour out all of the liquid at once; you must take seven days. You are magickally linked to the entity, and there exists an etheric energy link between you and the familiar. A portion of your essence bleeds off when you dissolve the entity. It will replenish itself later, but you want to avoid the shock of draining energy off by suddenly pouring all of the magickal liquid out.

CHARGING A PROTECTIVE PENTAGRAM FOR YOUR HOME

It is always a good magickal practice to hang a pentagram in your bedroom. Having a pentagram over a doorway into the home is also a sound practice. Also, energy-trace the pentagram symbol across doors and windows using your athame. This helps seal your home against negative energy passing into it. Don't forget to trace a pentagram on the ceiling and floor as well.

The pentagram is an ancient symbol of protection. The symbol itself represents the power of the divine spirit bringing the four elements of creation into balance and harmony. In this context, the pentagram is a sigil that brings chaos into order. Because thoughts manifest as things, upon the astral plane, the pentagram acts as a tangible presence to spirits rather than a symbolic concept. It becomes a reality instead of a principle. Just as we instantly react to a traffic light turning red in front of us, so too is the trigger effect of the appearance of a pentagram to astral beings.

To prepare a home protection pentagram, begin on the night of the Full Moon and place the pentagram on your altar along with a cup of water. Take the metal lid from a medium size jar and half-fill it with a flammable liquid such as Everclear. Light the mixture with a long fireplace match and suspend the amulet over and above the flame with a chain. Trace the star pattern with the tip of your athame, then trace the circle.

Next, dip the pentagram into the cup of pure water, then hold the amulet in your left hand, and with the tip of the athame, point at the center of the pentagram and say:

"I call upon the Source of All Power to empower this pentagram as a protection against all that is evil, negative, or unbalanced."

Again, suspend the pentagram over the flame and say:

"I call upon ye spirits and Guardians of the North, East, South, and West to empower this pentagram, lending your force against all that is evil, negative, or unbalanced."

Dip the pentagram in the cup of water again, and then lay it upon the altar. Complete the charge by placing the tip of the athame on the center of the pentagram and say:

"I bind here, by all of these powers and forces, this unyielding Pentagram of Protection. To thee, thy course by lot hath given charge and strict watch, that in the presence of this pentagram, no evil thing may approach or enter in."

To activate a pentagram to full power in times of psychic or magickal attack, start at the top of the star and trace down to the bottom right corner. Visualize a blue flame flowing with your movement. Next, trace to the left middle point of the star, then across to the right point. Continue down to the left corner and conclude by tracing back up to the top of the star. At this point, visualize a flaming blue star in its entirety. Make sure that tracing the star out is performed in one continuous and unbroken motion. When this is complete, point at the center of the star and say with conviction:

"By the powers of Earth, Air, Fire, and Water, joined together with divine Spirit: strict charge and watch I give thee, that to this place, no evil thing approach or enter in."

Magickal and Ritual Correspondences

Planetary Influences

- **Sun:** Purification, strength, victory, banishing, valor. Vitalizes the blood, heart, and circulation. Linked to the will.
- **Moon:** Transforming, blending, persuading, hidden forces, emotions. Subconscious stimulation.
- **Jupiter:** Material possessions, status, legal matters, authority. Optimism, freedom, inspiration.
- **Venus:** Relationships, love, beauty, appearances, seduction. Blends the heart.
- **Mars:** Competition, victory in conflict, turmoil, motivation, aggression, perseverance.
- **Saturn:** Binding, limiting, confining, correcting, repairing. Disharmony, condenses, collects.
- **Mercury:** Communication. Links the mind to other planes. Bridges minds.

Herbal Associations

- **Sun:** Peony, angelica, sunflower, saffron, cinnamon, laurel, wolfsbane
- **Moon:** Selenotrope, hyssop, rosemary, watercress, moonflower, moonwort, garlic
- **Jupiter:** Basil, mint, elecampane, henbane, betony sage
- **Venus:** Lavender, vervain, valerian, coriander, laurel, lovage, foxglove
- **Mars:** Wolfsbane, hellebore, garlic, tobacco, capsicum
- **Saturn:** Dragon's wort, rue, cumin, hellebore, mandrake, aconite, hemlock
- **Mercury:** Fennel, mint, smallage, marjoram, parsley

Planetary Colors

- **Sun:** Gold or yellow
- **Moon:** White or silver
- **Mars:** Red

- **Mercury:** Violet
- **Jupiter:** Blue
- **Venus:** Green
- **Saturn:** Black

MAGICKAL COLOR SYMBOLISM

- **White:** Purification, protection
- **Pink:** Love, friendship
- **Yellow:** Drawing (pulling/compelling)
- **Green:** Growth, abundance, renewal
- **Red:** Passion, vigor, sexual energy
- **Orange:** Concentration, psychic energy
- **Purple:** Power over obstacles, magickal forces
- **Brown:** Neutralizing
- **Gold:** Drawing (strengthens other candles)
- **Blue:** Peace, spirituality, spiritual energy
- **Dark Blue:** Depression
- **Black:** Crossing, suppressing, ending

RITUAL COLOR SYMBOLISM

- **White:** Purity, transmitting
- **Green:** Nature magic, love, receptive fertility
- **Blue:** Peace, spiritual forces
- **Red:** Life force, sexual energy, vitality, active fertility
- **Brown:** Earth magic, neutralizing/grounding
- **Yellow:** Mental energy
- **Black:** Drawing, absorbing

ELEMENTAL ASSOCIATIONS

- **Earth:** (Yellow) strength, fortitude
- **Air:** (Blue) intellect, healing, freeing, inspiration
- **Fire:** (Red) sexual energy, life-giving, cleansing, force, desire
- **Water:** (Green) emotion, subconscious, love, fertility, adaptability

TREES

- **Sun:** Laurel and oak
- **Moon:** Willow, olive, palm
- **Mars:** Hickory
- **Mercury:** Hazel
- **Jupiter:** Pine, birch, mulberry
- **Venus:** Myrtle, ash, apple
- **Saturn:** Elm

AROMATICS

- **Sun:** Cinnamon, laurel, olibanum
- **Moon:** Almond, jasmine, camphor, lotus
- **Mars:** Aloes, dragon's blood, tobacco
- **Mercury:** Cinquefoil, fennel, aniseed
- **Jupiter:** Nutmeg, juniper, basil
- **Venus:** Myrtle, rose, ambergris
- **Saturn:** Myrrh, poppy, asafoetida

NUMERICAL VALUES

- **Sun:** 6
- **Moon:** 9
- **Mars:** 5
- **Mercury:** 8
- **Jupiter:** 4
- **Venus:** 7
- **Saturn:** 3

STONES

- **Sun:** Diamond, topaz
- **Moon:** Moonstone, opal, clear crystal quartz
- **Mars:** Bloodstone, ruby, jasper
- **Venus:** Emerald, green tourmaline, aquamarine, rose quartz

- **Jupiter:** Amethyst, chrysocolla, chrysoprase
- **Mercury:** Chalcedony, citrine, topaz
- **Saturn:** Black onyx, jet, black jade

When formulating a work of magick, or embellishing one that already exists, it is important to consider any correspondences related to the work at hand. Go over the list in this chapter and work in as much as possible. Consider the numerical value of the planet connected to the magickal intent. An example of this might be to add seven roses to a spell for love since seven is the number of the planet Venus and roses are sacred to the goddess Venus.

Remember that colors, scents, and symbols are all necessary as they stimulate the senses of the person performing a work of magick. This stimulation creates a vibration which then causes a reaction within the subconscious mind, then in turn within the etheric substance of the astral plane. As we know from the law of physics, every action causes a reaction. So is it too with the law of metaphysics.

Now that we have examined the art of magick, in the next chapter, we turn our attention to a more personalized approach. Although magick is an occult science based upon metaphysical principles, there is a great deal of personal adaptation available to the Witch. Let us now explore the next chapter dealing with personal power.

⤳ CHAPTER 7 ⤶

ℙERSONAL ℙOWER

For the Witch, personal power is developed from two sources. These sources are experience and rapport. Experience is the accumulation of the time and effort put into one's training and discernment. Rapport arises from the building of a relationship with spirits or personal deities. Both sources reflect, within the Witch, their personal devotion to the art.

When a Witch makes a ritual declaration such as *"and as my word, so mote it be,"* this is a statement reflective of their personal willpower. The Witch must always keep their word whenever possible in order for this ritual statement to have any real force or meaning behind it. The Witch must also finish any project they begin. This builds up within the aura "the energy of determination" which will be readily recognized by a spirit or deity. Just as we can read facial expressions and body language, spirits can read energy patterns.

The establishment of rapport created by a Witch between a spirit, Watcher, or deity, indicates the acknowledgment of the Witch as a practitioner of the Old Ways by such an entity. This recognition brings the entity into favor with the Witch, and therefore, a willingness to assist the Witch is evoked. This basic principle is the same on the mundane plane regarding friends and loved ones, as it is on the astral plane regarding entities. This is another example of the occult principle "as above, so below."

To build rapport, the Witch must practice evoking the Watchers (Guardians of the four quarters) and begin the practice of giving offerings to deity. Ideally, icons should be placed on the altar. To be "recognized" at the four quarters by the Watchers is essential in a magickal sense. The Watchers have the power to negate a magickal work, preventing it from passing into the astral realm. The astral realm is the dimension from which energy is transformed into something tangible on the physical plane. The Watchers can also allow magickal energy to freely pass from the physical dimension into the astral, wherein transformation can begin.

Repetition of such things as evoking the Watchers, casting ritual circles, setting an altar, and performing seasonal and lunar rites establishes the experience necessary for rousing personal power at will. In the Old Religion, it is taught that Witches maintain their personal power by immersing themselves in the eight sabbats of the year as well as the lunar rites. These lunar and seasonal energies permeate the aura of the Witch, condensing into the personal power centers of the body.

THE CENTERS OF POWER

According to the ancient teachings, the human body contains various centers of power associated with internal organs and linked to the endocrine system. In Eastern mysticism, there are seven centers in the body known as *chakras*. In the Old Religion of Europe, only three of these personal power centers appear in the teachings. The first one is located at the forehead, centered about an inch above the eyebrows. The second center lies at the breastbone area, and the third resides in the genital region.

In the Old Ways, these three points are called the *three knots of magick*. They symbolize the *Higher Self* and the *Lower Self* balanced by the *Middle Self*. In this relationship, the personal will (forehead center) and the primal energy (genital center) are joined in partnership through compassion (breast center). The mind by itself can do harm through emotional detachment and the primal energy of the body can do harm by unrestrained desire. But the spirit dwelling within the heart can invoke empathy through the second power center, thereby creating balance and harmony between the power centers. The three knots of magick function to ensure that no abuse of magickal power will take place.

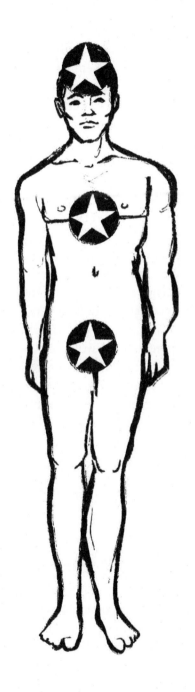

The Tree Power Centers symbolize occult zones of energy that utilize mind, body, and spirit.

To vitalize and align these centers, it is helpful to draw lunar energy down into them when the Moon is full. To accomplish this, simply perform the following technique. Remove all clothing and anoint the forehead, breastbone area, and genital area with a dab of camphor oil. Most pharmacies carry it, but if you cannot obtain camphor oil, then obtain a Moon oil or lunar oil from an occult shop. Once each center is anointed, either sit or stand beneath the Full Moon and perform the act of Drawing Down the Moon.

DRAWING DOWN THE MOON

This technique is designed to draw upon the astral substance of moonlight. For Witches, there is energy and magick in the Moon's subtle light. Lunar energy can also be used for psychic development and to aid states of meditation. In the Old Ways, the practice of *Drawing Down the Moon* is not the same concept that modern Witches employ when seeking to invoke the Goddess during the Full Moon ritual. The old term for invoking the Goddess within a human female vessel is referred to as *Calling Down the Goddess*. The first act is connecting with lunar energy, while the second act is designed to connect with Goddess energy. These are two different and yet related sources of power.

TECHNIQUE FOR DRAWING DOWN THE MOON

Sit quietly and visualize the Full Moon hovering a foot or two above your head. Close your eyes and mentally picture the Moon slowly descending down into each of your three body centers. Beginning with your head, visualize each center glowing with the Moon's light as the Full Moon pauses a few moments at each point. Picture each center within you emanating a miniature Full Moon. Concentrate on each point for at least a minute before moving on to the next, breathing in slowly and deeply. When finished, open your eyes and, beginning with the bottom center, touch each point with the fingertips of your left hand.

This technique, and those that follow, can be enhanced by playing soft music in the background. Audio tapes of drumming can also help to empower the techniques, as can burning an incense containing herbs associated with the Moon. Soft candlelight is beneficial for lighting, or you can simply sit in the dark. Employ anything that you feel will help you shift from a mundane state of consciousness.

TECHNIQUE FOR CALLING DOWN THE GODDESS

This technique is designed to invoke the Goddess into the consciousness of one's body. It can be performed either standing or laying down. In either case, the participant needs to assume the star position immediately following the invocation.

To begin, you will need several items: a flower, a bud, a leaf, and three white candles along with an incense burner, a cauldron, a bell, and a small bowl of clear water. Ideally, the act of Calling Down the Goddess should be performed in the nude, but you can also wear a light robe. In such a case, the material needs to be thin enough so that you can feel the touch of the flower, bud, and leaf through it.

Place the three candles so that they form a triangle large enough to enclose the cauldron. The triangle should be inverted, the tip facing you, as this represents the open vessel receiving and containing the emanations. Set the incense near the base of the outer center edge of the triangle. Position the bowl of water at the tip of the triangle and set the bell next to it. Place the flower, bud, and leaf in the cauldron. Light the candles and the incense.

Begin the invocation by ringing the bell three times over the cauldron. Three is the number of manifestation; the joining of time, place, and energy. Then take the leaf from the cauldron and dip it in the water. Anoint your left nipple with the leaf, followed by your right nipple, then the genital area, and once again anoint the left nipple. As you do so, speak these words:

"By sacred leaf, and bud, and flower,
I invoke my Lady now in this hour,
I call upon the Goddess of the Moon,
Come ye now to the bell's gay tune,
Maiden, Enchantress, Mother, and Crone,
Within my body now make thy home."

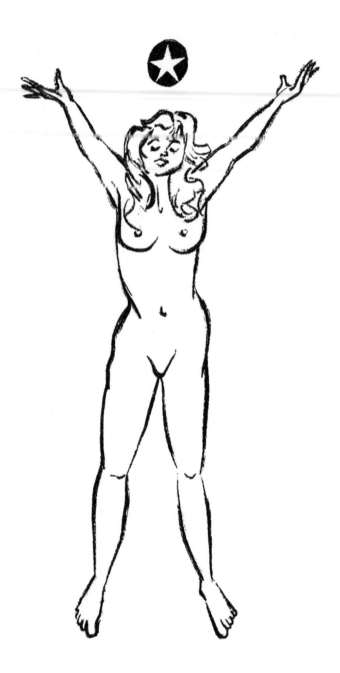

The Star Posture symbolizes the open and receptive vessel into which the Goddess may descend.

Ring the bell prior to repeating the above invocation as you anoint yourself in the same manner with the bud, followed by the flower. Place each item back in the cauldron after the anointing. Once the anointing is completed, pour the bowl of water into the cauldron. This represents the birthing fluid within the womb. In effect, the cauldron acts as the womb gate to the invocation. Dip your left hand into the cauldron, anoint yourself as you did, then immediately assume the star posture and chant the names of the Goddess three times:

Selene, Pertunda, Diana, Hecate.
Selene, Pertunda, Diana, Hecate.
Selene, Pertunda, Diana, Hecate.

Once completed, take three slow, deep breaths, visualizing yourself as you might imagine the appearance of the human form of the Goddess.

Remain in the star posture for as long as you like. Allow your thoughts and feelings to come and go of their own accord. Do not force anything, but rather, simply experience the moment. With practice, this technique should become a very potent tool for merging with Goddess energy. Work with it each Full Moon and note your experiences in a journal. Reflecting back upon what you've written after a full-year cycle should prove to be interesting.

When you wish to end the ceremony, you will need to release the Goddess energy. To accomplish this, place the fingertips of both hands into the cauldron water and anoint each of the three power centers. This is a separate act for each center. Speak the following words each time:

"Retire now, My Lady, into the night,
Reclaim thy home of sacred light,
Amidst the stars and sacred Moon,
Til' the bell again doth sing its tune."

Then extinguish the candle at the tip of the triangle. This closes the vessel gate. Leave the other two candles lit for lighting. Do not replenish the incense. To conclude, you will now need to perform the grounding technique.

GROUNDING EXERCISE

This technique works to drain off excess energy from ritual or magickal work, restoring one's previous state of consciousness. To begin, sit directly upon the bare earth, if possible, with your legs folded in front of you, palms of the hands pressed down upon the ground. A grass lawn will work also, or if absolutely necessary, you can use the floor of your home. In such a case, try and use an area of wood or tile, and avoid synthetic material.

Imagine your arms to be two hollow hoses. Envision yourself filled with light. Mentally pour out the excess/unwanted energy within you out into the earth. Breathe slowly and deeply, picturing the energy moving out through your arms with each exhale. Once you feel the energy is sufficiently drained, then quickly get up and leave the area. It is best not to return to the spot for a few hours as contact may create a magickal link, reconnecting you with the drained-off energy. The earth soon will neutralize the energy you discharged there, and the area will be as it was before you performed this act.

INHERENT POWER

Techniques that link one with God or Goddess energy can be identified as drawn power. In other words, the Witch evokes or invokes power from a source other than their own body. Another technique, different in nature, is known as *raised power*. This is energy generated from the body and spirit of the Witch. It is an inherent power rooted in the divine spark that animates the physical body.

The physical body is capable of generating an electromagnetic energy field, mixed with heat and vapor escaping from the flesh. This can all be condensed into an etheric sphere that, in turn, can be impregnated with a formed thought generated by the directed consciousness of the mind. To accomplish this requires the use of a simple design such as a spiral, or a sigil of one's choosing. The desired outcome of your magickal intent is first visualized while allowing the emotions to rise with the imagination. Then you begin to concentrate on a symbol representing what you desire. Next, you mentally transfer this symbol into the energy sphere, and thus, you have impregnated the etheric substance of magick with a thought-form representing your desire. The following section provides the basic formula for employing this technique.

RAISING THE ENERGY SPHERE

Sit comfortably, close your eyes, and imagine a white sphere of light about six inches above your head. Imagine it flowing down through your head, neck, shoulders, chest, arms, and so on. Let this energy flow through every inch of you until it has completely saturated you inside and covered your body along the outside. Imagine that your entire being is glowing white. At this point, you are in touch with the essence of power and you may proceed with an act of personal power, such as raising a sphere.

To raise a sphere of power, place your hands in front of you, about ten inches apart, palms facing each other. Now begin to move your hands slowly back and forth like playing the accordion. Gradually move your hands closer together but never allow the palms to touch. Experience the sensations of warmth, pressure, and magnetism. At some point, you should feel a soft balloon-like sphere between your hands.

Once you can sense or feel the sphere of power, you can then pass a mental sigil into it, or project a thought-form, thereby giving the sphere its purpose or magickal intent. To increase this energy, use your concentration and imagination to visualize a glowing force of power. At this point, mentally direct the sphere, visualizing it entering an object you wish to charge, or floating off to a place, situation, or person.

CLEANSING THROUGH PERSONAL POWER

This is a simple technique for cleansing and repairing the field surrounding the physical body. It is designed for working on another's body. First, raise your sphere of energy as you did in the previous exercise. Next, slowly glide your hands along the form of the body, palms facing the flesh. Avoid making direct physical contact, keeping your hands about four or five inches away.

Starting at the head, completely cover it with graceful sweeps of the hands, moving downward. When you complete this area, shake your hands toward the ground as though you were shaking off some water. Another technique is to use a small branch with leaves instead of your hands. In this case, you would dip the branch into a bowl of salted water.

Continue moving down the body a section at a time. Follow along the natural curves of the body as you proceed. Remember to "shake off" the energy after working on a section, as this helps to remove astral debris contaminating the aura. After completing the general sweep of the body, run your hands along the aura sensing for "gaps" in the structure. You should be able to feel the person's aura much like you felt the energy sphere formed between your hands in the previous exercise. Gaps typically feel cool or hollow, and sometimes they have a slight drawing feeling. If you sense any gaps or holes, then raise a sphere and "patch" it into the gap by pushing the sphere in and blending it. Use clockwise circular motions much like giving a massage. Let your intuition guide you as you go along.

SEX MAGICK

The use of sexual energy in magick and ritual was an essential ingredient in the fertility cults of pre-Christian Europe. In ancient India, sexual energy was the foundation upon which tantric magick and kundalini yoga were developed by Eastern mystics. Many of their techniques can be found in a book known as *The Kama Sutra*. In ancient Western culture, sexual themes of a magickal nature appear in cave drawings and in primitive iconography.

Our ancestors connected sexual intercourse to life and vitality. It was an act shared by the animals that humans hunted, and through this, a magickal connection existed between the hunter and the hunted. When our ancestors came to understand that sexual intercourse caused impregnation, then the fertility connection arose and was marked by symbols of human genitalia found in association with ancient rites. Before this connection, both impregnation and sexual intercourse were mysterious forces.

Eventually, rites, including sexual intercourse, were performed for the dead in order to give them life again. The dead were also anointed with menstrual blood to magickally connect them with the womb for rebirth. In one aspect or another, human sexuality and human reproductive organs have long been an intimate part of ritual and magick.

With the knowledge of how impregnation actually came about, women discovered the use of plants as contraception. This knowledge most likely arose during the time of raising herds, as many farmers have seen the reproductive cycles of their livestock disrupted by the ingestion of such plants as ivy. Ivy contains estrogenic compounds, as do many other plants associated with Witchcraft, such as the willow. Other plants employed in Witchcraft are effective for aborting pregnancy. These include acacia, madder, wormwood, and pennyroyal among others. Ancient Roman women used lemons (common in the Aegean/Mediterranean after the fifth century BCE) cut in half and inserted into the vagina. Later, borrowing from the Egyptians, they also employed the juice of stinging nettle mixed with honey, then inserted into the vagina on a piece of linen. Acacia and stinging nettle are now known to be very effective spermicides.

Not only was contraception important for the sacred sex workers who served their gods by bringing in money to support their temples, but also for the magick users who employed sexual stimulation in order to raise energy. Sexual energy is not only the most powerful and most concentrated force generated by the physical body; it also has the most profound psychological effects upon states of consciousness. Therefore, it can be harnessed for magickal purposes and directed towards specific goals. It was not uncommon for some female Witches to become wet nurses since frequent nursing is known to greatly reduce the chance of pregnancy. This allowed them to continue their sex magick practices without too great a risk of pregnancy.

In the Old Religion, Witches practiced sexual rites during the solstice and equinox periods. This was done to ensure fertility to fields, crops, and herds. Other rituals such as the May rite and the October rite employed sexual themes as part of an ancient mythos connected with the courtship of the God and Goddess. Some sects, such as the Benandanti and Malandanti of old Italy, fought ritual battles during the *ember days* over the fertility of crops and herds.

In modern times, some Witchcraft traditions employ sexuality only in such initiation rites as the third-degree level, a rite that marks one as a high priestess or high priest. This aspect of magick uses the energy of sexual union to create a link between the divine source, the high priestess/priest, and the individual being initiated. This is often referred to as the *Divine Marriage* or sometimes as the *Divine Incarnation Rite*. In this type of ritual, a couple connects with the divinity within themselves, portraying themselves as gods or goddesses interacting with each other. Through the intimate union arises the realization of the higher self.

Like the various stages of life itself, sexual initiation is a learning experience, a mystical setting that introduces something new, enhancing if not altering old perceptions. Immersion into the awareness of the duality principle through sexually altered states of consciousness creates a doorway to the full understanding of an old occult principle: the bringing together of two partners, through the introduction of a third element (the isolated consciousness of the initiate) creates a new element made of all three, one that is neither of the other two separately. This is the bestowing of a state of consciousness, a direct awareness of the divine spark within one that can serve as a conduit for the outpouring of divine consciousness. The act of *Calling Down the Goddess* into the body of a high priestess is one such example of such an ability.

At the base of the spine lies an inherent source of power known as the *serpent force*. In Eastern mysticism, it is known as the *kundalini*, a powerful force whereby humans can advance themselves magickally and spiritually. It is said that the ancient Egyptian headdress (often worn by pharaohs) depicting a serpent extended from the forehead was the sign of the kundalini power under the conscious control of the individual. It is interesting to note that the Egyptians believed their pharaohs to be demigods, which fits in with the teaching of how sexually-altered states of consciousness links one to divine power.

The goal of working with serpent energy is to draw it up into the *third eye* region. This is one of the power centers mentioned earlier in this chapter, a point between the eyes just above the bridge of the nose. Buried deep within is the pineal gland. Once the serpent power can be housed there, a great amount of occult power then lies at the command of the Witch. There are several methods of arousing this power. The usual method involves sexual stimulation of the genitals, usually by members of the opposite sex.[1] During this time, the serpent is visualized as moving up through the chakra areas, coiling at each point, and then proceeding to the next. When the serpent is roused by this method, it energizes the occult centers of power within the human body as it is drawn upward. This technique must be performed gradually, working on only one chakra point each session, on different days.

The serpent center is directly linked to the astral level and has its own cycles, each influenced by the four lunar phases. The New Moon, associated with Cancer, Scorpio, and Pisces, emanates the vital potential of the lunar current, unawakened and untainted. This is an excellent time for meditative practices and energy bathing. The first quarter Moon marks the building up and concentrating of energy arising from the potential state of the New Moon. Here, energy becomes magnetic and sensual. The first quarter is associated with Taurus, Virgo, and Capricorn. In the latter sign, magnetic energy is transformed into magickal power.

The Full Moon is the time of the alchemical process, the distillation and completed transformation of accumulated energy into the material of magickal desire. It is associated with Aries, Leo, and Sagittarius. The fourth quarter, or waning Moon, is associated with Gemini, Libra, and Aquarius. This is the time of energy release, the magickal orgasm whereby the seed of the body is emanated outward into humanity. Through the energy of the greater good over the self-centered consciousness (Aquarius versus Aries), the gods reach down and embrace humankind.

Ejaculated semen transmits energy that contributes to the creation of either a material or astral form. If the semen enters the womb, then its magickal energy is neutralized and absorbed into the mundane forces of procreation. This typically occurs after fifteen minutes of contact within the vaginal walls. If semen is produced through masturbation, fellatio, or sodomy, then the energy attracts the astral current where it is drawn into the astral dimension or is fed upon by

---

1　EDITOR'S NOTE: Though acts of sex magick were, at one time, traditionally preformed between a cisgender man and a cisgender woman, we now know and embrace wholeheartedly that queer, same-sex, and non-binary expressions of sex magick are valid and powerful.

entities dwelling either on the elemental or astral levels. The latter is an example of why fantasies do not manifest as they never root in the astral dimension before the energy is depleted.

Vaginal secretions are also very valuable fluids in sex magick. They contain the excretions of various endocrine glands in a purer form than those produced in scientific laboratories. Vaginal secretions transport chemicals from the cerebral spinal fluid and the endocrine glands. Fluids from the pituitary and pineal gland contribute chemicals during an act of sex magick when nerves governing urination in the floor of the third ventricle, and nerves directly connecting that center with the bladder, are employed during the sexual union.

The method of producing a magickal charge is to simply focus upon genital stimulation while imagining the desired magickal outcome of the rite. Then, just before allowing orgasm, the mental image representing the desired effect is mentally transferred into a sigil. Then the sigil is focused in the third eye and visualized at the time of climax, and thereby, the body fluids are imprinted with the formed thought. The actual sigil can be drawn beforehand so that one can simply stare at it, or it can even be painted on the body of one's sexual partner in a place readily viewed at the time of orgasm. The most common areas are the forehead, tailbone, or chest.

Once produced in such a fashion, the charged body fluids can be used to anoint any object one wishes to magickally charge. This will transfer the magickal charge through what I call *contagion magick*. The item can then be put into contact with a person, place, or situation in order to take effect. Charged body fluids can also be mixed with scents in order to transfer the charge. Some scents by themselves evoke sensual energies that can be employed for magickal purposes. They can be burned as incense or added to massage oil. The following are some examples.

- **Civet:** A sweet and musk-like scent that awakens the base chakra energy of the serpent energy residing in the genital region.
- **Clary Sage:** A relaxing scent, which, in turn, creates an atmosphere of ease. It is said to relieve impotence, as well as increase warmth, and make one more emotionally open.
- **Jasmine:** A traditionally romantic scent. It is said to ease emotional constriction and impotence. It is conducive to igniting passion.

- **Marjoram:** A scent that is said to calm the sex drive. It can be used to ground energy and restore normal sexual appetites following sex magick work.
- **Musk:** A sweet, sensual scent that adds a seductive quality to one's personal energy.
- **Orange Blossom:** A soothing scent that creates an atmosphere of romance. It is said to relieve stress and anxiety.
- **Patchouli:** A stimulating scent. It has an erotic quality linked to animal sexual scent signals.
- **Rose:** A gentle aphrodisiac, a symbol of love (elegant, romantic, enchanting), eases impotence, helps smooth and soothe relationship difficulties, and enhances creativity.
- **Rosewood:** A gentle scent—mildly stimulating. It is said to ease anxiety and depression.
- **Sandalwood:** This scent has an effect similar to patchouli but to a lesser degree. It is therefore better to use in situations where someone is more timid or anxious.
- **Ylang-Ylang:** A relaxing scent conducive to sexual union. As a tea, it has a mild aphrodisiac effect when combined with Yohimbe. Damiana steeped in a coffee liqueur is more effective, however.

METHODS USING OILS

If you want to make your own oils, some good base oils are almond, grapeseed, and jojoba. Olive oil is good if you add several drops of benzoin as a preservative. Otherwise, it will turn rancid. A primitive way of extracting fragrance from flowers and herbs is to heat them in oil, allow them to steep for twenty minutes, and strain the mixture through cheesecloth.

- **For Massage Oil:** Ten to twelve drops of the desired essential oil per ounce of base oil (2% dilution). Heat the massage oil slightly before applying, and rub your palms together briskly to warm the skin.
- **As Bath Oil:** Add three to eight drops of essential oil to bath water.
- **As a Scent:** A small dab of oil can be placed on top of a light bulb, and will smoke as the bulb heats. Metallic or ceramic light bulb rings are sold for this purpose as well. Skin can be scented with

oil when you know that you will be in close proximity to another person. Incense can be burned in a setting where the smoke will not be a deterrent to the sensual atmosphere.

Some Sample Blends:

- **Aphrodite's Bath:** Jasmine (one drop), sandalwood (four drops), ylang-ylang (1 drop)
- **Aphrodite Oil:** Jasmine (4 drops), rosewood (13 drops), ylang-ylang (8 drops)
- **Liberating Oil:** (to ease impotence) Clary sage (6 drops), jasmine (1 drop)

Achieving altered states of consciousness is one of the primary elements of the Witches' magickal ability. Let us turn now to the next chapter and explore this concept in greater depth.

> CHAPTER 8 <

ALTERED STATES OF CONSCIOUSNESS

IF THE ART OF WITCHCRAFT can be reduced to one aspect, it would be the achieving of altered states of consciousness. The simple act of setting an altar is one basic example, as well as casting a ritual circle or even the wearing of a ritual robe and occult jewelry. On a deeper level, we can add trance (induced by whatever means) and psychic development. Such states of consciousness allow the Witch not only to perceive things behind their veneer but also to reshape reality in an experiential sense. In other words, the Witch is capable of creating an alternative reality that is neither fantasy nor self-delusion. However, care must be taken to balance the mental, spiritual, and physical worlds in order to avoid the types of psychological damage previously mentioned.

The Witch has always been associated with herbs, amulets, and potions. Such "hands-on" activities ground the Witch in material and practical practices. A serious and devoted study of herbs, potions, amulets, and spells (along with their practice) provides the Witch with self-discipline. Through studying occult sciences such as divination and magick, the Witch develops the mental attunement and properties necessary to raise and wield personal power. Adherence to the Old Religion provides the Witch with spiritual goals and principles (a creed, if you will), arming the Witch with a clear vision of their place in the scheme of things. Such personal beliefs and practices gave rise to the so-called signs of the magus: to know, will, dare, and be silent.

Knowledge is aligned with Earth magick and represents the physical realm. The personal beliefs will reflect the disciplined mind. "To dare" is to hold to a set of beliefs, and to walk a personal path against all obstacles. When a person can do this, they have no need to boast or to demonstrate; there is only the silent witness of the person's presence. Such presence is unmistakable, reflected quietly like the light of the Full Moon glowing in the night sky.

ATAVISTIC RESURGENCE

The term "atavistic resurgence" was popularized by Austin Spare, an occultist who lived in the first half of the twentieth century. Spare claimed to have been taught the Witches' Craft by a Witch he called Mrs. Paterson, whom he met sometime around 1903. According to Spare, Paterson claimed to be descended from a line of Salem Witches. Paterson taught Spare how to reach altered states of consciousness in which he reportedly experienced "the Witches' sabbat" within another dimension. Spare explained that the accounts of the Witches' sabbat portrayed in the literature of the Middle Ages and Renaissance periods were a "debased and grotesque parody" of the actual event, which took place on the astral plane.

Some people have described atavistic resurgence as a form of sexual sorcery because it employs sexual stimulation as a base of energy. Spare spoke of atavistic resurgence as the *"evoking of latent memory clothed in new flesh."* He believed that the subconscious mind of a human was connected to past events experienced by all of their ancestors, going back even to pre-human form over the entire history of evolution.

To invoke and evoke the primal power slumbering in the genetic memory is one of the keys to the Craft of the Witches. The traditional images and icons of the Old Religion are themselves memory imprints. For example, the image of Pan depicts the base animal nature of humankind merged with the higher nature of human intellect. Together with Pan's traditional sexual nature, his image reminds us of the primal drives that empower our will and our desire. So, in Pan, we see the fertile sexual energies transmuted into divine creative energies.

During the period of the Inquisition, one of the allegations made against Witches was that they copulated with goats and with the Devil of Christian theology. The goat has been, since the cultures of ancient Mesopotamia, linked with regenerative powers and atavistic consciousness. What modern people might likely equate with bestiality was, in ancient times, a means of awakening primal occult power among certain select Pagan sects. There is an old myth, related to this concept, arising from Italian Paganism connected to the Sabine culture. According to the legend, after the Sabine women had been sexually assaulted, they were left sterile. The Sabines then went to give prayer and offerings to the goddess Juno. Juno spoke through the sound of the winds rustling the trees and told them their women must willingly submit to intimacy with a goat in order for their fertility to be restored (the goat was one of Juno's sacred animals).

Lacking the desire to do as Juno had decreed, the Sabines turned to the Etruscans, who were famous for their occult knowledge. One of the Etruscan priests told them to bring a goat offering. He then slew the goat and offered it to Juno. The priest cut the hide into straps and had the women appear before him and bare themselves. Then, the priest had each woman pass by him as he lashed her across the back and buttocks with the goat strap. The lash penetrated the skin and thus were the women joined in intimate contact with the goat. Juno's decree was thereby honored, and fertility was restored to the Sabine women.

This ancient myth carries not only psychological elements related to the assaulted women's cure but also elements of endocrine physiology associated with endorphins. Endorphins are peptide hormones that bind to opiate receptors primarily in the brain, affecting both the perception of pain and the experience of emotions. Flagellation and physical bindings restricting blood circulation are very ancient techniques for creating altered states of consciousness. Some Craft traditions still incorporate such elements in their initiation rituals. One of the secrets of successful initiation is to link pleasure, pain, apprehension, fear, or whatever catalysts the tradition employs to the emotional experience of the initiate (as well as to the scents, sounds, and other things particular to the ways of the sect). See the section subtitled "Myth and Metaphor" in this chapter for further information.

Trance

Trance is an altered state of consciousness created through a variety of techniques, including drugs, rhythmic sounds such as drumming, chanting, meditation, sensory deprivation, fasting, flagellation, dancing, and ecstasy. Other related techniques can be useful as well, such as magickal or shamanic practices involving visualization, controlled breathing, and sexual stimulation. Most of the involved studies in these areas appear in published texts related to tantric practices

One of the simplest techniques for inducing a trance state in modern Witchcraft practices centers around vibration. Vibration can be created through drumming or chanting. The sound waves introduce both physical sensation and auditory stimulation. It is difficult for the conscious mind to stay focused on more than one sensory input at a time. Therefore, by creating several stimulating factors, other areas of the mind take over awareness. For example, if you have incense burning while listening to repetitive drumming (especially a deep bass sound), while at the same time experiencing sensual touch as you hum a single musical note, the conscious mind cannot hold it all in full awareness. At this point, another aspect of consciousness begins to share awareness, and in effect, an altered state emerges.

Sound resonates within the abdominal cavity, which is where the personal power chakra is located. This area is an erogenous zone and responds erotically to light stroking of the skin or soft licking by a tongue. This general area begins to show the first signs of sensual response when music is introduced. In other words, people start to move their hips to strong musical beats. Although people may begin bobbing their heads to the rhythm of music, when the hip actions begin, we often use the phrase "they're really into it."

Music alters the relation of the self to the world, modifying the psyche both internally and in relation to the external space/ time environment. We often imprint upon a song, connecting it to a setting or experience, so that years later, when we hear it, the song instantly recalls the memory of a place or person. Music can also invoke emotions and even cause the endocrine glands to secrete chemicals in response to sudden changes in the intensity or rhythm of sound.

Music and dancing can produce feelings of energy and power. Dancing, in and of itself, can transform sensory awareness, leaving one with a feeling of physical lightness. A skillful dancer can even in- duce trance in others through their perfection of the art, as witnessed in the fact that people are willing to pay money just to see other people dance (as in ballet or professional ice-skating competitions). There is something transfixing and compelling in dance; perhaps it may even evoke the genetic memory of a primal courtship dance from our primitive days.

Dancing, and the consumption of a drug, combined with music, is a very powerful catalyst for creating trance. In such trance states, an individual can connect with things that cannot be perceived by the analytical mind nor by awareness of the five senses. This is, in effect, a reflection of the spiritual or mystical experience itself. In ancient times, it was used to bring the ritual celebrants into contact with the group mind of the clan, as well as into alignment with archetypes in general.

Trance can equate with personal liberation, which is one element addressed in "The Charge of the Goddess," that Witches must be free, and as a sign that they are truly free, they must sing, dance, make music, and love all in praise of the Goddess. Such a mentality frees the celebrants from the constraints of mundane reality allowing them to transcend space and time. The fantastic accounts of Witches' sabbats reflected in the records of the Inquisition are quite likely derived from such altered states of consciousness.

Drugs, dancing, chanting, and even listening to music affect our rate of breathing. In occultism, there is a correspondence between the breath and the spirit, and therefore, a correlation between techniques for conscious control of the breath and inducing altered states of consciousness related to the mystical spiritual experience. On a magickal level, the breath can be used to collect and condense Odic energy, about which I have written at length in my books *Wiccan Magick* and *Wiccan Mysteries*.

One of the most practical uses for states of trance by Witches lies in the ability of trance to repress the conscious mind. This results in the temporary extinction of the ego which, in turn, allows the Witch access to inspirational states of consciousness not contaminated by self-imposed limits nor self-delusions of the personal ego. Here, the mind can perceive a deeper understanding of self as it relates to the higher self and its connection with the divine. The rite of "Drawing Down the Moon" is one such example of ego displacement in trance, and the desire to merge with the spiritual or divine consciousness. In such a rite, the mind, body, and spirit become one in a holistic relationship with the Divine.

RITUAL FLAGELLATION

Flagellation, also known as scourging, is a technique of inflicting pain as both a purifier and a catalyst to induce states of trance. Flagellation appears in ancient times in connection with various Mystery Traditions, including the Eleusinian rites of Greece and the Dionysian rites in Pompeii, Italy. Scourging was a common practice among priests and priestesses in the Aegean and Mediterranean Mystery Traditions. Gerald Gardner mentions viewing the Mystery Murals at Pompeii and noticing the depiction of flagellation in connection with initiation themes there (*Witchcraft Today*. Secaucus: The Citadel Press, 1973).

Flagellation can induce an altered state of consciousness, known in modern times as the *alpha state*. In response to the pain signal, the brain causes the release of certain chemicals designed to relieve pain. Some of these chemicals can cause a feeling of pleasure and ecstasy, which is why flagellation is sometimes used in sexual settings as well. The release of chemicals within the body minimizes sensory awareness, allowing the mind to separate its full attention from the pain signal.

Examples of this type of control are well-documented in such feats as people walking barefoot across hot coals, shamanic body piercing rituals, as well as the Eastern disciplines of laying on a bed of nails, and so forth. In such a state of altered consciousness, the higher self emerges in the conscious mind, temporarily displacing the ego. As the predominant force of will during trance, the higher self merges with the Universal Force through which it creates a separate reality (where there is no pain, bleeding, or blistering).

Flagellation, like the binding of body parts with rope or cord, causes changes in the blood supply to the brain. Reduced blood supply to the brain induces an altered state of consciousness. The rhythmic strokes of flagellation are not unlike shamanic drumming and have the same effects upon the mind and body as discussed in this chapter concerning music. Pleasure and pain can become one and the same experience, the polarities of one energy. When fear and anticipation are added, such as a blindfolded initiate may experience in a ritual setting, additional chemicals are released by the endocrine glands in response.

The experience of being scourged is not unlike the feeling of plunging into cold water, rather than wading in. A combination of shock and invigoration is quite common and serves to heighten mental and emotional awareness. From a magickal perspective, the sting of each rhythmic lash can be mentally transformed from the sensation of pain to the sensation of penetration. In this mentality, the act becomes sexual and procreative, resulting in the impregnation of mind and spirit with the magickal child. The magickal child in this context is the desired altered state of consciousness and its goal in the magickal transformation.

To accomplish this, the recipient creates a sigil of the desired goal and concentrates upon it during the height of the flagellation experience. In a metaphysical sense, the equivalent of an orgasm in flagellation is the climax of shifting consciousness while fixing one's gaze upon the sigil. Thus, it is the moment of the conception of the magickal child.

RIGHT- AND LEFT-BRAIN CONSCIOUSNESS

The human brain can be divided into right and left hemispheres, functioning quite differently in the way they process information. The left hemisphere is analytical, logical, and linear. The right hemisphere deals with complex relationships, patterns, analogies, and configurations. The brain integrates both ways of processing information in order for us to discern our environment and the information provided to our senses.

The "strength" of the left sphere lies in its ability to focus upon specifics, but its "weakness" lies in the fact that this may make it more difficult to discern the holistic concept. The strength of the right sphere lies in its capability to translate the abstract, but its weakness lies in the fact that it has difficulty discerning specific individual images.

An artist employs more *right-brain thinking* during the creative process. But it is the left sphere's analytical properties that determine the mode through which creativity is made manifest. It is important, within the context of the magick, to understand the different ways that each brain hemisphere processes information. One example of how these spheres function differently can be discerned in viewing clouds. When looking at a cloud, the left-brain sphere perceives it as a cloud, perhaps even connecting it to the weather. The right sphere looks at the cloud and sees a dragon image or something else the cloud might resemble.

The suggestive shape taken on by a cloud, perhaps that of a bear, is one of many examples of how people experience altered states of consciousness in everyday life. In the *waking state,* the conscious mind controls the priority of discernment, while in altered states of consciousness, the subconscious mind shares (or can even govern) the role of director. Dreams are examples of this shift because the sequence of events in a dream frequently follow no "logical" order and yet still make sense to the dreamer. One example is the dreamer driving a car that transforms into a bicycle. The dreamer does not typically question the event and the dream continues, uninterrupted by the absurdness of it all.

In some scientific circles, left- and right-brain function is divided into what is called "first- and second-order reality." So-called *first-order reality* is reflected in our response to any stimulation of the senses. We see a traffic light turn red and we are typically compelled to stop our vehicle. *Second-order reality* arises from the thoughts, feelings, and personal views concerning our first-order reality. Whether we do indeed stop our vehicle at the red light, or speed up and pass through the intersection, is a matter of communication between these two internal elements. In other words, our objective reality is in conflict with our subjective experience; we know we should stop at the light but we're running late for work.

Objective reality can be allocated to the province of the left brain hemisphere, and our subjective experience (second-order reality) can be thought of as residing in the right brain hemisphere. If indeed this is the case, then perhaps the origin of our behaviors lies in the right brain; while our left brain justifies our actions. So, in our example of the traffic light, the right brain perceives the situation in a larger sense of time management and decides to run the red light. The left brain analyses the specifics and creates a justification for giving priority to second-order reality, the subjective experience.

Acknowledging the ways and manners of the left- and right-brain function is not enough, in and of itself, to be of much value to us in shifting to altered states of consciousness at will. In order to begin to use the powers of these spheres, we must learn not only how they communicate with each other, but how we can communicate with them directly and independently. Fortunately, our ancestors pre-served these keys in the formulation and construction of myths and legends. As Witches, we employ metaphors in order to communicate and understand that which cannot be communicated or understood by the conscious mind.

MYTH AND METAPHOR

The two halves of our brain actually speak different languages and view incoming information about the world quite uniquely from one another. The left brain discerns through direct analysis while the right brain interprets through analogy.

As Witches, though, we do not underplay the importance of left-brain thinking; we tend towards a greater appreciation of right-brain function. We do this because it gives life, and greater meaning, to the mundane aspects of ritual and magickal work. It is not the ritual itself that is of such importance in the Craft, but rather the metaphor with which it connects.

A metaphor communicates through analogy. It is descriptive in nature and is the very core of Craft myth and legend. Myths, and the metaphors they wrap around, all appeal to right-brain perceptions of the world. Many of the great spiritual avatars, such as Buddha, Jesus, and Krishna, used analogy as the basis for their teachings. Today, we know this principle as one of "speaking in parables." The technique of the parable simply compares something the listener does not have personal knowledge of with something they do know.

Through analogy, the holistic concepts of right-brain under-standing can be analyzed by left-brain examination. Both aspects of our consciousness are vital to making practical use of whatever stimulates our senses. Even though we may not be consciously able to fully appreciate the metaphor, we can embrace it consciously for discernment. What the conscious mind cannot unravel stimulates the subconscious mind to join in the process of resolution.

Metaphor is a form of symbolic language that has been used for countless ages as a teaching method. The parables of the New Testament, the koans of Zen Buddhism, and even old fairy tales are good examples of the use of metaphor to convey concepts in an indirect, yet more meaningful way. As Witches, I think we can agree with folklorist Joseph Campbell that myths are not vehicles for seeking answers to the meaning of life, but rather, for understanding the experience of life itself. For it is through our microcosmic connection with the macrocosm that our experiences within the physical dimension strike resonance with the divine spark within us (given to us by that which created us). Such an experience is foretold in the Craft verse from "The Charge" which reads: "…*let thine innermost divine self be enfolded in the rapture of the infinite.*"

In the Craft, we do not so much *learn* about the tenets of our belief as we *participate* in (and therefore, experience) the mythology that forms the structure of our religion. I refer here to the mythos that is carried throughout the year within the sabbats centered around the solstices, equinoxes, and the cross-quarter days. The mythos of the Wheel of the Year contains metaphors connecting us to nature and, by extension, to that which created nature itself. This is the power of myths, for they carry significant meaning directly into the listener's consciousness and subconscious mind.

Left-brain consciousness grasps the meaning of the moral of a myth or fairy tale while right-brain consciousness experiences the event itself. These two types of consciousness allow the images and details of the story to resonate respectively within the mind. The left brain matches similar experiences related within the story, while the right brain integrates elements that speak to that part of us that already *knows* somewhere deep inside us. For myths are valuable teaching aids, creating metaphors that address both what is common to the human experience (our trials and tribulations) as well as what is heroic (what we can reach or strive to reach in our finest moments).

In order to discern the meaning of myth and metaphor, we need to somewhat understand the operation of the brain's spheres in the process of integrating information. However, the key question is, how do myth and metaphor operate as catalysts to this process? The answer lies in the relationship between microcosm and macrocosm, how our inner world connects with the outer world. Everyone has an individual worldview influenced by the unique experiences a person has while growing up. For example, each of us can agree upon a basic understanding of what a fence is, but our personal experiences with fences affect our personal views. In other words, when I used the word "fence," did you think of a wooden fence or perhaps a stone wall? Was it a small fence or a large fence? A fence is universal to our "community knowledge" or "group mind," if you will, but its image and character are unique to the individual.

Each of us, therefore, colors our perceptions of even basic things because of our personal experiences. Yet, from an occult perspective, it is the mind's search for connection and correlation that is important in achieving altered states of consciousness. In other words, it's the mechanism itself that alters consciousness and not the end result. It is the process of discernment itself. In our example of the fence, the brain searches through past experiences retained in memory cells in order to identify what a fence is and what its presence indicates. Then it connects how we feel about it, and communicates how we should react to its presence. Is it safe, helpful, an obstacle, an advantage, or what?

It is this exact process of relating sensory input to one's personal worldview that makes metaphors within a myth such a powerful catalyst and magickal key. When we listen to a story, our mind searches through our memory cells in order to make sense of the story. If elements of the story match something of significance in our personal experience, then these elements take on new meaning because of the new context in which they are presented. Seemingly unrelated data within our brain can be joined to create knowledge we never knew was already contained in fragments simply awaiting the connective metaphors to evoke enlightenment. It is an ancient Mystery teaching that it is not so much the information relayed, but rather the context in which it is presented, that leads to enlightenment.

To be effective, a mythical tale must contain elements comparable to the listener's own experiences, even though the setting and conditions might not relate to personal experience. For example, a character within a myth might have to fight a dragon, something none of us have ever done. But we have all been afraid at some time in our lives, and as adults, most people have faced serious life-altering situations, so we can relate to the character facing the dragon.

The ancient myths and legends contain information that is useful to the process of left- and right-brain function. This is not surprising, because left- and right-consciousness minds created them to begin with. Embedded within the ancient tales are catalysts, commands, imagery, information, and other data, all of which have been preserved for us by our ancestors. But what has been lost to the public are the keys to activating the metaphors.

In ancient times, storytelling was an art in and of itself. By changing voice pitch, tone, or tempo the storyteller gave life to the tale, communicating important information about what was happening or was about to happen. It is very similar to a musical score woven into a movie; we are not fully aware of it but it sets the tone for danger, romance, suspense, or whatever as the story unfolds before us. To watch the same movie without the background music is quite a different experience, lacking in the richness of full sensory communication.

Additionally, and parallel to the concept of background music, the storyteller uses non-verbal communication through posture, facial expression, and other conceptual images. All of this combines to "get past" left-brain defenses and speak directly to the right brain. For the left brain is the guardian who stands in the way of transformation. The left sphere questions phenomena and looks for alternative explanations. Often, the left sphere can talk us out of believing in something we just experienced because the event defies left-brain reasoning. But as Witches, we understand that ritual and ritual phenomena are metaphorical communication. This is why our rituals form around myths representing the seasons of the year, and through them, we communicate with divinity residing within nature.

In order for a myth to successfully transmit through metaphor, it must do several things. First, it must contain learning situations resembling our own dilemmas in life (thereby keeping the left sphere interested), while establishing the stage in "other world" settings (thus proving a focus for right-brain function). Next, it must connect us to the hero, transforming us by enabling us to relate to them. Typically, the hero represents what is most noble within us, yet still remains undiscovered or unrealized. In other words, we do not know what it is we really know about ourselves, but the hero speaks to it loudly.

The next phase in the myth is to present a metaphorical conflict in the story resembling our own struggles with right and wrong, failure and success, etc. The tools/weapons and magickal objects carried by the hero represent the conscious and subconscious processes respectively, through which resolution of the conflict is possible. This is followed by presenting within the tale various parallel learning situations to which we can relate our own microcosmic experiences. Typically, the myth will incorporate both individual and cultural images and connections. As the myth continues, a metaphorical crisis develops. It is one which the hero (our newly transformed sense of personal identification) must attempt to resolve or conquer in some manner symbolic of our own higher nature. Whether the hero succeeds or fails is a vital element of the altered state of consciousness intended. We see altered states of consciousness invoked every time an audience is moved by a film, event, or play. Sadly, the power of the metaphor in modern times often sells T-shirts, figurines, toys, posters, and other merchandise related to popular movies.

PSYCHIC AWARENESS

In my experience, some of the most psychic people I have ever met were people who suffered from some traumatic event in their current life experience. I have found that emotionally and/or physically abused individuals tend to end up with pronounced psychic abilities. Sometimes people who have clinically died and then returned to life will display psychic powers they did not demonstrate previously. I believe this is because psychic powers are one of the survival mechanisms humans naturally possess.

Intuition is one of several manifestations of the psychic nature. People, especially women and children, who are subject to abuse at home, become very astute at reading the environment for signs of pending danger. In the case of physical abuse, these people develop a keen ability to discern the mood of the abuser even without the obvious signs of anger or agitation readily apparent. It is another sense at work, one that is beyond the five senses perceived by modern science.

Science relies upon rationalism and materialism as the only legitimate means of discerning reality. The conscious mind, which is only one-half of our human consciousness, is given reign over our perception of reality. In fact, we tend to think of ourselves as the conscious mind, and our subconscious mind is relegated to dreams and fantasies, things that are not "real" in the sense of our "waking" consciousness. Yet, there are still some, such as the poet and the magician, who continue to embrace both the analytical and the conceptual aspects of the mind.

The fact that Witches can easily shift consciousness, communicating with both the analytical left sphere of the brain as well as the conceptual right sphere, allows the Witch to commune with both the mundane and the spiritual world. Altered states of consciousness are apparent in tales of Witches flying to their ritual sites, speaking with familiars, and foretelling the future. All of these are repeated themes related to Witches dating back to pre-Christian times in Rome and Greece.

Altering one's consciousness can be used to evoke primitive patterns within the mind. The constraints of rational thought can be loosened in order for the primal animal nature to commandeer the waking consciousness. Thus, the Witch removes that which separates them from other realms in which animals can be directly communicated with and spirits can be contacted. This is a separate reality belonging to mystics and Witches that can never be understood nor realized by the scientific mind.

Primitive shapeshifting rituals are good examples of transcending mundane reality. This involves the use of animal masks, costumes, and mimicry. To wear an animal mask, and to possess its fur or feathers, is to embrace the spirit double of the animal. This is a mental and spiritual merging of both human and primal animal essence. To this is added the imitation of the animal through sound and movement. Such a joining of primal and higher nature results in an altered state of consciousness. In some respects, this state of mind is a meeting place wherein mediation of animal and human communication can occur on common ground.

Primal communication of the type described here is the essence of the relationship between a Witch and their familiar or *power animal.* Such communication is an expansion of the constraints of mundane reality, allowing the Witch awareness of things that are invisible to the physical senses. In some cultures, the smoking of hallucinogenic herbs aided in primal evocation. The employment of drugs or alcohol in ancient occult societies was a very common practice, and quite likely, ergot mold played a part in the Witches' sect of Old Europe.

DRUGS AND ALTERED STATES

Beginning as early as the fifteenth century BCE, an agricultural cult of the goddess Demeter flourished in Greece. From it arose the great Mystery religions of the Aegean and Mediterranean, which were to later influence the Craft traditions of northern and western Europe. Initiation into the ancient Mysteries was designed to create a change of mindset and consciousness through direct experience of the sacred. Such Mystery cults as those of Dionysus, Orpheus, Mithras, Cybele, and Isis had a tremendous impact upon European Paganism. However, the most profound influences on European Witchcraft are traceable to the Mystery tradition of the goddess Demeter and her daughter Persephone, especially within the Eleusinian Mysteries.

In it, we find the familiar tale of Persephone, who, while gathering flowers far from her mother Demeter, was captured by Hades, Lord of the Underworld, and carried away into the depths of the earth. Sick with grief, Demeter causes the earth to become barren, and thus we have the myth of the first winter. The gods grow concerned that should humankind perish, there would be no one to offer worship. Zeus orders Hermes into the Underworld realm of Hades to retrieve Persephone. The mother and daughter are joyfully reunited, and Demeter lifts her curse on the earth and life returns to the planet. In these myths, we find the Craft mythos of the descent and ascent of the Goddess.

The rites of the Greater Mysteries at Eleusis were held at the autumn equinox each year. There is much speculation that consciousness-altering drugs were employed in the Mystery rites of this ancient cult. Albert Hofmann proposed in a 1978 study that the sacred meal with which the initiates ended their weeklong fast contained a hallucinogenic compound. In 1964, author Robert Graves published an essay suggesting the Eleusinians had discovered a variety of hallucinogenic mushroom that could be baked into offering cakes and still retain the psychedelic potency. We know from ancient records that the sacred meal of the Eleusinian Mystery Cult was made of pennyroyal leaves or a related plant, water, and barley grain.

As mentioned in a previous chapter, barley, wheat, rye, and other cereals are known to be subject to the parasitic fungus ergot (*Claviceps purpurea*). Ergot contains a number of alkaloids, several of which are psychoactive, including ergine (lysergic acid amide) and ergonovine. Ergine is the botanical source of one of the most powerful psychedelic compounds known, the modern synthetic LSD, and produces similar effects. It is not unlikely that the priestesses of Eleusis had discovered the psychedelic properties of ergot and that the Mystery rites enacted there were enhanced by powerful hallucinogenic experiences directed by the initiators.

Ancient writers of the period, such as Plutarch, describe that the initiates awaited the ceremony in an initially agitated state of confusion. They appeared to tremble with cold while at the same time perspiring. The physiological effects of ergonovine are similar to those of LSD as it begins to take effect within the first hour of ingestion. The first signs are dilatation of the pupils, and increased heart rate, blood pressure, and body temperature. Following this is the onset of mild dizziness or nausea, chills, tingling, trembling; slow deep breathing; loss of appetite; and insomnia. Along with these effects is an increase in both perspiration and blood glucose levels.

Aristotle, Proclus, and Plutarch relate that the Mysteries of Eleusis were experienced, not explained. The transcendent nature of the experience defied attempts to communicate it in words. What the initiates learned during the Mysteries was accomplished by sight and without explicit verbal teaching. The initiate was shown various cult objects and presented with various themes, all enhanced by the flickering light of torches.

The altered state of consciousness provided through the hallucinogenic properties of ergot heightened visual and emotional perceptions of the ritual, adding seemingly spiritual significance to them.

It is specifically the perception of visual stimuli that is most affected by psychedelic compounds. The subject's perceptions are magnified in contrast and intensity. Cross-sensory perceptions occur and the individual perceives the "sight of sound" or the "texture of a color." Aristides the Rhetor, who witnessed the Mysteries at Eleusis, wrote:

"Eleusis is a shrine common to the whole earth...it is both the most awesome and the most luminous. At what place in the world have more miraculous tidings been sung, and where have the dromena called forth greater emotion, where has there been greater rivalry between seeing and hearing?"

An initiate whose perceptions had been altered with ergine or ergonovine would no doubt feel that deep meanings had suddenly and inexplicably become transparent. The psychic changes that arise from altered states of consciousness induced by hallucinogens are so radically different from ordinary experiences that they cannot be described or related through mundane analogy. Thus, the initiate feels that something very mystical transpired and that their own mental capacities were expanded, which indeed they were.

Added to the experience of an altered state of consciousness is the initiate's understanding of the religious and magickal basis of the sect in which they were a member. The Mysteries of Demeter and Kore were transmitted through the utilization of naturally occurring ergot mold appearing on the heads of grain, which were sacred to these goddesses. To the ancient mind, what we now know as the pharmaceutical properties of a substance, were viewed as the indwelling spirit. Wine, for example, contained the spirit of Dionysus. Through this reasoning, the grain contaminated by ergot mold held the spirit of Demeter and Kore. To partake of the grain was to enter into communion with one's deities. In many Craft traditions, the ceremony of cakes and wine is a form of communion with the God and Goddess. This ceremony involves the blessing and consumption of a ritual meal consisting of red wine and a grain cake.

There comes a time in the magickal career of the Witch when altered states of consciousness can be attained at will. This is due in part to the memory path or memory path nature of the brain/mind. Any specific strong element of the memory chain, when concentrated upon, can evoke the onset of the entire previously experienced pattern. One example is the so-called LSD flashback experience. The sudden viewing of a distorted image, for example, can create similar visual and audio distortions that one experienced when they were on LSD. This is because the brain/mind, triggered by the sudden visual shift, is replaying a recorded memory pattern, or memory chain association, superimposed over the current setting in which the individual finds themself.

The Witch can enter various altered states of consciousness at will by evoking their memory chain associations. One of the techniques commonly employed during such altered states is known as *merging*. Let us turn now to the next chapter and learn about merging, raising a cone of power, and how to perform various acts of magick.

CHAPTER 9

THE WORKINGS OF POWER

IN THIS CHAPTER, we will explore a method of employing states of consciousness for magickal workings. I offer the following material in honor and in memory of my friend and teacher, Mel Fuller, who shared these concepts with me so long ago. Magick as a work of power is produced by the combination of several factors: the tools with their symbolic meanings and prescribed manipulations, the ritual stages and expectations, chants, and the mental and emotional state of the practitioner. All of these create a momentum of power and greatly enhance a work of power.

The concept of *oneness* is the basic foundation from which all the laws and principles of magick are derived. In metaphysical terminology, the concept is called *pantheistic monism*. This refers to the belief in one divine being who is present in many forms. All creatures, objects, vibrations, forms, energies, levels, gods, plants, and awarenesses (human or otherwise) are manifestations of that one being. This is the uniting factor, the single thread running through all religions.

The mental and emotional state of the Witch is an essential ingredient for creating magickal energy. An important step in becoming a master of the Witches' Craft is the direct realization that the Witch and the Divine Source share an alignment. The spirit within the Witch is the indwelling spark of divinity bestowed by the creators. Because of this creative divine spark, the Witch can also generate and transmit creative sparks of their own energy. The realization of this unifying factor allows the Witch to merge their own consciousness into objects and other conscious beings.

When in a merged state, the Witch has the awareness that they and the creators are one through the union of the creative spark, the indwelling spirit. Therefore, whatever expectations are expressed while in that state will become a reality. This is because the creative spark of one's own consciousness then becomes amplified by merging with the greater consciousness that created all things. Identification with the one becomes the reality of the other. The greater the depth of merging, the greater the degree of power that can be drawn upon in this shared consciousness.

A Technique for Merging

A very simple and effective technique for learning how to merge involves the use of clouds. Look up into the sky and select a small wispy cloud for practice. Later, once you have built up your confidence, you can tackle larger clouds. Lay down and relax, looking directly up at the cloud. Breathe deeply and slowly, pushing all thoughts from your mind. Fix your gaze on the center of the cloud, and mentally picture yourself as being the cloud itself. Each time you exhale, feel yourself pouring or spreading out into the sky. At the same time, mentally see the cloud doing this as well.

If this is too difficult at first, try just concentrating on the cloud, focusing your thoughts, and visualizing the cloud dissolving into the blue sky. Eventually, you will need to make the connection between you and the cloud, a true sense of oneness. Merging is becoming one with the object and not simply imagining that you have done so. Once you *are* the object, you can make changes within your consciousness that will, in turn, change the object. In the deepest levels of merging, there is no difference between you and the object.

With practice, you should find that you can easily and quickly disperse larger clouds, or even bring clouds together. This was one of the old techniques that Witches used for weather magick. The Witch is still reliant upon nature, and one cannot produce rain without the presence of clouds, nor cause clouds to appear when the conditions are not conducive to cloud formation. The art of Witchcraft is not mumbo-jumbo, but rather a metaphysical science based upon time-proven formulas in accord with the forces and ways of nature.

FORMULA MAGICK

The factors that bear on being able to tap magickal energy through states of consciousness are as follows:

- **Visualization:** The nature, character, and circumstances of the thing you want.
- **Desire:** The degree of intensity, the need, and the personal will to possess.
- **Expectation:** The realization that you and the goal are united through the same indwelling creative energy, and therefore, "like attracts like."
- **Merging:** Not simply *to know*, but to realize that you are one with the Source of All Things. In merging, one's ego-awareness decentralizes or diffuses into the higher self. It is not unlike a cloud diffusing into the vast blue sky that envelops it.

The following work of magick is set up in a manner that, if performed properly, will incorporate the necessary factors listed earlier for you. In other words, they are built into the framework of each work of magick. The difference in how effective a work will be is reflected in one's ability to control these factors without external aid. There is one rule that must be remembered when you're performing a work of magick: *an error in one or more of the formula factors will result in an error or lack of manifestation.* Be sure you know what it is that you really want, how you want it to be, and that you really need it.

A WORK OF POWER

In magick, we begin with the premise that salt is naturally cleansed and therefore is a purifier in and of itself. With this understanding, take a bowl of water and put three pinches of salt in it. Light an incense, the ingredients of which are appropriate in nature to the intent of the magickal desire. Next, take a sprig of evergreen and dip it in the water. Sprinkle the area that is to be used for the setting. As you do this, simply say these words:

"With the purity of this salt and with the dissolving power of this water, I dispel all that is negative and counter to my intent!"

Set an altar with all the instruments, tools, and various items that are required for the work at hand. If you are going to use specific chants, set them where you can see them plainly so that your concentration is not broken by having to search for things. Place an image of the Goddess and God on your altar as a reminder of the higher nature with which you desire to merge. Direct your chants and gestures to the images. Perform the magickal work as prescribed in the following sections, and afterward, purify yourself and the ritual setting with the salt water. Finish by carefully cleaning up any ritual debris such as melted wax and incense ash, then put everything away.

PREPARING THE PENTACLE

Select a large poster board or sheet of paper, about two feet by two feet in size. Draw a large five-pointed star on it. Depending upon how you map out your spell, you may need to draw a six-pointed star, as explained further in this section. Mark the inside triangles of the pentacle, numbering them as indicated in the drawing. Hang the pentacle drawing on a wall at eye level.

On a separate piece of paper, make a symbol for each concept in a draft you will create. For example, you may wish to express *I want a car.* These four words are simply two concepts: "I want" and "a car." Turn these into two symbols. Continue doing this through the whole draft as outlined in the next paragraph. If a concept is repeated, then you may use the same symbol for it each time. Make up your own original symbols. It is very important to memorize them so that whenever you look at a symbol, the concept will instantly flash into your mind.

Images condense concepts into symbols representing one's desire. Here, the symbols express the desire: "I want a car." Sigils representing these needs, and the steps contemplated to achieve them, are placed in the points of the pentagram in this magical working.

In your draft, state clearly and concisely what your desire is on a sheet of paper. Logically map out the situation, the manner of obtaining the goal step by step, and the goal itself. Choose a symbol to represent the following: yourself as the intended focal point of

THE WITCHES' CRAFT

the desire manifested, the summation of the situation, the necessary steps to achieve the desire, and the desired manifestation itself. It may be necessary to redraft this several times until you can express what you want, and how you want it, through symbols. Reduce the wordage into simple concepts and then sigilize each concept.

Once the sigils have been created, place the symbol chosen to represent you into area number one on the pentacle. Into area number two, place the summation of the problem. In areas three and four, place the steps of how you want it solved. In area five, place the desired outcome. Your draft must contain all of these aspects.

When ready, enter a merged state via emotion or whatever method you prefer. Point your wand or index finger at each symbol beginning with the symbol in area number one. Pause briefly and let each symbol flash into your mind. Continue to the last symbol and then clap your hands sharply together; turn and leave the area until your mind has returned to normal.

CHARGING A TALISMAN

Thoughts that are joined to concepts in merged states of consciousness can also be housed in a talisman. The talisman may be made out of any object. However, stones and metals are traditional materials. Specific feelings and attitudes can be implanted in an object through this technique. For example, a feeling of love or peacefulness, or an attitude of confidence may be transmitted. Once joined to an object, feelings become an aura energy; a field of energy influencing others with which it makes contact.

Having chosen the desired concept and the talisman to carry it, you must decide on the size of the aura that will surround the talisman (such as an area of three feet, ten feet, or whatever is appropriate). It is within this distance that the talisman will have influence through the magickal energy it emanates. Therefore, whoever or whatever you wish to work your magick on must be within, or pass within, this field of energy.

When you are ready to proceed with the magickal charge, set the altar with two candles and lay the talisman directly in front of you where you can gaze upon it easily. Enter a merged state and fill your mind with the feeling or attitude you wish to implant into the object.

Then direct the feeling into the object and see it being implanted within the very atoms of the object. Visualize the field of influence it is to have. Clap your hands sharply together and leave the work area until your mind returns to normal.

MAGICKAL BINDING

Unfortunately, there are times when an individual, a group, or a situation needs to be restrained from doing harm. In the modern Craft, most Witches have a strong aversion to interfering with the free will of another person. Yet, we understand that sometimes this is necessary, as in the case of a murderer or a rapist. It is the free will of the rapist to rape, or the murderer to murder. However, because we understand that these actions are not to be tolerated, as a modern society, we condemn perpetrators of these actions to prison cells and deny them their free will to harm others. Regretfully, there are times when the magickal equivalent must be employed.

Before binding someone with a magickal spell, it is wise to first prepare yourself. Go to your altar and call upon your deities, seeking their guidance. Meditate upon the situation so as to assure yourself that it is necessary to take this course of action. Prior to the work at hand, and after its completion, cleanse yourself with sage smoke, and anoint yourself with a protective oil. Wear a charged pentagram for one complete cycle of the Moon. This will help shield you from the natural links and rebounds commonly associated with spell casting.

A binding spell is best cast on the night of the Full Moon or any time following this as the Moon wanes. Prepare a poppet doll to personify whatever needs binding. Anoint it with an oil and name the individual, group, or situation as you do so. For example, you can dab an oil on the doll saying:

"With this oil I name you _____ and link this image to your essence. Be now _____ in name, body, and spirit."

After this, you will want to collect the items you need in order to cast the spell, and you will also want to write the words of evocation for the magickal binding.

Objects Needed:

- A yard of twine, cord, or yarn (choose a symbolic color)
- A handmade doll (cloth is best)
- A chant of binding (composed for your specific needs)
- A black or dark brown candle (to seal)
- A piece of ivy (the magickal binding link)
- Binding incense (such as Saturn incense)
- Mercury incense

Things to be addressed in the evocation:

- Name of the person
- Why they deserve to be bound
- How long they will be bound

The words of the binding are to be chanted as you slowly and carefully wind the yarn around the doll, binding the image. Then, drip candle wax on the ends of the yarn to secure it in place. Next, place the piece of ivy on the area of the doll that symbolizes the intent of the binding. For example, if someone is a sexual predator, then the ivy is placed on the genital area of the image. Once the ivy is in place, then drip candle wax on it.

At this point, simply hold the doll up with both hands and pass it through the incense smoke. Speak the words of binding once more, this time directly into the incense smoke. With the proper mental alignment, the smoke will carry the vibration into the ether, lifting it to the astral level where it will take root.

At some point, you will want to remove or unbind the spell. To do this, simply cut the bindings away carefully with strong, deliberate snips of the scissors. Scrape off the wax that holds the ivy and melt the patch so as to release the ivy. Burn the cords in a planetary incense of Mercury. Then, bury the ivy in the earth along with the ashes left from the cords and incense. The doll must be cleansed at this point in order to break the magickal link. Pour some salt water over the doll and proclaim that it no longer bears the name of the person, group, or situation. You can say something like:

"With this cleansing water, I wash away the link of magick. No longer are you named _____, *no longer are you mind, body, and spirit. Now you are but cloth and thread again."*

Using the Mercury incense smoke, speak these words:

"I no longer bear the mind, body, and spirit of _____. *I bear only a doll of cloth and thread. To the four winds, I release my spell, and I free that which was bound."*

Complete the unbinding process by burning the doll and pouring the ashes into running water.

A Procedure for Raising the Cone of Power

In the art of Witchcraft, a cone of power is raised or drawn in order to create raw energy into which a thought-form or desire can be implanted. Once charged with the magickal seed of intent, the cone can be released and directed toward achieving the goal of the work at hand. A cone of power can be raised by an individual or by a group, although typically, group energy will be more effective.

Preparing to raise a cone is similar to creating the pentacle spell in a work of power. Go back over that section in this chapter and map out the idea and the plan according to the prescribed formula. When you are ready to begin, prepare your altar. Draw out a triangle about six to twelve inches high and place it on the center of the altar. Purify the area and yourself with incense and salt water.

Then, enter a merged state. Imagine yourself without physical form. Visualize a great violet light filling your mind.

Turn to each of the four quarters, holding up your wand in your left hand, and point upward. Turn three times to each quarter, mentally and emotionally drawing more energy with each turn. Slow, deep breaths will enhance the sense of empowerment.

Next, stand facing your altar. Keep the wand held upward while the right hand is extended toward the center of the altar. Point the index finger into the middle of the triangle on the altar. Speak the words: *"Ayea! Ayea! Ayea!"* and then lower your wand, joining both hands together. Point the wand directly center into the triangle, and in your mind's eye, see a shaft of white light descend into it. Visualize it growing brighter and brighter until it is a cone of vibrant power.

With a shout, thrust the wand upward and release the energy. To do this, take in a deep breath and then forcefully exhale it as you hold the wand outward. If you know what direction the target of the cone lies in, you can send the cone off into that specific quarter. Once completed, put the wand down on the altar and sharply clap your hands together three times to break the energy link between you and the cone. If you maintain a connection, you will bleed energy off the cone and diminish its effectiveness.

STRING MAGICK

String magick is a technique for inducing a mild to moderate altered state of consciousness. With practice, this technique can take you to deeper levels since it is related to self-hypnosis. It is a very old method and is related to the magickal themes of weaving and sowing reflected in myths of the goddesses of fate. Examples to practice can be found in any children's game incorporating string, such as the cat's cradle.

To begin a work of string magick, cut a length of thick cord or yarn about a yard long. Spend about five minutes centering your inner self through slow, deep breathing. Then, tie the ends of the string together with a good strong knot. Focus clearly on the desire in your mind, defining what it is that you want. Loop the cord in and out of the fingers of both hands. It doesn't matter how you do it; simply use your intuition.

Begin to move your hands and fingers with the cord in slow graceful movements as if you were performing a ballet with your hands, fingers, and the cord. Concentrate and become absorbed in this action. Let your whole awareness turn to what it is that you wish to obtain. This is very important. Create a mini-drama symbolizing the situation just as a ballet dancer tells a story with the movements of their body. Let the actions of your hands, fingers, and cord correspond with the circumstances of the situation that you are holding in your awareness.

The words, your hands, fingers, and the cord tell the story of what you desire. Magickally speaking, they are what you desire and you merge with all of it mentally and emotionally. It is vital to become so absorbed with the identification between the circumstance of what you want and the movements of your hands, fingers, and cord, that you are aware of no difference between them. Whistling or humming can be added to a performance of string magick to enhance the work, and you simply whistle or hum a tune of your own inspiration along with the movements of your hands and the cord.

Since string magick is a work of the mental sphere, it is best to burn the cord in incense after casting a spell. However, the string can also be given over to another element that corresponds to the nature of the magickal work. In this case, you might think of Earth as binding, flowing Water as emotion, Fire as transforming, and Air as transmissive.

SLIP-KNOT MAGICK

There is another work that is performed with string or cord. It is called *slip-knot magick*. It is used to rid or dissolve something that you want removed or undone. In this technique, you do not tie the ends of the string together. Instead, you make a slip-knot in the middle of the cord. Quiet your mind and employ deep breathing as before. Take hold of each end of the cord in each hand. Pull tightly but not enough to pull the slip-knot out.

Fill your awareness with what it is that you wish to remove or undo. Become completely absorbed in this, focusing on the knot as the circumstance itself. Let the identification become complete in your mind, heart, and spirit. When the identification has become complete, pull the string hard and know that with the disappearance of the knot that the circumstance ceases to be.

SCRYING

Scrying is the employment of dark reflective surfaces or a crystal sphere for the purposes of divination. It is one of the most ancient forms of the Witches' Craft. It was once considered so important that special priests and priestesses were trained in the art of scrying, serving in the temples of countless gods. Ancient historians tell us that the Etruscans were unequaled throughout the known world in their knowledge of the art of divination.

Scrying is another form of establishing altered states of consciousness. By temporarily diminishing the awareness of our physical bodies and the physical dimension, our spirit can focus upon the discernment of etheric patterns of energy. Each day, these energies are generated by the thoughts, deeds, and desires of everyone on the planet. They collect within the astral level and stimulate the creative forces there, which will, in turn, direct such things toward manifestation. Divination, through whatever methods, simply allows us to catch a glimpse of what is about to manifest in the physical dimension.

It is important to understand that not everything that enters the astral level will result in a physical manifestation. Some energies, such as those generated by daydreams, lack the focus of will that is necessary to keep the energy cohesive. The thought-form entering the astral level must be cohesive in order to maintain its existence long enough to attract the astral forces that will act upon it. In a sense, we can liken this to individual sperm that enter the womb, competing for the goal of entering into the creative egg. Weak or malformed sperm have little if any chance of reaching the egg.

Divination allows us to perceive simply the patterns that are likely to manifest. Many factors can alter or negate those patterns. Magick is one factor, the conscious reshaping or redirecting of reality. Another factor is the introduction of opposing thought-form energies generated by other people. Winning the lotto is one good example: many wills focused on the same desire but competing for a different manifestation of that one desire. Nature restores imbalance and disharmony, and to accomplish that often means one thing gives way to another.

Scrying is best performed in a quiet place with one or two candles employed for lighting. Hold the scrying object or arrange it to ensure that no images are reflected in it. Allow your eyes to go off focus slightly, and gaze past the reflective surface, looking *into* it but not at it. Allow your mind to calm so that you are in a state much like that of drifting off to sleep.

When images appear either in your mind or are reflected back to you on the dark surface of the scrying object, don't focus on them but look at them as a casual observer. Becoming excited will disconnect you from the process. Always allow the images to appear; never force them or react to them. Simply watch them and let them speak to you symbolically. Do this for a few minutes in the beginning. You can increase holding this altered state longer once you are more experienced.

WORKING WITH MAGICK MIRRORS

The magick mirror is one of the oldest tools employed in the art of both divination and spell casting. The classic magick mirror is a dark concave surface of reflective material. You can construct one for yourself by using the curved glass face of a clock and painting the convex side with glossy black paint. Antique stores are a good source for old clocks with rounded glass faces. The traditional preparation of a magick mirror begins on the night of the Full Moon. It is particularly effective to do this when the Moon is in the sign of Pisces, Cancer, or Scorpio. Consult an astrological calendar for the days and times within any given month.

Once you have painted the glass and it has thoroughly dried, then bathe the mirror in an herbal brew of equal parts rosemary, fennel, rue, vervain, ivy, and walnut leaves or bark. If you want to hold to the oldest of traditions, then pour some sea foam into the mixture. If you are unable to obtain these items, consult a book on magickal herbs and substitute other herbs associated with psychic vision, oracles, or divination. While the glass is still bathing in the potion, hold both your hands out over it, palms down, and say:

"I awaken the sleeping spirits of old,
Whose eyes reveal all that in darkness is told,
Give to me visions within this dark well,
And make this a portal of magickal spell."

Visualize a silver mist forming around the mirror. Take a deep breath and then slowly exhale outward upon the potion. Mentally envision that your breath moves the silver mist into the mirror. Repeat this three times. Next, remove the mirror from the potion and dry it off thoroughly. Prop the mirror up vertically with a sturdy object and make sure the support does not obscure the mirror. Hold your right hand out in front of you so that your palm is facing the convex side of the mirror. Then, place the left palm facing the concave side, about three inches away from the glass surface. You are now ready to magnetize the mirror to your aura. With the left hand, begin making a circular clockwise motion staying within the dimensions of the mirror. Do this for a few minutes and then perform the same motion on the convex side of the mirror with the right hand. The opposite hand is always held still while the moving hand circulates.

Once completed, take the mirror out beneath the Full Moon so that its light falls upon the concave side. Slowly fill the glass to the brim with the herbal potion. Hold it up towards the Moon, almost level with your eyes. Don't worry about any spillage that may take place. While looking at the Moon, allow your eyes to unfocus slightly. If you are doing this correctly, you will see three lines of light seemingly emanating from the Moon. Continue to squint until the vertical line coming from the bottom of the Moon seems to touch upon the mirror.

Once the moonbeam is touching the mirror, speak these words:

*"Three are the lights
Here now that are seen
But not to all
The one in between,
For now, the Enchantress
Has long come at last
To charge and empower
This dark magic glass."*

Quickly close your eyes so that you break eye contact. Open them again, looking down towards the glass. Kneel and pour out the potion upon the earth in the manner of libation. Then, rinse the mirror off with fresh, clear water and dry it thoroughly. The final step in preparing the mirror is to glue a strip of snakeskin to the back (convex) side. The snake is a symbol of the Underworld, which has long been associated with divination, oracle, and fate. Once the glue has dried under the snakeskin, wrap the mirror in a silk cloth to protect its lunar magnetism. Never allow sunlight to fall directly upon the mirror. The mirror is now ready to be used for divination or spell casting. The technique is a very ancient one common among shamanic traditions.

Divination is the ability to see what patterns are forming toward manifestation. What you see is actually what is likely to occur if nothing changes the pattern being woven in the astral material. The following technique will provide you with the basic foundation for performing the art of divination known as *scrying*. Place two candles as your source of light so that the light does not reflect directly upon the mirror (off a foot or two, in front of you. Flanking the mirror should work fine).

Next, you will perform a series of hand passes over the mirror, slowly and deliberately. Magickally speaking, the right hand is of an electrical nature/active charge, and the left hand is of a magnetic/receptive charge. A left-handed pass will attract an image toward formation and right-handed passes will strengthen or focus the image. Begin by making left-handed passes over the mirror, in a clockwise circle, just a few inches above it (palms open and facing down). Stop and gaze into the dark reflection; not at it, but into it.

You will need to repeat these passes as you await the vision. Alternate between the left hand and the right hand. This requires patience and time. Use your intuition as you sit before the mirror. Make sure the setting is quiet without distractions.

The magick mirror can also be used for spell casting. This is a simple technique involving reflections or sigils. Light two candles and set them off to each side of the mirror about three inches away. Place a photograph, image, or sigil of the target of your spell so that it reflects in the mirror. Gaze into the mirror and imagine the desired effect. Make up a short rhyme if you like so you can state your desire without breaking your concentration. If you desire to be rid of an influence or situation, you can sigilize it and then burn the sigil, gazing into the reflected flames in the mirror.

Another effective method is to gently blow incense smoke onto the mirror as you gaze at the reflection. Allow yourself to stir your emotions, then deeply inhale, and slowly exhale across a stick of incense. Imagine the smoke to be a magickal vapor carrying your will. As it touches the mirror, imagine the target responding as you wish it to. Do this a total of three times. Creating a short rhyme for your spell can be helpful in this technique as well.

Once you are finished, combine the melted wax, ashes from the incense, and the photo or image you used. Dispose of this in a manner in keeping with the elemental nature of your spell. Matters of love and feelings generally belong to Water. Creative or artistic ventures belong to Air. Situations of loss, separation, or destruction can be associated with Fire. Endurance, strength, fertility, and stability are typically linked to Earth.

When disposing of ritual remnants, bear in mind that to toss something into moving water will merge it with the Water element, thus connecting it on a macrocosmic level with the higher nature of the spell. This helps to empower your act of magick. For Earth-related spells, you would bury the object in an area connected to your target. Spells related to the element of Fire involve burning the links. Finally, for an Air related spell, you use steam or smoke.

Now it is time to turn to the next chapter and explore the Old Ways of Witchcraft and how they apply to the daily life of the Witch.

CHAPTER 10

The Old Ways in Modern Witchcraft

To understand the Old Religion of Witchcraft, we must understand something of the mentality of our ancient ancestors.

Picture a time when people did not know what the Moon was, how it changed shape, or why it disappeared for three days every month. The Moon was a complete mystery, a glowing sphere seemingly rising from beneath the earth. The Moon drifted across the heavens and returned from whence it came. Over the course of its daily journey, it would change shapes, growing larger and then smaller in an endless cycle.

Today, we know that the Moon is a physical object orbiting around our planet, and because of this knowledge, we have lost some of the magick. But we can recapture this when we gaze upon the Full Moon and realize that we are seeing the very same Moon upon which every Witch who ever lived has looked upon. It is there in that one moment of this realization, beneath the Full Moon, that the past and present come together and touch in a sphere of light.

Early Witches viewed the world around them with what may be called a *peasant Pagan mentality*. What this means is that the Witch believed in a world filled with spirits that animated nature. The Witch also believed in another world just beyond this one, which was a place of renewed life for the dead. Everything good or bad that took place in the world of the living was due to the influence of a spirit. Therefore, the Witch knew that it was necessary to possess the knowledge of how to effectively work with these entities. A very common theme in European folklore is the kindred relationship between the fairy and the Witch.

According to oral tradition, the village Witch was sought after for cures both magickal and medicinal. Their knowledge of herbs and rapport with the spirit world was both respected and feared by the villagers. The village Witch grew their own herbs, made their own charms, and perfected the art of the Witches' Craft through adherence to the ways handed down from generation to generation. The art of Witchcraft was also taught "on the voice of the wind" which reflects the teaching that spirits convey the Old Ways to those they deem worthy. Such individuals are "spirit taught" and often believe they are acting upon intuition.

Being prepared for any eventuality is the hallmark of the experienced Witch. This includes having oils, potions, incense, charms, and other items readily on hand. In this chapter, we will explore how to put together everything you are likely to need in case of an emergency. In addition, we will learn how to create protections for the home and how to establish an astral temple for magickal and spiritual work.

Please note that most of the techniques discussed in this chapter are primarily what I call *folk magick*, which to me means simple spells employing a basic charm or talisman and words that rhyme in some fashion. I have, however, also included some more involved spells that employ advanced concepts and methods. With minor adjustments made as necessary for this type of book, the spells in this chapter reflect an older authentic form of Witchcraft pre-dating popular modern Wiccan material. It is my hope that this will provide some additional balance for the magickal work of modern Witches.

Magickal and psychic work tends to attract and draw spirits, both in this world and the next. From time to time, there are also other practitioners of the art that may send negative energy your way, for whatever purposes. This requires taking measures to protect yourself and to either negate or return what is sent to you.

In the following section, I have provided a list of herbs that will enable you to serve as the local "village Witch" of your community. It is the way of things that as you grow in the knowledge and wisdom of the Witches' Craft, people will come to you for aid and advice. Without having a "stock of energy" in supply, you can too easily become depleted by meeting the needs of others on a constant basis. To avoid being drained of your energy by others, you should set up a supply of charged herbs and oils to have on hand.

THE MAGICKAL CUPBOARD

There are several main staples of herbs, oils, candles, elemental condensers, parchment paper, a writing tool, a carving tool, and various charms that every Witch should have on hand. This saves time when something is suddenly needed or an emergency presents itself. In addition, the Witch should also have a mortar and pestle, some herb jars and potion vials, a funnel, a cauldron, a pentagram, and a Witch ball. With this fundamental equipment, the Witch can begin working on whatever presents itself.

It is very helpful to obtain a nice herb jar cupboard or a spice rack to hold some of your herbs and oils. They are fairly affordable if you find them at a garage sale or an antique store. The ones with drawers are the best to obtain as this prevents sunlight from weakening the potency of your herbs and oils, and also allows for some privacy when people are around.

The traditional magickal herbs of the Witch were: aconite, belladonna, foxglove, hellebore, henbane, and hemlock. All of these plants have chthonic associations and draw their power from the Underworld. They have been used for healing, binding, and producing altered states of consciousness for magickal training and astral journey work. I have grown all of these plants and worked with them for several years. Because they contain deadly poisons and are extremely dangerous, I've decided not to discuss them in any detail within this chapter. I list them here strictly for historical reference and strongly discourage any experimentation with these herbs without personal training from a certified herbalist.

As a modern Witch, your basic herb supply should consist of the following thirteen herbs: asafoetida, rue, dragon's blood, Solomon's seal, mistletoe, rosemary, periwinkle, ginger, lady's mantle, vervain, mugwort, mandrake, and pennyroyal. Let's look at the ascribed powers of each herb:

Asafoetida (*Ferula foetida*) is essentially an herb of exorcism or banishment. It is associated with the Underworld. Asafoetida has a very foul odor when burned and is believed to drive away negative and evil energy. Use this herb to dispel unwanted forces and to cleanse areas in which trauma has occurred.

Rue (*Ruta graveolens*) is an herb of protection and counter magick. The plant naturally divides into three branches, said to symbolize the triformis goddess. The ancient Etruscans made charms depicting a simple spring of rue, which were sacred to Atimite/Artimiti who was the Etruscan equivalent of Artemis/Diana. In Tuscan Witchcraft, a charm called the *cimaruta* (meaning a sprig from the top of the rue plant) bears various symbols hanging from the budding ends of the rue branches. Use this herb to protect against psychic/magickal attacks and to return such an attack back to its sender.

Dragon's Blood (*Daemomorops draco*) has a variety of uses, including cleansing and banishing. It is also an herb associated with transition and shapeshifting and is used for astral work and to help those who have recently crossed over from physical life to spirit form. Burn some dragon's blood incense for astral travel, and to aid the release of someone's spirit that has recently died.

Mandrake (*Atropa mandragora*) is an herb associated with the human body, its sexual nature, its fertility, and its flesh in general. It is also attributed to the magickal power to enhance psychic abilities. This is an extension of the mundane faculty of sight, meaning that the mandrake turns "normal" vision into "second sight" or psychic vision. Use mandrake root as a healing herb, incorporating it into a poppet, sealing or attaching the herb to the part of the body in need of healing.

Mistletoe (*Viscum album*) is an herb that has a conflicted history. In its lore, the mistletoe was responsible for slaying a god and thus became likened to war and death. This legend originated perhaps from the fact that mistletoe saps the strength of the host tree upon which it grows.

In the same legend, the mistletoe was given to the goddess of love for safekeeping. She ordained that anyone who passed beneath mistletoe must then kiss as a sign of peace and love. Place mistletoe in a pouch and use it to bring harmony to troubled relationships and households.

Mugwort (*Artemisia vulgaris*) is an herb associated with dreams. It is sacred to the goddess Artemis/Diana. Therefore, it is attributed with the power to keep one safe against the forces of darkness, just as the Full Moon makes it possible for the traveler to see in the darkness (when artificial light is not present) and therefore, makes the night safer. Use mugwort to stuff a dream pillow when one seeks answers or solutions to problems. It should also be used as an offering to the Moon Goddess, thereby strengthening the rapport between Witch and Goddess.

Rosemary (*Rosmarinus officinalis*) is an herb associated with a variety of powers. One of its main attributes is the ability to strengthen memory and recall. Brew in a tea or burn with incense to awaken the ancestral memory within you, and retrieve the knowledge and wisdom of your ancestors.

Periwinkle (*Vinca major* and *Vinca minor*) is also known as *sorcerer's violet*. In the old magickal books, periwinkle was used as an herb to bind people. It appears most frequently in love spells, drawing and uniting people together. Use this herb in spells of attraction; to draw compatible people together in matters of love.

Pennyroyal (*Mentha pulegium*) is an herb used in ancient times as the base for oils of initiation. Pennyroyal is attributed with the power to open the psychic centers within the human body and connects one with the inner Mysteries of rebirth. Use an oil or tincture of pennyroyal to anoint the third eye of a student before beginning a teaching session, or anoint yourself when meditating or studying the inner Mysteries of the Old Religion.

Solomon's Seal (*Polygoatum multiflorum*) is an herb used in ancient magick for consecration. Burn some of the dried herb on a charcoal block and pass ritual tools through it to consecrate them to a specific deity and/or purpose.

Ginger (*Zingiber officinale*) is an herb associated with restoring good health or preventing illness in general. The root is ascribed with healing power and can be used as a talisman. Place some of this herb in a pouch and wear it as a healing herb.

Lady's Mantle (*Alchemilla vulgaris*) is an herb attributed with the power to aid in the transformation of any object. Its botanical name points to the principle of alchemy, the ancient science of transmutation. Add this herb to incense to enhance the effects, or make a tincture to add to potions. This herb may be considered the "magickal activator."

Vervain (*Verbena officinalis*) is an herb strongly linked to the fairy race. It is attributed to the power to grant "second sight" or psychic vision. A vervain blossom appears on the Witch charm known as the *cimaruta*. Burn this herb with incense to enhance divination.

SACRED TREES

In the Old Religion of Witchcraft, there reside the sacred trees used for blessings and spiritual focus. Twigs from these trees can be used to make symbolic charms and talismans. Some examples are "the Witches' Tree" and the "Celtic Need-Fire Tree," which form a spiritual connection for the Witch. The trees commonly associated with Witchcraft are ash, oak, hawthorn, birch, sycamore, rowan, elder, yew, and willow. Some commentators have tried to link the nine sacred trees that were burned in the ancient need-fires of pre-Christian Celtic religion with traditional Witchcraft: oak, pine, holly, hazel, juniper, cedar, poplar, apple, and ash.

Let us look at the symbolism of the trees that commonly appear in the literature on Witchcraft. The ash tree (*Fraxinus excelsior*) is one of the three sacred woods referred to in Wicca along with the oak and thorn. The ash is attributed to the powers of divination due to its appearance in the myth of the god Odin. Odin is said to have hung from an ash tree in order to gain enlightenment. He was then able to read and interpret the sacred runic script that appeared in a vision beneath him. His ability to do so transferred the gift of divination to the ash.

The Witches' Tree Charm.

The Oak Tree (*Quercus petraea*) has long been revered and worshipped as a deity throughout most of continental Europe and the British Isles. In Greek mythology, spirits of the forest known as *dryads* favored the oak tree, and offerings were given to secure their favor and obtain their occult knowledge. Oak was the traditional wood used for the Yule log, and oak was burned in the midsummer balefires. The goddess Brigid was associated with oak groves, and Egeria (a water nymph of the sacred spring at Lake Nemi) was ritually wedded to the Oak God. The ancient writer Herodotus reported that oaks possessed oracle powers.

The Hawthorn Tree (*Crataegus oxyacantha*) is associated with May Day, heralded by the opening of the hawthorn blossoms. Sprigs of hawthorn and hawthorn flowers were collected on May Day and then placed within one's house upon the dresser to banish evil from the home. In Teutonic lore, the hawthorn was a symbol of death and its wood was used for funeral pyres. In ancient Greece, crowns bearing hawthorn blossoms were made for the wedding couple, and the wedding party carried torches of hawthorn wood. The ancient Romans placed hawthorn leaves in the cradle of newborns as protection. In Celtic lore, the hawthorn was associated with Blodeuwedd, the wife of Lleu.

The Elder Tree (*Sambucus ebulus/Sambucus nigra*) was once called the "Old Woman Tree" because the spirit of the Earth Mother was said to reside in the elder. For this reason, it was long considered bad luck to cut wood from an elder tree. Witches, as worshippers of the Great Mother, came to be associated with elder. In European folklore, Witches were said to transform themselves into elder trees. One legend tells of a Witch who turned a group of knights into stone (the Rollright Stones of Oxfordshire) and then transformed herself into a nearby elder tree. Legends are still told of midsummer rites in which Witches danced around this elder tree. Because the elder is also associated with fairies, there is some suggestion that "hollow" may refer to the elder as a doorway into the fairy kingdom. Legend holds that if one stands beneath an elder on midsummer's eve and breathes in the scent of the tree, that one will see fairies.

The Rowan Tree (*Sorbus aucuparia*) is also known as *mountain ash*. In ancient times, it was the custom on May 1 to pass animals through a large hoop made of rowan to protect them and ensure fertility. The tree was believed to be the home of benevolent fairies, and having one near one's home was believed to bring good fortune. The red berries of the rowan were considered sacred and were connected to themes of blood, life, death, and renewal. The rowan tree blossoms in May and is in fruit in August.

The Sycamore Tree (*Acer pseudoplatanus*) bears fig-like fruit that grows upon the stalk of the tree rather than on the branches. It is therefore associated with Artemis of Ephesus, the many-breasted Mother Goddess. The fruit of the sycamore produces a milky fluid, and the tree has been called the *Mother Tree* and the *Tree of Life*.

The Willow Tree (*Salix alba*) is associated with the Underworld and such goddesses as Proserpina and Hecate. The willow was also associated with the serpent, perhaps due to its slender branches. The willow is a tree found near streams, rivers, and swamplands. Its connection with water has linked it to the Moon and thereby to the Moon Goddess. It was an ancient practice to place willow branches in the beds of women who were infertile. This was believed to draw mystical serpents that would help with impregnation. From the time of antiquity, the willow was used to make wands to be employed in Moon magick. It also has a long history of being used to make straps for flagellation. These were used both in rites of initiation and purification as well as in sex magick rituals incorporating pain and pleasure. A length of willow was also traditionally employed to bind together the materials for a Witches' broom, the willow being sacred to Hecate.

The Birch Tree (*Betula pendula/alba*) has an old connection with the spirits of the dead. An old English folk ballad known as "The Wife of Usher's Well" speaks of souls returning from the realm of the dead wearing hats and clothing made of birch. This may be a remnant of the association between the birch and the Underworld. According to oral tradition, the Witches' broom was made of birch twigs tied around an ash branch with strips of willow.

The Yew Tree (*Taxus baccata*) is associated with death and the goddess Hecate. It is also associated with rebirth, as its branches grow down into the ground and from them, new growth arises. When the main trunk of the tree dies, it decays and is renewed by the growth of a new trunk.

OILS AND CANDLES

In addition to a collection of herbs, the Witch's cupboard should also contain a stock of magickal oils and colored candles. The Witch should collect an oil for each of the planets: Mercury, Venus, Mars, Saturn, Jupiter, Pluto, Neptune, and Uranus. Most occult shops carry some version of these oils. Candles of the following colors should be on hand as well: green, blue, red, yellow, black, white, pink, silver, gold, orange, purple, and brown or gray.

The symbolism of each candle is as follows:

- **Green:** Fertility, prosperity, growth, health
- **Blue:** Peace, loyalty, truth
- **Red:** Passion, sexual lust, life force, blood matters
- **Yellow:** Communication, activity, vitality, initiative

- **Black:** Decline, restriction, loss, separation
- **White:** Cleansing, consecration
- **Pink:** Friendship, relationships, love
- **Silver:** Lunar energies, Goddess energies
- **Gold:** Solar energies, God energies
- **Brown:** Neutralizing, grounding
- **Purple:** Intuition, psychic power, spirituality
- **Orange:** Success
- **Gray:** Neutralizing

The attributions of each oil are as follows:

- **Mercury:** Communication and transmission
- **Venus:** Love and relationships
- **Mars:** Assertion and initiative
- **Saturn:** Discipline and focus
- **Jupiter:** Expansion and luck
- **Pluto:** Transformation and secret processes
- **Neptune:** Mysticism and intuition
- **Uranus:** Innovation, invention, creative thinking, and magick

USING CANDLES AND OILS

Before using any candle for ritual or spell work, make sure that the candle is free of any debris on its surface. In preparation for employing a candle, it should be blessed in the names of your deities or spirits and anointed with oil. The oil should be dabbed on each end of the candle and rubbed into the center. During this act, the mind must be focused on the desired effects of the spell. The greater one's concentration, the greater the strength and purity of the transmitted energy will be.

Candles can be customized to enhance the intent of the spell by marking them with a symbol. An etching tool such as a needle, pointed quill, or thorn can be used to carve symbols into the wax. Words or names can also be etched into the wax. Most occult shops carry candles shaped to resemble people, creatures, and other symbolic representations. Image candles usually come in various colors to fit the nature of any spell. These can be used to help increase the symbolism and therefore strengthen the spell by helping the mind more easily visualize.

Sometimes a spell will require that the work be done in segments over a period of hours or even days. The "seven-knob" candle is ideal for such situations, and the candle can be allowed to burn down to each knob, which will represent an hour or day per the spell's requirements.

In addition to anointing candles, an oil can be used to charge any ritual tool with an intention. The oil is dabbed on the ends of the object and then rubbed into the center, just as one does for the candle. Oils can also be dabbed on letters and envelopes to convey a charge or blessing. An old technique for creating alignments using an oil is to select a scent that will only be used for one single intention, which for our purpose here will be to invoke a state of consciousness linked to a word of power.

Once you have the oil, then concentrate on a feeling you would like to have. For example, perhaps there is a scene in a movie that makes you feel a strong sense of justice, happiness, or empowerment. Try watching this part of the movie, and inhale the scent of the oil at exactly the moment of emotional impact from the scene. Give the feeling a word, like "justice" or "relief" and say the word in your mind as you inhale. Try not to think of the event or of the characters in the scene, but think only of the feeling that swells up inside you. Used correctly, this technique creates a memory chain association between the feeling and the scent.

In the older practices of Witchcraft, the memory chain association was an important part of the Witches' Craft. Oils of initiation were charged using a similar technique so as to convey the spirit of the Old Religion, which brought about a change in consciousness as any valid initiation experience must. Memory chain associations were established with great care by the elders of the Old Religion.

This was accomplished by the teacher creating a mystical experience for the student beneath the Full Moon, using tone of voice and everything else the teacher can bring to bear in order to heighten the emotions of the student. Then at exactly the right moment of receptivity within the student, the teacher softly whispers a word into the ear of the student. This word then becomes a "word of power" for the student. Each and every time the student hears this word, then they are aligned to the magickal moment when the word was first whispered. This results in an immediate altered state of consciousness. Techniques like this one have preserved various elements of the Old Religion, allowing the Old Ways to be preserved and passed down through many generations.

CHARGING OILS AND INCENSE

In the old days, Witches grew their own herbs for incense and made their own oils. The herbs were planted and harvested at the prescribed times, according to occult lore. The oils were created using time-honored methods and in accord with the seasons and phases of the Moon.

Today, most modern Witches rely heavily upon occult shops or other Witches in order to secure the incense and oils needed for the Witches' Craft. Although many occult shops and Witches that make their incense for sale do place a magickal charge on the herbs, not all do. The latter feel that this should be done by the purchaser.

If you need or want to charge your own oils and incense, you can do so using a simple technique. On the night of the Full Moon, draw a triangle on the ground or on a poster board. Make sure that the size of the triangle is large enough that the oil and incense can be set down inside the lines of the borders. Place the jars/bottles inside the triangle area and set a lighted candle on each tip of the triangle. Choose candle colors that correspond to the general magickal nature of the oil or incense, such as pink for love and so forth.

Next, take some colored cellophane that symbolizes the magickal intent that you want to impart to the oil or incense. Cover the incense or oil with the cellophane and leave it under the Moon for three hours. You can also use stained glass in this same manner, and a stained-glass box works nicely for charging substances beneath the Moon.

To complete the charge (before leaving the substances beneath the moonlight), point to the Moon with the index finger of your left hand, and to the oil or incense with the index finger of your right hand, and holding this position, recite these words:

"Sacred Moon and sacred light
To these things your magick bright,
I pray thee now that you impart."

Visualize power flowing from the Moon down through you and into the triangle.

You can charge several different oils and incenses using different colors with this technique if you wish. You should add words of your own to the charge that state your desire before you recite the rhyme. This will help focus your mind on what your desire the charge to accomplish or impart.

GROWING MAGICKAL HERBS

If you are fortunate enough to be able to grow your own herbs, here are some magickal tips to help empower them. Bless the seeds or herbs before planting them with this prayer:

"Blessings be upon these seeds/plants.
Grow in power and knowledge,
Drawing from the earth,
The deep Mysteries that reside.
Spring forth and dance with the elements,
And the spirits of the field will come
And shed their light upon you,
Imparting to you secrets strange.
Grow, and keep for me
The Mysteries hidden within you,
And I shall care for you
And protect you.
I ask that in return
That you shall share with me
The powers and Mysteries,
In stem, and leaf, and bud, and seed."

Now plant the seed/herb in a place where it will thrive, making sure that you care for it as promised. Check the plant each day and remove anything harmful that might be on it. The water that you give the plant must be charged water. To charge this water, use the same method as described for charging oils with colored cellophane. Since you can only charge this water beneath the Full Moon, make sure you have enough to last for a month and keep this in a sealed jar. Keep the main supply out of the sunlight after it is charged. When needed, pour out enough for watering into a separate cup or watering can.

Talk to your plant each time you water it. Tell it what powers are attributed to it, and remind it about the covenant you have with it. You may even want to repeat the prayer. When it comes time to harvest, tell the plant that it is time now to share its power and its secrets as agreed. Cut the part of the plant that is needed with a sharp blade, and do so quickly. The kindest cut is a quick, clean cut.

MAKING POTIONS

Potions are useful for adding power to something, transferring a thought-form, or transmitting a desired effect. Potions can be drunk (if safe to do so) or used to anoint. If the potion is oil or alcohol-based, several drops can be added to melted wax for candle making. Potions can also be dabbed onto cloth or baked into ritual cakes. Always make sure that all of the ingredients in a potion are safe to use if the potion will come into contact with skin or be swallowed. Never use a potion without knowing the effects of each ingredient.

Herbal potions can be easily made in the form of tinctures. To make a tincture, simply grind about four ounces of herbs in your mortar and pestle, and then put the herbs in a jar that can be sealed with a lid. Slowly pour in eight ounces of vodka, and then four ounces of clean water. Next, close the jar with the lid firmly in place and then shake the jar a few times. Any liquor can be used that is from seventy-five-proof to ninety-proof but bear in mind that some have various herbs already mixed in them such as gin, which is made with juniper berries. Leave the mixture in the jar for two weeks, gently shaking the contents once a day. When the required time has passed, strain it through linen, cheesecloth, or if necessary, even a coffee filter. Pour the filtered liquid into a separate bottle that can be tightly sealed to avoid evaporation, and label the bottle so the contents are known.

Another method of creating a potion is to make an infusion. An herbal infusion is much like a tea. A standard infusion is prepared by adding one to two teaspoons of dried herb (or two to four teaspoons of fresh herb) to a cup of boiling water. Infuse for ten minutes before straining. If the herb is left too long, the infusion will become bitter. It's best to use a ceramic pot with a lid. Never prepare the infusion more than twenty-four hours in advance. Never ingest any herbal brew without full knowledge of the effects it may have.

Another type of infusion is an oil infusion. Oil infusions are for external use only. They can be prepared by hot or cold methods. For the hot method, fill a jar with fresh herbs and cover with olive, sunflower, or almond oil. Place the jar up to the neck in a saucepan of water and bring to a medium temperature. Simmer for up to three hours. Strain through filter paper or cloth into a brown glass bottle. Follow the same instructions for the cold method, except that the oil should be placed on a sunny windowsill instead of heated. The process can be repeated with a strained oil infusion and a fresh supply of herbs to make a stronger oil.

Here's a simple recipe for infusing your favorite herb or botanical into an oil. This method takes about two weeks to complete:

- 2 cups or 16 oz of olive oil
- 8 ounces of the desired herb

Place the herb and olive oil in a pot and heat to 100°F (37.7°C). Remove from heat and cover. Repeat this procedure daily for the next week or two. Strain the mixture through a cheesecloth. Fill a glass container with the infused oil. The oil will keep indefinitely if the container is tightly closed.

Another method of creating potions is to make an herbal decoction. Decoctions are used for herbs that are stringy, rough, woody, or are roots. Take one ounce of the dried herb (torn or cut into pieces) and 1.5 pints of pure water. Put the herbs into an enamel, glass, or stainless-steel pan, then add the water. Do not use aluminum or any other type of container as it may affect the herbs. Bring to a boil and simmer for about ten to twenty minutes or until the liquid has reduced by about one-third, then strain. Generally speaking, it should be used while it is still hot.

An herbal wine can also be made for special occasions. Use a sweet red wine with an alcohol content of at least 12%. Cover four ounces of herb with three cups of wine. Leave for a week before straining.

PROTECTION, COUNTER-MAGICK, AND BINDING

Unfortunately, the day will come when you will either need to protect yourself or someone you care about from magickal or psychic attacks. It may come from another practitioner, or it may come from the Otherworld. Defending yourself with your magickal abilities is a reasonable alternative to victimization. In the following sections are provided some methods that can help you deal with things you may encounter from time to time. Before turning to them, it may be helpful to discuss the philosophy and the mechanism of counter-magick.

What many people do not consider is that all magickal and psychic attacks leave a trail back to their originator. There are certain techniques that can "cover the tracks" or increase the difficulty in tracing the source. Obviously, it would be unwise to reveal such techniques here, but fortunately, very few practitioners know them, and those who do are advanced enough that they have no need or desire to launch an attack, to begin with.

Energy directed in a spell or ritual leaves what is called an *etheric thread* or *cord* trailing behind it. You can think of it as a vapor trail. This connection back to the sender is the mechanism by which one's "karmic return" is attached. It is, in a manner of speaking, a homing beacon. This beacon can be used to rebound the energy of a magickal or psychic attack. A specially designed artificial familiar (see Chapter Five) can be created to send out along the beacon and to make contact with the perpetrator. An image of a bird, a winged dragon, or a winged gargoyle is ideal.

Whether to launch a defensive counter-attack is a matter that you must give a great deal of consideration to. While you can instead keep putting up and charging protections, this will eventually deplete your energy, which will only create more problems for you. Sometimes, if the attacker is persistent, you may need to give them a magickal zap. Only you can decide whether you will live as a victim or a participant in the affairs of your own life.

Let's look now at some techniques you can use in your arsenal of defensive weapons.

SETTING THE WARDS

Whenever you suspect an attack of any nature, first cleanse the area by burning some sage and/or dragon's blood. Open all windows to allow the smoke to drift out. Following this, sprinkle some coarse salt around the area and then sweep it out through the front or back door of the home.

If sweeping is not practical, then you can vacuum the area. However, in this case, you must toss the vacuum bag away in the trash outside of the home.

Once the area has been cleansed, then place a piece of carnelian stone on each window ledge of the home and over each door leading into the house. Suspend it from a cord or use a piece of tape to adhere it in place, if necessary. To activate the carnelian, tap it three times with a crystal of any type. During periods of attack, and especially while you sleep, wear a piece of jet. Jet absorbs negative energy and neutralizes it better than any other substance.

To help block the energy of an attack, use one of the protective pentagram/pentacle techniques described in Chapter Five and trace a pentagram across every window and doorway in the home. Do this with your athame, or index finger, leaving an "imaginary" energy imprint of the pentagram. If possible, place an actual pentagram in the window and on the door, and charge it with the technique described in Chapter Five.

If you need to be secretive about using pentagrams in your home, the following may be of help. Obtain an inexpensive set of chess pieces that are hollow. Take each of the "castle" pieces and stuff some modeling clay in the bottom and then smooth over the surface.

Next, take a toothpick and etch a pentagram into the clay. You can also fill the chess piece with a protective herb before using the clay. During periods of attack, charge the pentagrams and then place the chess pieces, one in each corner of the room. Place a small piece of carnelian on each of the turrets of the castle pieces.

THE WITCH BOTTLE

The Witch bottle is a very old spell that has stood the test of time. It is designed to draw in and trap any negative energy directed against you. To make one, you will need thirteen pins with colored heads. Most stationery stores or fabric stores will carry them. You will also need a bottle or vial at least six inches deep, a piece of parchment paper, and a lodestone or small magnet. In the bottle, put three white pins, two blue, three yellow, two red, and three orange pins. Now add thirteen drops of a protection oil and then fill the bottle with a magnetic condenser such as lodestone oil. To make your own magnetic oil, heat a magnet in oil for twenty minutes.

Consecrate the bottle in this manner: take your writing tool and write these words on the parchment using dragon's blood ink:

"Witch bottle with pins, with pins and with oil, and with oil in you. I consecrate you to the four elements: Earth, Air, Fire, and Water. You have the powers of the four elements to protect my person, family, house, and all. You shall capture all the evil sent to me. Be it in the form of a curse, a thought, a wish, a secret desire, or a hex. Nothing evil will be able to pass you, for you will magnetize it and draw it into yourself, and disintegrate it, that it be no more.

This I do in the name of She who is from everlasting to everlasting. Little bottle, I charge you to bring me protection from every side, height, and depth. I shall hang you in open view, and all this work you shall do. I am safe now you see, as my word, so mote it be."

Once the ink is dry, roll up the parchment paper into a thin rod shape (words facing outward) and either tie it with string or seal it along the edge with some glue so that it does not come undone. Next, take some string and tie the parchment roll onto the bottle securely. Now, hang the bottle somewhere in plain view. According to ancient belief, no evil thing can then enter your home or touch any person in your home at any time. It is said that if hung in a child's bedroom, the Witch bottle will protect the child even when they are away from home.

THE WITCH BALL

The primary purpose of the Witch ball is to protect one against the "evil eye" which today might be called *ill wishes*. Traditionally, the Witch ball is green in color, although today, it can be found in various colors. According to tradition, the Witch ball was hung in the window of one's home. One legend that continues to be told is that the modern Christmas ornament ball is descended from the Witch ball. According to this tale, the ornament was placed on the tree to dispel a visitor's envy over the presents left beneath the tree. It is a common theme in folklore that envy can cause bad luck. In many European countries, bright objects were used to deflect the evil eye and even appear on horses and other animals that were used to haul supply carts through village streets.

Witch balls can often be found in antique stores, but are often very expensive. In seaport cities, you can find the fisherman's net-float balls, which are identical to the old witch balls common during the nineteenth century. During the Yule season, you can sometimes find a very large ornament ball in the local shops of most major cities.

Once you have obtained a Witch ball, bathe it in water set out beneath the Full Moon. Then, dry it off thoroughly, and recite the following words:

"All who gaze upon this ball
Their evil wishes do withdraw.
In my window, shining brightly
Protect within
Both day and nightly."

Then, simply hang the witch ball in your main window. You can place the ball in a fine net to suspend it from.

THE TROUBLE DOLL

The purpose of a trouble doll is to bring about a change in your life if things are going badly for you. Make a little rag doll and stuff it with dried moss or grass. Go to a quiet place and calm your mind. Take up the doll and, looking at it with all your focus, anoint it with Mercury oil and say these words:

> *"You are the trouble in my life.*
> *I name you this trouble (and here you describe the problem)."*

Looking intently at the doll, and picture all your troubles going into it. Be very absorbed and emotional about this. You can pace back and forth, vent your feeling on the doll, or do whatever it takes to get your emotions to a pitch. When you have poured all your troubles into it, throw it from you with all your might, shouting:

> *"Be gone from my life!"*

This is essential to the work; you must be fully invested in your emotions. The more worked up you get, the better the results will be.

To complete this work, take the doll into the woods (to a spot where you will not return again) and either nail it to a tree or hang it from a branch. If you are unable to do this, then you can throw the doll into a river or over a cliff. Another option is to bury it in a field far from where you live. When you have completed the task, simply say:

> *"You are gone from my life.*
> *I sever all connections,*
> *And I walk away from you!"*

Leave the scene and do not look back.

THE WITCHES' LADDER

The Witches' ladder is a very old and very powerful tool in the Witches' Craft. Various mentions of the Witches' ladder appear in folklore transcripts of the nineteenth century in both England and Italy. Charles Leland describes a type of Witches' ladder in his book *Etruscan Roman Remains*, published in 1892. He includes the traditional black hen feathers and magickal knots.

Traditionally, the Witches' ladder functioned with two primary purposes, both of which served as a type of binding magick. One use was to bind the Thirteen Moons of the Year and capture their power. This allowed the Witch to work weather magick, and nature magick, and to open the doorway to the Otherworld. The second purpose of the Witches' ladder was to bind enemies through the casting of a spell.

Preparing a Witches' ladder takes a year and a day. It requires a length of cord long enough to tie into thirteen knots as described in the method, and thirteen feathers from a black hen. The cord can be of cloth or hide strips, but it cannot be made from any synthetic material. The symbolism of the Witches' ladder is highly chthonic. Black hens were sacred offerings to the goddess Hecate, and so the feathers of the hen were of great value in the casting of spells and other works of magick. Black was also the color of night and was associated with the Underworld.

In ancient times, the Moon was believed to dwell in the Underworld, from which it journeyed up into the world of the living, crossing the night sky, and returning back into the Underworld where it was at home. The magickal goal of the Witch was to capture the light of the Full Moon in a knot each month until thirteen knots were obtained. In modern terminology, this would bind the energy of the Wheel of the Year into the cord. The process was begun on the Full Moon following the cross-quarter now commonly called *Samhain*.

The ancient method of collecting moonlight was to use a bowl of water in which the Full Moon was reflected. In this method, the Witch places a bowl of clean water beneath the Moon and stands in a position from which the Moon can be seen reflected on the surface of the water. The best time for this is when the Moon is directly overhead. Once the Moon can be easily viewed on the water, the Witch forms a loop in the cord in preparation for tying a knot and then looks at the image of the Moon through the open loop with their left eye. The Witch then quickly draws the loop into a knot, closes their eyes at the same moment, and imagines that the Moon has been captured in the knot. The following chant can be recited just before drawing the cord into a knot:

"With the Witches' cord
In this time and hour
Encircle I
The Moon's bright power.

A fairy eye to see
When Mystery we find,
And thee o'Moon
Hung in the dark
I here and now do bind."

Before opening their eyes, the Witch turns their head away from the bowl. In this way, when the eyes open again, the Moon cannot be seen in the water. According to Old Ways magick, if you see the Moon in the bowl as you open your eyes, the power will flow back into the water. In accordance with this teaching, the Witch avoids looking at the Moon until the cord has been safely put away in a pouch.

The entire process is performed again, making a new knot each time, until a total of thirteen Moons have been secured. Traditionally, nine knots occupy the center of the cord, followed by a space on each side of the string of nine knots. Each end of the cord (to each side of the nine knots) is tied with two knots. The cord is then presented up to the Moon, holding one end in each hand.

Once the last of the thirteen knots have been tied, on that same night, the thirteen black hen feathers are inserted into the knots. With the black feathers laid out before you, recite the following:

"Thirteen feathers
Black do lay
Sacred each to Hecate.
Thirteen seasons,
And thirteen doors,
Open to these magick swords."

Now it is time to add the feathers to the cord. The process of attaching the feathers begins with the knot on the left end of the cord, which will simply be the end you held in your left hand when you raised the cord up to the Moon. Insert and secure the feather into the knot, working down each knot to the other end of the cord. As you insert each feather, say:

"Feather to knot
Bring or send
Join complete
Or wholly rend."

KNOT CONFIGURATION

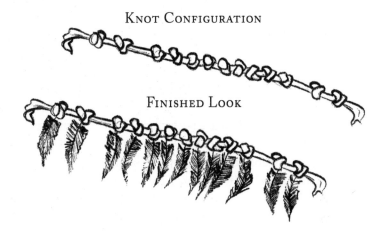

FINISHED LOOK

When all of the feathers are in place, the Witches' ladder is complete. For the final incantation, recite the following:

"Powers of the Witches' cord,
Come ye to the Witch's word.
Forces of seasons, and forces of night,
Be bound to the Witches' knot here tight.
By Hecate and these black feathers of hen,
All I desire and will, shall thee bend."

Whenever you need to use the Witches' ladder after this charge, simply repeat the final incantation and add words stating what it is you desire to manifest. To bind with the Witches' ladder, use a personal link or poppet image, and either encircle it with the cord or tie the cord around it. Try and make your wording rhyme if possible when you state the desired effect.

THE ASTRAL TEMPLE

The astral temple is a relatively modern concept, but in essence, originates from what Witches referred to as "traveling in spirit" or "traveling without the body." References to this concept among Witches appear in many writings including historian Carlo Ginzburg's books dealing with Witchcraft during the sixteenth and seventeenth centuries.

The purpose of the astral temple is to provide a doorway or gateway into a place between this world and the Otherworld, a magickal corridor or anteroom. In this realm, you can perform directly within the astral material for devotional and magickal work. One of the older techniques involves using a painting or a picture of some type, which reflects a place or setting that suits your taste for a mystical or magickal place you would enjoy being in. The picture must have one of the following things in it: a door, a path, a well, a pool, a lake, or a stream/river. This will be called your *inner gateway*. For your first experiment, avoid pictures with people or deities in them. You can choose another picture later on as you progress.

Once you have the image you desire, then place it in a glass-covered frame to protect it. Do this on the day of the New Moon. When the Moon is full, anoint the glass with the four elemental condensers described in Chapter Five, and then dry thoroughly. Next, trace a pentagram over the glass with your athame or index finger, beginning at the top and working down to the lower right point and continuing clockwise. As you trace the pentagram, recite these words:

"I call upon Spirit,
The elements to bind,
Doorways to open
And Mysteries to find."

Then sit or kneel beneath the Full Moon, facing away from it. Position the frame so that the Moon is reflected in the glass. You will most likely need to prop the frame, for even the slightest movement of your hands will be distracting since it will make the Moon's reflection wobble on the glass surface. While looking at the picture in the frame, center the Moon so it is either directly in the middle or is in a position of significance appropriate to the portrayed image (such as on the door of a castle). Once everything is in position, recite the following as you gaze upon the Moon's reflected light:

"Moonlight here, I hold you fast,
A gateway of magick
Through which to pass,

(pause)

To realms and places
Shown in glass and Moon
I pray thee, Goddess,
To grant this boon."

Now it is time to wrap the frame up in a cloth. From this point on, never allow the sunlight to fall upon the picture. If this happens, you will need to repeat the process over again. When you wish to work with your doorway, place it on a stand or on hang it on the wall. Use only candlelight or an oil lamp for light and make sure that you cannot see the flame reflected in the glass.

To use the portal, sit comfortably in a position that allows for a full and long-term view of the picture. To enhance the experience, you can anoint yourself with Mercury oil. Gaze into the picture and take three slow, deep breaths, exhaling each time. On the last exhalation, imagine that you are going out with your breath and passing into the picture. To leave the setting, repeat the breathing technique, and on the last exhalation, rub the palms of both hands back and forth on the floor/ground several times, and then sharply clap your hands together three times. This will affirm your return. If you feel disoriented in any way, have something to drink and a small snack.

Take a few moments and imagine yourself there in the picture. Mentally walk about, looking around and getting a feel for the place. Look at everything and imagine how each of your physical senses would experience the props within the setting. At first, this may seem totally imaginary, but in time, the reality of this "world between the worlds" will become very apparent. As with everything in life, you will get as much from this method as you are willing to devote the time and energy to making it manifest.

After exploring the setting several times, you can then proceed to use the picture as a portal into the astral realm. You may want to set an alarm clock for one hour when you first use this method. Begin by employing the same technique to enter the image as you did before. Once you are mentally within the image, you will need to make some magickal adjustments. Look at your inner gateway (mentioned earlier in this chapter) and trace a pentagram over it, saying:

"By the power of Spirit
Hear my call,
Bound to this place
With the image I draw.
Earth and Water
Fire and Air,
Joined with Spirit
As I declare.
Heed the call,
Both great and small,
The elements four
Do open the door."

The inner gateway is now open for you to pass into and through to the other side. Do this in whatever manner is appropriate. For example, if you chose a well for your inner gateway, then you would want to lower yourself down into it with a secured rope. If you selected a river, then you want to have a raft. If a door was your gateway, then simply open it and step through.

What you experience on the other side will be unique to you. It is best at first to simply imagine the same setting on the other side as appears in your picture. Grant yourself the magickal powers required to alter anything there. With your "imagination," you can wave a wand and have anything appear, disappear, or transform into something else. You can command blocks of stone to move and form into a castle or whatever you want.

Whatever you end up creating, remember that the goal is to establish an astral temple. Therefore, you will want to create an altar in your temple, and your temple will require four windows of some type through which you will pass your magickal and ritual energy. Seal all openings to your temple with a protective pentagram of blue fire. Decorate the temple as simply or elaborately as you wish. In this temple, you are the master magician, master ritualist, and master Witch of your realm.

Whatever works of magick you perform in your astral temple, visualize a "cone of power" into which your desire passes and is contained. Then visualize the cone passing out through the quarter window that is appropriate to the elemental nature of the spell or ritual. If you're unsure, then create a skylight in the ceiling of the temple and pass the cone out into the night sky, where the Moon will receive it.

Once established, you should go to your astral temple at least once a month. If you have artistic ability, you can paint or draw the temple you've created, which will enhance your visual image of it and make it stronger in your mind. If you work in clay, you can even make a model of the temple. The astral temple is ideal for practicing the Witches' Craft as a solitary, and for situations in which privacy is important.

Now it is time to turn to the next chapter and examine some of the ancient concepts of the Old Religion as they appear in modern Witchcraft.

~ CHAPTER II ~

Ancient Principles in Modern Craft Tenets

Like any system or religion, Witchcraft has its basic tenets or principles that color, shape, or define it. In this chapter, we will examine each of the main principles generally connected to modern Witchcraft. This is not to imply that Witchcraft as a religion is something modern, for as we saw in Chapters One and Two, there is a reasonable argument to the contrary. However, it must be noted that through the centuries, Witches have indeed added or merged various beliefs from non-European sources with European Witchcraft. Sometimes this was done to enhance an already existing belief, and sometimes it was done to fill in the missing pieces lost to various traditions during the time of the Inquisition or the dying out of some family traditions. Although the vast majority of people put to death for practicing Witchcraft during the Inquisition were not Witches, some Witches did perish. In this case, and in the case of natural or accidental death, certain gaps were left in what was passed on prior to the death of any particular Witch.

The principles of the Old Religion are rooted in antiquity. They are found amidst many of the oldest known religions. Many of the modern elements now incorporated into Witchcraft can be traced to such individuals as Charles Leland, Gerald Gardner, Aleister Crowley, Doreen Valiente, Austin Spare, and several others. However, even in these cases, much of the material is based upon ancient concepts and practices that predated these individuals. In some cases, modern writers provided little more than a popular title to something that was already part of the ancient cultures, but which ancient people may never have put into such formal terms or categories.

Modern scholars and skeptics tend to view additions to the tenets of Witchcraft as being proof of either fabrication or purely modern construction. This approach denies Witchcraft the natural process of evolution within religious beliefs and practices. This standard of purity is applied to no other religion on earth that has undergone changes and modifications.

In the following sections of this chapter, we will look at the various fundamental aspects and elements that comprise modern Witchcraft. In doing so, we readily see that none of them are without references in Western literature dating centuries prior to the periods that modern scholars claim are the point of origin for such concepts in modern Witchcraft. Let us turn now to an overview of the tenets and concepts commonly found now in modern Witchcraft.

THE BOOK OF SHADOWS

The Book of Shadows is a term used to refer to the ritual and magickal book of a Witch. In it, the Witch records the rituals, laws, and spells of their particular tradition. In the case of a solitary Witch, the book is more often a collection of eclectic spells, symbols, ritual guidelines, and personal notes.

Traditionally, each Witch is required to hand copy their Book of Shadows exactly as it appears. Later, the Witch may add their own material to the book, and this may later be copied by their own students. This is how Witchcraft can be modified over the course of time.

A historical reference mentioning this type of book appears in the seventeenth-century trial of a woman named Laura Malipero, who was accused of practicing Witchcraft. This trial was recorded in the records of the Venetian Inquisition. The transcripts state that upon searching Laura's home, agents of the Inquisition found a copy of the *Key of Solomon* along with a private handwritten book of spells and rituals into which Laura had copied portions of the *Key of Solomon*.

Another historical reference to a Book of Shadows appears in the *Compendium Maleficarum*. This book was written by the Italian demonologist Francesco Guazzo during the seventeenth century as a

Witch hunter's guide. In it, Guazzo notes that Witches use a "black book" from which they read during their "religious rites."

These texts document that the basic concept of a Witches' Book of Shadows is not a modern construction.

THE RITUAL CIRCLE AND ELEMENTAL SPIRITS

Although many commentators believe that the use of a ritual circle by Witches is a modern Gardnerian concept, there are actually much older references. As early as the seventeenth century, we find woodcut illustrations depicting Witches gathered in a ritual/magickal circle. One such example, drawn by Guazzo in 1608, appears in *Compendium Maleficarum*. Here, Guazzo depicts several Witches gathered in a circle traced upon the ground. Outside of the circle appears a horned figure, possibly evoked to appear by the Witches. It is interesting to note that Guazzo also mentions that Witches work with elemental spirits of Earth, Air, Fire, and Water. In occult lore, the elementals are known as gnomes, sylphs, salamanders, and undines.

In the introduction to the book *Etruscan Roman Remains* (1892), author Charles Leland also mentions the elemental spirits in Witchcraft: *"Closely allied to the belief in these old deities, is a vast mass of curious tradition, such as that there is a spirit of every element."* Here we see that none of these basic concepts related to Witchcraft originate from the imagination of a retired civil servant named Gerald Gardner, as many scholars claim.

The Witches' circle, or Circle of the Arts, is, in effect, a microcosm of the Witches' magickal universe. The ritual/magickal circle is traced upon the ground, traditionally nine to eighteen feet in diameter. Properly cast, it becomes a place between the physical and spiritual world. Wiccans/Witches often refer to the ritual/magickal circle as the world between the worlds and as sacred space. Once established, the circle serves to contain the magickal and metaphysical energies raised within its sphere, condensing them enough to accomplish the desired magickal effect. The threshold of the circle, through which the celebrants enter and exit, is located at various points pertaining to the inner symbolism contained in each tradition. Many traditions use the North or the East quarter. In the Ancient Mystery Traditions, the Northeast point of the circle served as the doorway.

The North is the realm of the power of the gods, and the East is the realm of enlightenment. To enter and exit at the Northeast point was to symbolically meet with the gods in power and enlightenment. When a circle is established according to the mystical associations unique to each tradition, it becomes a grotto for initiation and spiritual rebirth, the sacred womb of the Mother Goddess.

The circle is first marked out physically so that a vehicle exists wherein the elemental spirits can be invoked. A space is marked out to separate the mundane from the sacred. The elements are then evoked at each of the four quarters of the circle according to their correspondence. Traditionally, the element of Earth is assigned to the North. Elemental Air is placed at the East, Fire at the South, and Water at the West quarter. Depending upon the climatic conditions of the region in which any tradition abides, these elemental associations may vary.

The ritual or magickal circle should be visualized as a sphere of energy rather than a wall of energy enclosing the area. The sphere serves to seal not only the circumference but also the top and bottom of the sacred space that one has established. Traditionally, beings known as the Watchers are evoked to each of the four quarters of the circle to magickally guard the sacred area against the intrusion of any forces not in harmony with the ritual itself. The Watchers also bear witness to the rites and can exert a great deal of influence over the nature of the work at hand.

Movement within the ritual circle is always performed in a clockwise manner when creating sacred space or magickal workings. When dissolving the circle or negating magickal energy, the movements are always counterclockwise (note that in the Southern Hemisphere, this is reversed). Wiccans refer to this as *deosil* ("sunwise") and *widdershins* (or *tuathal*, "against the shadows"). According to the Mystery Teachings, however, the clockwise movement within the circle is symbolic of the lunar/feminine energies emerging from the left-hand side, and displacing the solar/masculine energies associated with the right-hand side. It is the Moon rising to claim the Heavens as the Sun departs to the Underworld. Since Wicca is a matrifocal and lunar sect, it is only natural to find this association. The solar associations of movement within the circle stem from the Indo-European influences that usurped the matrifocal concepts, particularly in central Europe.

Once established, the ritual circle serves to accumulate energy. The participants within its sphere are immersed in the energies being drawn to or raised within the sacred sphere. Being attendant within the circle allows one to become aligned with the frequency or vibrational rate of the current of energy present within the circle. In ancient times, it was held that the power of a Witch arose from unbroken participation in the rituals of the year. Such participation aligned the Witch with the natural flow of Earth's energy. Becoming attuned to nature freed one's psychic abilities and made available certain insights that helped one to develop magickal powers.

INITIATION

Most modern scholars believe that the ritual of initiation into Witch-craft is a modern concept, and the favored stand is that it was borrowed from Freemasonry. However, the concept does appear in Guazzo's *Compendium Maleficarum* (1608) where we read that becoming a Witch requires a formal pact sworn by oath. In Book One, Chapter Six, Guazzo states that when someone wants to become a Witch, they are given a type of "baptism" and receive a new name. The new Witch is also marked with a small brand upon their body. Guazzo states that this is all performed within a circle traced upon the ground.

Charles Leland notes a tradition among Italian Witches in Chapter Ten of *Etruscan Roman Remains*:

> *"As for families in which stregheria, or a knowledge of charms, old traditions and songs is preserved...as the children grow older, if any aptitude is observed in them for sorcery, some old grandmother or aunt takes them in hand, and initiates them into the ancient faith."*

THE GOD AND GODDESS

As we saw in Chapter Three, Witch trial transcripts and other writings of this era related to Witchcraft depict Witches worshipping a male goat deity and his consort. She is sometimes referred to in this literature as the "Queen of the Sabbat." Historian Carlo Ginzburg, in Chapter Two of his book *Ecstasies: Deciphering the Witches Sabbat*, states that she appears in transcripts from several regions of Europe under such names as Diana, Bensozia Richella, Good Mistress, Habonde, Oriente, Satia, Cybele, and Donna Venus (see Chapter One for an interesting connection here to Venus). The concept of a mated pair appears largely in trial transcripts from Italy, France, and Brittany (the latter concerning Basque Witches).

Most modern Witches tend to look at the concept of deity in Witchcraft in a more "sophisticated" manner than did the Witches of old. The Source Of All Things is generally personified by modern Witches as a Goddess and a God. In other words, many modern Witches view divinity itself as a balance of masculine and feminine divine consciousness that can be individually addressed as a God and a Goddess. There are, however, some Witches who conceive of the "Great Spirit" as strictly a Goddess entity, one who contains the masculine and feminine polarities within Herself. Modern Dianic Witches are one example of those who hold such a view. Other Witches, influenced largely by Eastern mysticism, perceive of deity as a metaphysical concept of one type or another.

In ancient times, our ancestors perceived of the Ultimate Deity as a mated pair. They were the Great Goddess and Her consort, as seen in Greek and Roman religion with Zeus and Hera, or Jupiter and Juno. Some modern Witches believe that the concept of our deity evolved from Neolithic religion, and perceive a Great Mother Goddess and Her consort the Horned God, Lord of the animal kingdom. By the classical era, the Goddess appeared as a Triple Goddess reflecting the stages of a woman's life, what we now refer to as "Maiden, Mother, and Crone." This triple imagery was seen in the ancient iconography of Hecate who later merged with Juno and Diana and in the iconography of the Three Fates. The God-figure in Witchcraft evolved from His primitive form as the Horned God of the forests. He was commonly portrayed with stag horns during our hunter/gatherer era, bull horns during our pastoral era, and later with goat horns when we became sedentary farmers and herders. In such forms, the God represented the fertility aspect that impregnated the Great Mother.

Most scholars believe that the Witches' concept of a mated pair of deities originated with Gerald Gardner and his cohorts. However, as we have seen a mated pair (goat deity and Sabbat Queen) appear in Witchcraft literature during the early seventeenth century. Over half a century before Gardner's writings, folklorist Charles Leland described a God and Goddess mythos discovered during his field studies on Italian Witchcraft. These deities bore the name of the Roman god Lucifer and the goddess Diana.

In Leland's *Aradia: Gospel of the Witches* we read:

"Diana was the first created before all creation; in her were all things; our of herself, the first darkness, she divided herself; into darkness and light she was divided. Lucifer, her brother and son, herself and her other half, was the light."

In this myth, Leland presents the tale of how Diana seduced her brother by changing herself into the image of his favorite cat and crawling into his bed one night. The story concludes with some text connecting the God and Goddess to the power of fate over humankind:

"Lucifer was extremely angry; but Diana with her wiles of Witchcraft so charmed him that he yielded to her love. This was the first fascination; she hummed the song, it was as the buzzing of bees (or a top spinning round), a spinning wheel spinning life. She spun the lives of all men; all things were spun from the wheel of Diana. Lucifer turned the wheel."

Leland next writes of this legend:

"The ancient myth is, to begin with, one of darkness and light, or day and night, from which are born the fifty-one (now fifty-two) weeks of the year. This is Diana, the night, and Apollo, the sun, or light in another form..."

Goddess worship, a major tenet in modern Witchcraft, is also a strong focus of Leland's research accounts. Two examples appear in *Aradia: Gospel of the Witches*. In Chapter Four, Leland records one of the Witches' prayers:

> *"Diana, beautiful Diana!*
> *Who art indeed as good as beautiful,*
> *By all the worship I have given thee,*
> *And all the joy of love which thou hast known,*
> *I do implore thee…"*

In Chapter Ten, Leland recounts the words of the Witch Aradia:

> *"Why worship a deity whom you cannot see, when there is the Moon in all her splendor visible? Worship her. Invoke Diana, the goddess of the Moon, and she will grant your prayers. This shalt thou do, obeying the Gospel of (the Witches and of) Diana, who is Queen of the Fairies and of the Moon."*

THE WATCHERS

The Watchers are beings who guard the portals linking the physical world with the spirit world. In some traditions, the Watchers are viewed as a spiritual race, a set of deities, or as the elemental spirits of Earth, Air, Fire, and Water. The Watchers are intimately connected to the four quarters: North, East, South, and West. Many traditions extend this association to include the Watchers as spirits having power over the four elements.

In old occult lore, the Watchers were also linked to each solstice and equinox, as well as to a specific star. Within the early stellar cults of Mesopotamia, there were four "royal" stars (known as Lords) which were called the Watchers. Each one of these stars "ruled" over one of the four cardinal points common to astrology. The star Aldebaran (when it marked the vernal equinox) held the position of Watcher of the East. Regulus (marking the summer solstice) was Watcher of the South. Antares (marking the autumn equinox) was Watcher of the West. Fomalhaut (marking the winter solstice) was Watcher of the North.

In many of the Witchcraft traditions dating from antiquity, the Watchers were known as *The Old Ones*. They have long been viewed as an elder race pre-dating humankind. In *Aradia: Gospel of the Witches*, Leland presents the tale of "The Children of Diana, or How the Fairies Were Born" in which it is stated that Diana created *"the great spirits of the stars."* In another legend titled "How Diana Made the Stars and the Rain," Leland writes that Diana went *"to the fathers of the Beginning, to the mothers, the spirits who were before the first spirit."* It is not difficult to see a reference to an elder race in this text.

In many Witchcraft/Wiccan traditions, the Watchers are the Guardians of the portals to other realms, protectors of the ritual circle, and witnesses to the rites that have been kept down through the ages. Each of the four ruling Watchers oversees an individual Watchtower, which is a gateway protecting the ritual circle. Each Watchtower is associated with one of the four quarters of North, East, South, and West.

NATURE

Witches view nature as a conscious, living being, and personify Her as the Great Mother Goddess. Witches venerate nature and, generally speaking, feel a strong sense of stewardship. When we consider a painting, we can see that something of the nature of the artist can be discerned from the use of color, character of brush stroke, sense of composition, and so forth. In much the same way, Witches discern things about the nature of the gods who created the Earth and the forces we call nature. This is accomplished through alignment with, and the veneration of, nature.

In the earliest writings concerning Witches, they are associated with groves and hilltops. Homer writes of Circe "within the forest glades" and Ovid speaks of Glaucus going to the "herb-clad hills" of the Witch Circe. Homer also writes in *The Odyssey* of the handmaids of Circe as being "children" of the *"springs, groves, and of sacred rivers that flow to the sea."* Later in Western literature, we find stories of Witches that live in the woods or in caves. There are also many tales of Witches living in cabins or cottages outside of rural villages. The general theme is one of isolation from "civilization" and points to two elements. First is the preference for living in a more natural setting, something better attuned to communion with nature. The second element reflects the refusal to accept the Witch within common society.

The ancients believed that Witches possessed power over nature. Ovid wrote that Witches could make streams run back to their fountainheads, stir up the sea, move clouds, cause earthquakes, uproot trees, and draw the Moon down from the sky. In reality, Witches do not master nature but instead share a relationship with Her. The Witch does not have "power over nature" but instead has power *with* nature. It is the Witches' alignment with nature that allows Witches to become channels for natural forces. Witches do not master nature; they live in common cause with nature. To celebrate nature, and to create and maintain alignment with nature, Witches gather to perform rituals at the eight seasonal sabbats of the year.

RITUAL

Ritual is both a means of worship and a method of communicating with deities or spirits. It is a symbolic language that can gain access to other dimensions or states of consciousness. Ritual also allows us to step out of our mundane personalities and become something larger than ourselves. This is because properly constructed rituals, based upon time-proven techniques, serve to evoke the momentum of the past. What this refers to is the occult principle:

> *"When an act is performed, which has been performed in the exact manner, time and time again, century after century, it gains a momentum of energy that flows from the past."*

In Witchcraft, the sabbat rituals have been created to connect us with the energies of the seasonal shifts of our planet. These periods of energy flows are marked by the solstices and equinoxes. The other times of power exist at exactly the mid-points between these times of power and constitute the other four sabbats. The ritual circle serves as a pool that collects the energies flowing into it. The celebrants who gather within the circle are bathed in this energy and begin to resonate with its vibratory nature.

Many Craft traditions have different names for the ritual sabbats depending upon their cultural influence. Generally speaking, the sabbats are known by the following popular relatively modern names:

1. Imbolg or Candlemas (February 2)

2. Spring Equinox or Lady's Day/Ostara (March 2)

3. Beltane or Roodmas (April 30)

4. Summer Solstice or Midsummer/Litha (June 22)

5. Lughnasadh or Lammas (July 31)

6. Autumn Equinox or Mabon (September 21)

7. Samhain or Hallowmas (October 31)

8. Yule or Winter Solstice (December 22)

PERSONAL POWER

It is an ancient teaching that the human body contains zones or areas of energy. These zones can be applied and accessed in order to generate personal power towards a magickal goal. In Eastern mysticism, these centers are called *chakras*, and it is taught that there are seven such zones of power within the human body. In the old Witchcraft systems, it was taught that three centers existed. These were located at the forehead, heart, and genital area. Most modern Witchcraft traditions share the Eastern view, but the chakras are often referred to as *personal power centers* instead of chakras.

The first center is located at the crown of the head and is perceived as the meeting place between human and divine consciousness. The second is located in the center of the forehead just above and between the eyes. It is often referred to as *the third eye* because it is believed that the sum of the five human senses is amplified within the pineal gland located there and that this produces a sixth sense of psychic sight or extra-sensory perception.

The third center is located at the throat area and is involved in the influence of tones and vibrations that in turn affect energy patterns. It is this center that conveys energy within chants and invocations. The fourth center is located at the heart area and is concerned with feeling energy patterns. Thus, it is often associated with our feelings toward others and our feelings toward places and situations. The fifth center is located at the solar plexus and is the center through which the soul and astral body derive nourishment from etheric energy within the physical dimension.

The sixth center is located just below the navel and is known as the *personal power center*. It is here that we relate to our own power or lack thereof. This is often experienced as a feeling in the pit of the stomach when we are confronted with something challenging (like an important job interview). The seventh center is located in the genital area and is associated with energy in a pure form; in other words, it is raw or unrefined energy. This center makes us vital and provides the drive and motivation that empower us.

THE AURA

The rate at which the power centers in the body vibrate and the degree of harmony existing between them create an energy field around the human body known as *the aura*. The aura is comprised of bio-electromagnetic energy and heat vapor. It is the "energy representation" of who and what we are, a sort of spiritual image painted in our energy field. The aura is an etheric energy pattern surrounding not only a living creature but any natural physical object as well. In the case of living things, the aura reflects the spiritual, mental, and emotional state of that which it surrounds. Psychics can perceive vaporous colors within the aura, indicating various things about the state of an individual.

It is an old teaching that whatever manifests within the body was first present in the aura. This is one of the reasons why feeling good about yourself makes you look good to others. The mental energy penetrates into the physical form through the aura surrounding the body. From an occult perspective, "thoughts are things," and therefore, it is important not to allow negativity to remain within one's consciousness. The aura should always be strengthened with positive thoughts, words, and deeds.

The aura is comprised of seven bands or layers of energy. Each one is linked to a power center in the body which is associated with specific internal organs. These power centers are linked to one of the seven realms of existence. Through this system, the soul is connected with the lower, middle, and higher self. The self is perceived as existing within various states of consciousness separated by its integration into the planes of existence. The soul is functioning simultaneously on different levels with different states of awareness. On a mundane scale, we can liken this to someone driving a car. They are operating the vehicle, talking to a passenger, and watching the traffic and surroundings all at the same time. Each is a separate awareness representing a different focus and a different expression of what the individual is experiencing and projecting into the world.

THE PLANES OF EXISTENCE

Occultism teaches that there are seven planes or dimensions that comprise existence. The highest dimension is the Ultimate Plane (unknowable from our human perspective). The lowest is the Physical Dimension. In essence, these are the highest and lowest frequencies at which energy vibrates or resonates in a metaphysical sense. In reality, they do not occupy space as we understand it, and their relationship to each other is not literally one above or below another. It can be said that they occupy the same space at the same time, but exist as different states of energy.

The traditional order in which these dimensions are placed is as follows:

- Ultimate
- Divine
- Spiritual
- Mental

- Astral
- Elemental (or Plane of Forces)
- Physical

The Ultimate Plane is the realm in which the Source of All Things dwells. This is what some religions refer to as the "Godhead," the "Great Spirit," or the "Divine One." Nothing more can really be said about it because the ability to comprehend this is quite limited by our human condition.

The Divine Plane is where the gods and goddesses of our religions dwell. It is in this realm that the unknowable becomes personified into deities and reduced to concepts more understandable to human consciousness. In mythology, the Divine Plane is the home of the gods reflected in such realms as Olympus and Asgard.

The Spiritual Plane is the dwelling place of beings of light, the spiritual races known in some religions as spirit guides, angels, archangels, or Watchers. This realm is the dwelling place of enlightened beings who have joined with the community of souls and are no longer separated from the divine by a focus upon the self. Dwelling within each of us is the divine spark of that which created us. To isolate the spark and perceive it as being ourselves is to focus upon the self rather than the spark which unites us with all things.

The Mental Plane is the realm of pure thought, pure consciousness stripped of the limitations of physical sensation and awareness. In this realm, the mind is unlimited in its creativity and its ability to conceive and project. It is here that thoughts are uncontaminated by emotion and desire. They exist as pure concepts.

The Astral Plane is the realm of etheric matter, a "spirit material" capable of shaping thoughts and desires into visible forms. Everything that manifests in our material world is first shaped in the astral substance. The Astral Realm is where magick takes root, solidifying our desires into dense forms within the astral material. Once formed, these magickal images sink into the material dimension, manifesting our desire.

The Elemental Plane is a realm in which the creative forces of Earth, Air, Fire, and Water carry energy back and forth between the planes of existence. The forces within the Elemental Plane can be employed to add various vibrations to the energy we raise through ritual or magick. This is what we refer to as charging with Earth, Air, Fire, and Water. The Elemental Plane transmits our desires to the Astral Realm and then returns the astral thought-forms back to the physical dimension.

The Physical Plane is the realm of material objects, energy so dense and at such a low vibration that it is constantly visible and tangible. The Physical Plane is the most mundane expression of the principles existing and operating on the higher planes of existence. The laws of nature or the principles of physics are diminished expressions of a higher order of things. However, within their mundane patterns, we can discern something of the higher order.

AS ABOVE, SO BELOW

There is an ancient occult teaching stating that the higher nature is reflected in the lower nature and vice versa. This teaching addresses the issue of the physical dimension being the reflection of a higher non-physical dimension. Everything that exists within the physical world was first an energy form within a higher dimension that eventually manifested in the world of physical matter. The physical expression of this form or concept becomes denser (in all respects) as it passes into the physical dimension and yet still reflects the basic concept of the higher principle.

In the Egyptian Mysteries, it was taught that *"that which is below is like that which is above, and that which is above is like that which is below"* (creation is of the nature of the creator). This concept concerns not only the manifestation of physical matter but is also contained in the laws of nature/the principles of physics. This is why, within the Witches' theology, nature is viewed as the Great Teacher. It is through our understanding of nature and Her ways that we can understand the ways of the creators who brought all into existence. For the nature of the creators is reflected within their creations, just as the style of an artist can be detected within their art.

Like nature itself, the Old Religion contains certain established laws and ways, the very blueprint of the divine pattern within. Through a discernment of nature (which likewise reflects the nature of that which created it), the Witch can begin to unravel the Mystery of divine consciousness. This is one of the reasons why Witches hold such reverence for nature.

CAUSE AND EFFECT

Witches believe that both positive and negative energies return (in some related aspect) back to the originator of those energies. This is sometimes referred to as *The Three-Fold Law*. Essentially, this law addresses a magickal principle in which energy creates a cause-and-effect relationship. This energy reaction affects us on three levels: the mind, spirit, and body. This is why it is called the Three-Fold Law. In modern Wicca, this principle has been altered to mean that whatever energy one sends out, comes back three times that amount (in a cause-and-effect relationship). However, there is no corresponding law of physics to match this concept.

Our thoughts are energy forms that influence our aura. The state of our aura soon becomes the state of our physical well-being. Our physical condition then influences our mental state. This, in turn, influences our spirituality, and therein lies the law of three-fold return. In other words, our thoughts and deeds create energies that draw back to us energies of a like nature. Once absorbed into our aura, they penetrate into our mind, body, and spirit. This is the three-fold nature.

We experience this interplay of energy quite often, even in our mundane lives. Sometimes the mere presence of a person who is unknown to us can be disturbing and we do not want this person near us. Other times, we may not want to sit in a certain area or be in a certain place for no real apparent reason. There are times when we sense that a place or situation "feels wrong" and we want to leave. These are all mundane examples of how an aura receives energy that, in turn, causes changes within our consciousness.

ETHICS

Most Witches basically believe in a "live and let live" non-violent philosophy built upon the tolerance of differing beliefs and lifestyles. There is a basic gentleness of spirit within most Witches and a striving towards peaceful coexistence with those around them. However, most Witches do not generally "turn the other cheek" when attacked. Witches prefer to be left undisturbed, but if cornered and left no escape route, the Witch can be a most formidable opponent.

Witches do not avoid certain acts because they believe in some type of resulting punishment, but from a basic sense of right and wrong. It is wrong to steal, lie, or betray. It is wrong to needlessly take a life or to intentionally hurt another person without sufficient justification. Sexual conduct is generally seen as a personal issue and there is no judgment upon how one conducts themselves where sexual contact is mutually agreed upon between consenting adults.

Many modern Witches adhere to the popular text known as "The Wiccan Rede" as an ethical guide. This purely modern tenet reads: *"An as it harm none, do what thou will."* Some people interpret this to mean that a person can do anything they wish as long as no one is harmed by it, and thereby, that person is free of any repercussions. According to occult teachings, the inner meaning of the Rede addresses what "to will" means. Essentially, from an occult perspective, to "do as one wills to do" means to find one's purpose (one's True Will) and to fulfill it. This is to benefit the person but is not to serve as a detriment to another person. In a higher sense, this tenet is related to Eastern mysticism where it is the work of the neophyte to master their physical senses and to pass into non-attachment. Once the student has risen above the desires and needs of the flesh, then they can view the world with detachment and thereby discover their true will or purpose.

At this stage, there is no greed, envy, or jealousy, and therefore, the person can act through knowledge of their own pure will. No harm can be done to another because the personal will is not centered upon any relationship, personal status, prestige, or any personal gain within a society. It is the true will of the divine nature within the person, acting in accord with its purpose in this lifetime. Therefore, because one is acting in true accord with "the divine plan" (which includes all of us in the plan), one can then do as one wills without harming another.

The ethics of modern Witches differ from ancient ones. In ancient times, Witches used their powers to heal and to harm in accordance with their personal needs and the needs of those around them. The philosophy of not performing any act that can harm another is a relatively modern tenet, an evolution of spirituality over the centuries. It is clearly not reflective of any historical views held by any ancient society or people. This does not make ancient Witches evil. The Witch was a creature of nature, and like any untamed creature, the Witch preferred to be left unmolested. However, if cornered, Witches would defend themselves to the fullest measure. Like any person, the Witch viewed certain people as allies and certain people as adversaries. The Witch dealt with them as was appropriate to the situation.

MAGICK

Magick is the ability to bring about changes in accordance with one's personal will or desire. To accomplish this, one needs to understand how to draw, condense, move, and direct energy. The key to this understanding lies in a realization of how the inner mechanisms of nature work (the so-called supernatural). Added to this is an understanding of how a person can enlist the aid of a spirit or a deity.

True magick is a metaphysical science. It is the understanding of metaphysical principles and how to employ them in order to manifest one's wishes or needs. Magick typically requires the use of specially prepared tools and established states of consciousness. Such things allow the mind to access other realms wherein magickal forces await.

The tools of magick serve as conducting agents drawing energy in a manner not unlike a lightning rod. Under the direction of the Witch, these tools can channel energy toward a desired goal or effect. Once drawn and condensed, the Witch uses mental images and forms their thoughts into a desired goal. In magickal terms, this is called a "thought-form." The thought-form is then released and directed off to accomplish the desired outcome.

In 1608, Francesco Guazzo recounted one of the old laws of Witchcraft in the *Compendium Maleficarum,* stating that *"no one might thrust his sickle in another's harvest, according to the law which provides that he who binds must also unbind."* This addresses the Old Ways of the Witches' Craft when Witches did not interfere with one another. Among Witches, there was an understanding that one did not perform counter-magick against another Witch who used magick on an outsider. This not only served to minimize Witch feuds but also helped assure that non-Witches would not cheat or take advantage of the local Witch whose services were contracted by the village folk. If one could not pit one Witch against another, then it was best to stay on the good side of the Witch.

REINCARNATION

Reincarnation is the belief that a soul is reborn again into the physical world after death. Among the ancient Greeks, it was called *palingenesis,* a word meaning "to have origin again" and was a common teaching found in Orphism. Ancient historians recorded that reincarnation was also a belief taught by the Druids in northern Europe. It is an important concept in other religions such as Buddhism, Hinduism, Jainism, and Sikhism.

Essentially, the role of reincarnation is to educate and prepare the soul for its future existence as an enlightened spiritual being. In order to accomplish this, the soul must experience the joys and sorrows of physical existence. In this, the soul develops compassion and empathy. In the spiritual realms that await the soul, the soul will serve as a spirit guide for beings still encased in physical matter. The dissolving away of focus upon the self and the merging with the community of souls is essential to spiritual enlightenment.

The Mystery Cults of ancient southern Europe, established in Egypt, Greece, and Italy, taught that the soul survives bodily death and is later reincarnated in a human or other mammalian body. The teachings also addressed that the soul would eventually obtain release from the cycle of rebirth within the physical dimension. This release allowed the soul to move on to the three worlds that lie beyond; the lunar, solar, and stellar. In each realm, the soul took on a body appropriate to each new dimension, just as it once dwelled in material form on the physical plane. The labels of lunar, solar, and stellar were, of course, metaphors for spiritual states of consciousness.

The Druids reportedly taught that the soul passes into the realm of *Gwynvyd* if the deeds of the individual are positive. If their deeds are evil in nature, then the soul passes into the realm of *Abred*. In Gwynvyd, the soul enters into a state of bliss, and through Abred, the soul incarnates into an animal form best suiting its nature at the time of death. In either case, the Druids apparently believed that the soul could return again to a human body in a new lifetime.

In ancient Witchcraft, the belief was held that Witches were reborn within their own family bloodlines. Over the course of many lifetimes, the Witch grew more and more powerful. Eventually, the Witch could become a powerful spirit or demigod if desired. However, the Witch was also free to move from the Earth and dwell within the Otherworld, sometimes referred to as *the Summerland*.

Leland records beliefs in reincarnation among the Witches he encountered in Italy, known as the *Strega*. In Chapter Ten of his book, *Etruscan Roman Remains*, Leland writes:

> *"It is also believed in the Romagna that those who are specially of the strega faith die, but reappear again in human forms. This is a rather obscure esoteric doctrine, known in the Witch families but not much talked about. A child is born, when, after due family consultation, some very old and wise strega detects in it a long-departed grandfather by his smile, features, or expression."*

In the introduction, Leland writes: *"Also that sorcerers and Witches are sometimes born again in their descendants."* In Chapter Ten, Leland writes of a connection related to this theme:

"In this we may trace the process by which the Witch or sorcerer, by being reborn, becomes more powerful, and passes to the higher stage of a spirit."

Leland further states:

"Dr. O. W. Holmes has shrewdly observed that when a child is born, some person old enough to have triangulated the descent, can recognise very often the grandparent or great uncle in the descendant. In the Witch families, who cling together and intermarry, these triangulations lead to more frequent discoveries of palingenesis than in others. In one of the strange stories in this book relating to Benevento, a father is born again as his own child, and then marries his second mother. But the spirit of the departed wizard has at times certainly some choice in the matter, and he occasionally elects to be born again as a nobleman or prince."

THE SUMMERLAND

Like many belief systems, the Old Religion perceived the afterlife as a realm of eternal summer. Here, souls took their rest and were renewed, meeting with ancestors and all who had left behind the physical life before them. Some souls awaited rebirth back into the physical world or even some other reality. Among the Celts, this realm of eternal summer was generally known as *Tír na nÓg*, the Land of Undying Youth.

In the legends of King Arthur, we encounter the realm of The Isle of Apple Trees, also known as Avalon. Here, dead kings and heroes came to dwell at the end of their days. Among the Druids, it was taught that a similar realm existed called The Isle of Sein or The Isle of Seven Sleeps (*Enez Sizun*). These all bear some resemblance to the Summerland of Witches.

In Witchcraft, the doorway to the Summerland lies at the West quarter, the realm of the setting Sun and Moon. In ancient European mythology, gods and goddesses of the Sun and Moon often crossed the sky from east to west gathering departed souls and escorting them into the Underworld. One primitive belief held that souls were later taken to the Moon and that as the Moon filled with departed souls, the light of the Moon grew to fullness. As the souls reincarnated back into the world, the light of the Moon diminished.

HERBALISM

The use of herbs in modern Witchcraft is, of course, based upon an older folklore tradition of peasant Witchcraft. Herbal spells and potions that appear in many modern Witchcraft books are an expansion on the use of herbs in the Witches' Craft. This is further evidence of the natural evolution of Witchcraft over the course of time. However, most Witches still adhere to the attributes given to herbs that appear in the old grimoires of the Middle Ages and Renaissance periods. The old attributes reflect the knowledge and experience of our ancestors who lived closer to nature than most of us do today.

The old teachings tell us that there dwells within all things a living consciousness called *mana* or *numen*. Just as humans are souls encased in a physical body, plants also bear a divine spark within them (as do stones, trees, and all inanimate objects). It is the power of a plant's numen or mana that is employed in magick and spell casting. The ancients created a table of correspondences for various plants ascribing certain natures to them.

The collective energy of numen or mana within a setting such as a forest or lake, is responsible for the peaceful feeling we experience there. This is why many people enjoy camping and hiking. It is also what draws us to a particular area or influences us to choose a favorite place to sit or park our car. In such cases, we are responding to a harmonious emanation of numen or mana.

In ancient times, nature spirits were associated with meadows and woods. The power of various herbs was believed to derive from contact with fairies and other supernatural creatures. Certain planetary bodies were also believed to empower various herbs, including the Sun and the Moon. The etheric metaphysical properties of the Moon were said to pass power into herbal plants. This was one of the reasons why it was taught that herbs could only be gathered beneath the Full Moon.

FAMILIARS

It is an ancient teaching that a psychic rapport can be established between a human and an animal (or a spirit). Such a relationship is known as having a *familiar spirit*. This concept dates back to the early shamanic days of animal totems associated with human clans. Each clan believed in a certain animal spirit that protected or aided the clan. This is not unlike some of the American Indian tribes who named themselves after various creatures (such as the Crow tribe).

The wearing of a feather or animal pelt was believed to empower a person with the qualities of the animal from which they came. The wearer of such an object would mimic the mannerisms of the animal in order to awaken the power dwelling within the feather or pelt, etc. He or she was then becoming familiar with the spirit of the animal, and once this power could be easily invoked, then this person was said to possess a familiar spirit.

Eventually, this concept was extended to include establishing a psychic link with a living creature. The living spirit of the creature could possess the shaman, or be sent off in spirit form to aid them in some magickal work. During the Middle Ages, this was the most common relationship with a familiar and is the basis for the classic image of a Witch and her familiar as depicted in art.

Cats are one of the most common of the Witches' familiars mentioned in the old literature of Witchcraft. The black cat in particular was favored by Witches. In the old Witches' lore, any black-colored creature was associated with the powers of night and the forces of the Underworld. The cat familiar was also valued due to its ability to sense spirits or the "unseen" in general, which alerted the Witch to an immediate presence. Oral tradition states that Witches also used the purring sound made by cats to induce trance states. The croaking of frogs was also used in this way, and frogs likewise appear as familiars in literature regarding Witchcraft.

DIVINATION

Divination is the ability to discern what the future holds for us. Actually, it allows us to foresee what is going to happen if all factors remain constant. The tools of divination allow us to view the patterns that are forming which will, in turn, result in the particular manifestation of a specific situation. Thus, divination allows us to either prepare for what lies ahead or to take action to alter the patterns and thus, avoid the situation.

Some people believe that the future is fixed in time and they subscribe to the theory of predestination. If this were so, then everything would be on auto-pilot and no one would have the freedom of personal choice. We would all be just along for the ride, so to speak. Others believe that the major events of one's life such as marriage, children, injury, and death are predestined, but that in day-to-day life, a person has free choice. The Mystery Teachings tell us that the basic energy pattern of our life is pre-established (as reflected in the art of astrology), but that we can alter it (as in the art of magick and the gift of free will) as need be.

According to the old teachings, the future is not already decided but the pattern is established in the astral fabric and will manifest if nothing alters it. Everything that manifests in the physical dimension is first formed in the astral dimension. This is one of the keys to magick. Divination allows us to glimpse the astral pattern and see what has formed in the astral material. Astrology allows us an overview of what lies in store if nothing alters our course, and provides us with an understanding of the energies and forces that influence us. This knowledge helps us to strengthen our vulnerabilities and take advantage of our strengths.

The most common tools employed in the divinatory arts are tarot cards, rune stones, psychometry, crystal visions, and the reading of signs and omens. Techniques such as palmistry and phrenology fall under the category of psychometry.

THE AKASHIC RECORDS

The *Akashic Records* is a term referring to a realm or plane in which the memory of all that has transpired upon the Earth is imprinted (the energy patterns). In modern Witchcraft, the Akashic Records are said to reside within the Odic mantle of the Earth, an occult term for the etheric components of the Earth's magnetic field. This can be thought of as being similar to data being stored on magnetic computer disks. Occultists believe that the energy imprints contained within the Akasha Records can be read through magickal and psychic methods. Some psychics visualize the Akashic Records as an immense library containing the collective records of the ages that have passed on the Earth.

In the oral tradition of the old Witches' Craft, there is a concept known as the *voice of the wind*. This refers, in part, to the psychic ability to mentally receive teachings directly from an outside source. Spontaneous knowledge, and to a degree, even intuition, can be tapping into the Akashic levels of energy. This is related not only to interfacing with the Akashic Records but also to one's rapport with the spirits of the Old Religion.

Hearing the voice of the wind is sometimes said to indicate that a person hears the voices of spirits or fairies. It can also be an indication of the Witch's level of intuitive/psychic abilities. When a person feels directed, inspired, or *channels* (a spirit/entity speaking directly through a person), it is said that they hear the voice of the wind. In modern Witchcraft, one might simply say a person has accessed the Akashic Records and is tapping into ancient memories.

Throughout this book, we have looked at the modern and ancient aspects of Witchcraft revealed to us over the course of time. Now we come to the crossroads that have led us from the past to the present. Now we must look forward to where we go from here. Let us turn now to the final chapter before we part ways.

～ CHAPTER 12 ～

𝕿HE
𝖂ELL-𝖂ORN 𝕻ATH

JOSEPH CAMPBELL ONCE SPOKE of the "one deed done by many." What he was addressing was the mythos of the hero, the journey we must all take in order to reach our spiritual goals. Campbell wrote in his book *The Hero with a Thousand Faces* that the adventure is not risked alone because our mythical heroes have cleared a trail before us.

Campbell said that the pathways of the labyrinth through which we must pass in our quest are already known and that we need only follow the thread of the hero's path. Where we feared we might find a monster waiting to destroy us, we would instead find a god welcoming us into enlightenment. Campbell wrote that what we thought was a journey of outward exploration was instead a journey inward to the center of our own existence. He concluded that in the end, our sense of aloneness would dissolve away, and we would be united with the entire world.

Many years ago, when I made a full commitment to practice the religion of Witchcraft, I was told that before me lay the well-worn path. *The well-worn path* is a phrase that refers to all that has come before. This refers to the accumulation of the knowledge and wisdom of our ancestors. This was traditionally pictured as a long, winding footpath, crossing through a beautiful, high-grown field, and disappearing into the thicket. The teaching within this image is that each generation explores the path and clears it a little farther ahead each time, leaving a nicely-worn trail for others behind to follow.

I have walked the well-worn path for over thirty years at the time of this writing, and have hopefully learned something along the way. One of the most valuable lessons I believe I've learned is that there is no end to this road and that the great master who lives in the old cottage down the road is yourself in the making. However, there are many teachers along the way, and some of them are your own students. Some of the best teachers one will encounter are one's critics and adversaries. These individuals show us how we allow ourselves to be misunderstood by others.

Although there are elders, books, and life itself to help teach you, you will eventually come to the point when you must discern the path for yourself. The task left to the individual is to follow the well-worn path to where it ends, and then to blaze new trails. To walk the path that others have cleared before you allows you to begin further ahead on your own journey. By learning what others have learned and understood before you, you can be better prepared to venture into the unknown. Through you, the path is extended as the new walk begins, and the lineage is passed on to those who are walking up the trail just behind you.

Now let us turn to the time-honored oral history of the Witches, which is what scholars and skeptics call our mythical history.

THE OLD RELIGION

Throughout the writing of this book, I have thought a great deal about the question of what is the Old Religion. To understand this, we must consider what the Old Ways are. I have been a priest of the Old Religion for many years, and have tried to faithfully serve the old gods of my ancestors. One need only look upon the Full Moon at night to feel the living connection to ways that are ever ancient and ever new. The Old Ways are about the true veneration of nature and the forces that animate Her.

In the Old Ways, we see that everything is connected to every other thing. Life is like a spider web, and all the threads are important. Each thread vibrates to the movement of any other thread anywhere on the web. Through knowledge of the Old Ways, we come to understand that the seasons of nature are reflections of the cycles of our own life. The Old Ways teach us that everything is in transition, and there is comfort in knowing that winter does not last forever. The price for this release is to trade spring and summer, receive them back, and then trade them again. So too is it with the highs and lows of our own lives.

It is an ancient teaching that out of darkness, all things issue forth. This is one of the essential components to understanding the connection of the Underworld to Witchcraft. Take, for example, the seed of grain. To the ancient people who knew nothing about the internal structure of a seed and the inner biological process, the seed itself had no mystical power. They had observed that keeping a seed in a pouch or carrying one around would not result in the seed becoming a new plant. It was only when the seed was put into a hole in the ground and covered up in darkness with soil that the seed transformed into a plant. Therefore, to primitive reasoning, it must be the Earth itself that has the power to turn the seed into a plant and not the seed.

Other living things also issued forth from holes in the earth, such as snakes, weasels, and other creatures. To primitive minds, it must have seemed that something beneath the ground must be manufacturing these creatures. It was this sense of mystery that made the darkness magickal. In the greater sense of "darkness" itself, there was another Mystery, which we now call the Moon. This soft, ever-changing sphere of light arose from beneath the earth, climbed, and illuminated the night sky. It too had come up from the Underworld.

The Moon became the symbol of Mystery itself. Beneath its light, one could better look into the darkness in hopes of unlocking the greatest of secrets. Our ancestors traced the Full Moon upon the ground in an attempt to capture its magickal light, and stood within the large circle they traced into the soil to represent the Moon. Here, they took their first step toward the veneration of the Moon.

At night, the world seemed mysterious, and it was difficult to see the things that moved about and made noise in the darkness. Out of this arose the sense of magickal beings that inhabited this world of moonlight. In time, they were given such names as fairy, elven, and other various names of creatures belonging to the so-called supernatural realm.

Then, as now, there were certain humans that were attracted to this secret realm. Likewise, there were those who feared the darkness. Those who did not fear it, in time, came to better understand it. They built a rapport with the night spirits and were taught by them, and they came to favor the creatures of the night—the owl, the toad, the newt, and the bat. As these humans learned the secrets whispered beneath the Moon's light and came to understand them, they, in turn, taught others.

The knowledge of these individuals grew to include the secrets of herbs. They also learned to read signs and omens, to understand the weather, and the inner mechanisms of nature. Preferring to live away from the villages and towns, these individuals inhabited the hills and woodlands. The ancient Greeks called them the *pharmakeutes*. In time, they came to be called by many names: *pharmakis, saga, maga, striga, venefica,* sorceress, and Witch.

By whatever name, the Witch was a mediator between the world of humankind and the spirit world. The Witch was caretaker of the forest world. They kept the ways of the sacred places, blessed the Earth when the seasons changed, and rectified the offenses that humankind inflicted upon the spirits of the land. It was in this that the Witch and the fairy race became kindred spirits, joined together in the covenant of a common cause.

As we noted in Chapter One, the Witch became maligned over the course of history and came to be regarded as evil and dangerous among the common people. With the construction of laws against magick and Witchcraft, the members of this sect became a strictly secret society. They were relatively few in numbers by comparison to the population around them which helped them to go about unnoticed. In order to survive torture and death, most Witches put on the veneer of Christianity by attending church services and blending into the social order. Many of those who refused to do so became a renegade sect.

The renegades looked at what Christianity feared and discovered this to be the devil figure. From a magickal point of view, it only seemed logical to use this energy against the enemy. The renegades then set about constructing a counter-magick system, reversing the power symbols of Christianity and grounding the magickal energy currents of Christianity's power symbols. The latter was achieved by using such things as the communion wafer in a non-spiritual manner (what the Church then came to call *sacrilege*). As is always the case with human nature, the actions of a few members of this subculture sect were seen as a reflection of everyone. This is how Witches came to be viewed in the stereotypical images popularized in horror movies and fostered by many Christians today.

During the era of the Witchcraft trials, a few members of the Witches' sect were brought before the authorities, but the majority of these victims were not Witches by any definition. There are some examples of individuals that appear to have had knowledge of the Witches' Craft and may have been members of the Witches' sect. One individual is Isobel Gowdie, tried in 1662, who mentioned the "maiden of the coven" and was said to belong to a coven of Auldearn Witches. Another individual is Laura Malipero, tried in 1654, and at whose trial a Book of Shadows-style tome was found in her home and produced as evidence against her. A third example is Elena Draga, tried circa 1582, who performed magickal cures using the phases of the Moon and seawater. Historian Ruth Martin says this is an example of one of the few forms of entirely non-Christian aspects of healing still in use by this period. This is highly suggestive of the preservation of a tradition.

Over the course of time, those who knew the old arts of Witchcraft became fewer and fewer, due in part to the danger of teaching others and becoming known in one's community. The risk of being betrayed by a relationship gone bad was always a risk as well. This resulted in Witchcraft being preserved and taught largely within family lines, although a few isolated Witches living outside of the towns and villages may have taken on a vagabond student here and there.

Witchcraft continued on in relative anonymity until the early nineteenth century. As discussed in Chapter One, folklorists such as J.B. Andrews, Lady de Vere, Roma Lister, and Charles Leland discovered what they believed to be surviving sects of Witchcraft practitioners claiming to be practicing the "Old Religion." Over half a century later, Gerald Gardner believed he had encountered the same thing in England.

Beginning in the mid-1950s, public interest in Witchcraft grew with the publication of books by Gerald Gardner and others. By the mid-1960s, Gardner's version of the Old Religion spread to the United States and took root, particularly among the hippie generation. The 1970s saw the publication of a great deal of traditional Witchcraft teachings and material as more and more Witches came forth. In the early 1980s, books promoting a self-styled, non-traditional approach to Witchcraft began to appear. The next two decades accelerated the process and transformed the teachings into something less related to the Old Ways of traditional Witchcraft.

THE FORK IN THE ROAD

As mentioned in the introduction to this book, many of the time-honored and time-proven methods of practicing Witchcraft failed to be passed on by the majority of authors writing on this subject since the mid-1980s. This was due in part to the fact that popular authors of the period were opening up the Craft to the populace at large. Previously, the practice had been to directly teach and initiate only those individuals that the teacher felt were sincere, truly devoted, and ready to commit to being trained.

This resulted in a multitude of people being taught only from books, and by others who had read books, neither of which had any teachers that were initiated by someone trained in the older initiate level material. Having no other recourse, these individuals turned to their intuition, inner spirit, personal study, and research, and essentially created their own rituals, concepts, and so forth. It was at this stage that Wicca as we now know it arose.

I think it is important to know that the Old Ways have not totally disappeared in favor of the new. There are still those who practice and maintain the Old Religion of Witchcraft. Some people don't believe (or don't want to believe) that there ever was an older Craft. In talking with many of these individuals, I feel that, in part, this attitude stems from a fear of comparison. There appears to be a mistaken belief that if older rituals and teachings exist, and the new ones have little if anything in common with them, then the new ones are invalidated.

I've also experienced first-hand that some people are angry at the thought that others have something they don't and are not offering to give it to them just for the asking. In response, these individuals often join ranks with those who elect to believe that hereditary Witches don't exist, family traditions are bogus, and the "Old Religion" isn't and never was.

Whatever the reason, there does seem to be a growing trend in the Craft and Pagan community to dismiss the antiquity of our religion. During the early twenty-first century, it was reported that the administration in Washington DC did not recognize Wicca/Witchcraft as a religion, and, in accord, that Wiccan/Witchcraft organizations "need not apply" for any federal programs that fund or support other religious organizations. The reported reason Wicca/Witchcraft is not accepted as a valid religion by our government officials is that we do not have a central authority, a central doctrine, or a mutually agreed upon set of distinct beliefs that define our religion. Witches are collectively a tribal people, which is our greatest strength and our major weakness.

What is interesting is that this situation with the government is exactly the same one that Witches found themselves in back in the days of ancient Greece! As we saw in Chapter Two, the Greeks viewed Witches as practitioners of "illicit religion" and therefore did not recognize them as a religious people nor grant them the rights and privileges granted to other religious sects of the period. Here we are, 2,500 years later and we're still illegitimate!

As I've tried to demonstrate in this book, our religion is actually ancient and new all at the same time. We have evolved over the centuries and we are still here today. I personally believe that those Witches and Pagans in our own community that disavow our past serve only to support and give credence to the views of those who would deny us our equality among other religions today.

In all my travels as an author to various Pagan festivals, and among all the people I have met, I have yet to encounter one true Witch who ever stood beneath the Full Moon in ritual and did not feel the timelessness of our ways. It is to those individuals that this chapter is devoted. In an attempt to restore and preserve some of the things we've lost, I have put together the following traditional teaching with which to close this book. I hope you will find it to be of value to you in your study and practice of Witchcraft.

THE EIGHT-FOLD PATH

The Eight-Fold Path is a term referring to the eight traditional aspects of magickal and religious training that must be mastered in order to become an adept or master of the Craft. They appear here in their traditional listing:

1. Mental discipline through fasting and physical discipline.

2. Development of the Will through mental imagery, visualization, and meditation.

3. Altered states of consciousness and the proper use of substances such as alcohol.

4. Personal power, thought projection, raising, and drawing power.

5. The Keys: ritual knowledge and practice. Use of enchantments, spells, symbols, and charms.

6. Psychic development and dream control.

7. Rising upon the Planes. Astral projection and mental projection.

8. Sex magick, sensuality, and eroticism.

Let us look at each of the concepts.

Mental discipline is an important aspect of magickal training. One can develop this through learning yoga or even some form of martial arts. Mental discipline instills confidence and enriches the character of an individual. *Development of the Will* strengthens personal will and determination. It helps sharpen the powers of the mind. When a person possesses self-discipline and a strong will, then the phrase *"as my will/word, so mote it be!"* takes on powerful meaning. Once discipline is achieved, then the will can be further strengthened by a practice of visualization and meditation.

Altered states of consciousness and the related use of drugs and alcohol is a very controversial subject. As we have seen in previous chapters, in ancient times, alkaloid plants were used along with ergot mold to induce trance and altered states of consciousness. In modern Witchcraft, we still find the inclusion of wine, which itself was an intoxicant in the ancient Mystery Schools of Old Europe. The worship of Dionysus is one such example. Ritual cakes once contained herbal ingredients designed to provide coven members with a catalyst for the purposes of astral projection (flying to the sabbat). Since most modern Witches lack the knowledge of their ancestors in this field, the individual must make a personal decision as to what is appropriate and what is not. It is better to be safe and alive so you can continue your overall studies than to be dead, awaiting rebirth, so you can start over again.

Personal power is the ability to draw and raise energy. It is an integral part of magick and can be attained through several different methods. According to the old teachings, the Witch could obtain, develop, and possess certain powers by participating in each sabbat ritual of the year and by observing each Full Moon ritual of the month. This is because an individual is aligned and charged by the flow of energy concentrated in a ritual circle on such occasions as an equinox or solstice. Through such acts as practicing raising a cone of power and casting a circle by passing energy through one's blade, the Witch can become proficient at working with energy fields.

The Keys to the Witches' Craft lie in understanding the inner mechanisms of magick and the occult. Learning the various correspondences employed in magick is important to understanding the art of Witchcraft. A knowledge of various herbs, enchantments, charms, and spells helps to fine-tune one's ability to raise and direct energy. A working knowledge of how and why rituals function helps one to focus and to draw upon the momentum of concepts still flowing from out of the past. To become proficient in anything, practice is required in the Witches' Craft in order to become skillful. In the end, your personal magickal abilities will be equal to the time and energy that you have invested in the art of Witchcraft.

Psychic development is a very useful tool for the Witch in both magickal and daily life. Psychic abilities help you become able to better discern things of a nonphysical nature. This is important because the practice of Witchcraft will eventually bring you to an encounter with nonphysical entities. The psychic senses can help to perceive both the presence and the actions of various spirits and elemental creatures. To help increase your psychic abilities, try sitting beneath the Full Moon and gently inhaling camphor fumes for a brief period while gazing at the Moon. Having a cup of rosemary tea while you sit beneath the Moon will also aid in the development of psychic abilities. Dream control is another method that can be employed to train the psychic mind. This technique is advanced and requires much study and practice on your own.

Rising upon the planes refers to a phase of study that requires the use of trance and astral projection. Rising upon the planes allows you access to nonphysical realms and states of consciousness. The astral temple is a good starting place for such experiences. In the ancient Mystery Cults, astral projection was employed to negate the fear of death among initiates by proving that they could still exist outside of the flesh. The projection of the astral body is something that everyone does while they sleep. It is the dream body that we see in dreams and its senses are what allow us to see and to feel while in the dream state. Conscious projection of the mind into the astral body is the goal. In this way, we can operate in a conscious manner while exploring astral dimensions.

Sex magick is the employment of energy generated by sexual excitement and the magickal use of body fluids for their energy charges and chemical elements. The use of sex within Witchcraft is a very controversial subject in modern times. It is important to understand that Witchcraft evolved from pre-Christian European Paganism and therefore is constructed around the views, beliefs, and practices of an ancient fertility religion. Sexuality and sensuality were part of traditional Pagan rites intended to ensure a bountiful harvest or a successful hunt. Sexual energy was the source of the life force that empowered the old rites. It typically followed erotic dancing and provocative chants.

These eight traditional aspects of magickal/religious training within Witchcraft can be found in many Pagan magickal traditions throughout the world as well as in the mystical disciplines of Eastern practices. Tantric yoga is a good example of the Eastern practice wherein the kundalini force is evoked. The Eight-Fold Path is a guideline for those who are interested in what the ancients believed to be the necessary steps to personal power. A personal study of each of these aspects will provide you with the tools through which deeper levels of magickal knowledge can be obtained. The list of training phases given here in the Eight-Fold Path has supplied you with pointers toward future investigation, research, experimentation, and study.

We have now come to the end of our journey from the past to the present. The future of the Witches' Craft is in your hands. You are the seeds for the future harvest. I hope this book was fertile ground. I close now with the words always spoken in my own tradition whenever any ritual is completed: *as it was in the time of our beginning, so is it now, so shall it be.*

⅃HE ⅅOREEN ⅤALIENTE ⅬETTERS

THE FOLLOWING SECTION contains three of the many letters written to me by Doreen Valiente. She was the most gracious, humble, and beautiful spirit I've ever encountered in all my years in the Craft. I first began correspondence with Doreen in January 1997 and continued until a few months before her death in 1999. My initial contact with Doreen originated from a request for copyright permission concerning one of her poems. When she responded in a letter dated February 17, 1997, Doreen mentioned her interest in Leland's material on Aradia and expressed a further interest in learning more about Italian Witchcraft as I described my own writings.

My foremost interest in replying to Doreen's request was based upon a desire to learn more from her about how much influence Leland's material had been on her own writings. I was particularly interested in her version of the *Charge of Aradia* since it was clearly an expanded version of Leland's Italian Witchcraft material. Regretfully, Doreen was never to address the latter despite repeated attempts on my part. As a Witch, she no doubt sensed my questions were not fully designed to simply satisfy a personal curiosity on my part. As a friendship grew between us, I accordingly ceased my attempts to discover the full extent of the influence of Italian Witchcraft on Doreen's writings. I regret now the time I invested in trying to be a clever detective in my letters and in not being totally forthright in the phraseology of my wording. I wish I had simply spent my time learning more about this great Lady.

Letter of June 10, 1997

I did not keep any copies of my letters written to Doreen, and will therefore have to work from memory in trying to provide the context of Doreen's replies. Doreen's letter to me, dated June 10, 1997, was written in response to some questions and comments made by me concerning several topics. These included my questioning the appearance of "Lucifer" in the Aradia material, asking whether her name "Valiente" was Italian or Spanish, and my observation that Gardnerian Wicca seemed to be mixed with many Aegean/Mediterranean concepts. The importance of Doreen's various replies outlines her interest in both Leland's writings and Italian Witchcraft prior to helping Gardner embellish the Gardnerian Book of Shadows. Doreen also affirms her position, which I share, that Margaret Murray or Gerald Gardner did not invent the religion of Witchcraft.

6 Tyson Place
Grosvenor Street
Brighton,
East Sussex,
Bn2 2JQ

June 10, 1997

Dear Raven,

I've been trying to get around to writing to you since I received your letter back in April!

The trouble has been that my partner has been in and out of hospital, and now back in again, for the last two months. He is a member of the Old Religion, and 85 years old - one of the last witches in the country. I have been very worried about him, though he is a bit better now. His basic trouble is that he has a heart condition which badly affects his breathing.

I have always been interested in the witchcraft of Italy, ever since reading a copy of *Arcadia* in, of all places, the Public Library, way back when I was a young girl—and we won't go with how long ago *that* was! Anyway, it was years before I ever met Gerald Gardener. It

is certainly a very strange book, and I wonder if Maddalena deliberately delivered a "pied" version of the original material. The mixture
of Roman Catholic ideas with witch practices, as you described
among certain *streghe* today, is very odd, and reminds one of Voodoo.
One finds it also in the *brujheria* of Mexico, where La Guadalupena,
the Madonna of Guadalupe, is venerated as the patroness of white
witchcraft, and practically regarded as the Goddess Herself.

Personally, I do not object to the name "Lucifer" as being that
of the God of the Witches, because it just means "Light-bearer," as
opposed to Diana, the darkness, just like the Yin and the Yang of
Taoirt philosophy. It is the Christians who have given the name a
sinister significance, just as they gave horns and hoofs of Pan to their
idea of the Devil.

Since receiving your letter, I have got a copy of your book, *Ways of
the Strega*, and have been dipping into it—I haven't had time to read
it properly. I like it very much, however, especially the illustration by
Charles Godfrey Leland. He was a truly remarkable man, a pagan at
heart if ever there was one, and we owe him a debt of gratitude as one
of the forerunners of today's Pagan revival. Incidentally, he used at
one time to live here in Brighton.

I have some small letters of "Liguore Strega" made by Guiseppe
Alberti of Benevento. There is a lively little picture on the label,
of witches dancing round the old tree. It is a very pleasant liquor,
and I should think possibly quite a love potion. But I wonder why
a walnut-tree? One doesn't see many of these trees in England. Our
native sacred tree is the oak, beloved of the Druids and the subject
of many old legends and beliefs. So I suppose each country has its
own native tree which people of olden times used to revere.

I have Carlo Ginzburg's book *Ecstasies: Deciphering the Witches'
Sabbath*, though I found it far from easy to read; but it is certainly
interesting. He shows that there are many European traditions which
have some relation to the Old Religion, and hence it is not, as some
"authorities" have claimed, merely an invention of Margaret Murray
and Gerald Gardener. I knew old Gerald very well, and he was a
folklorist after the fashion of Charles Godfrey Leland himself—a
real personality who could breathe new life into the old traditions
and re-present them to the world.

I would certainly agree that "Gardnerian Wicca" is a blend of Mediterranean/Aegean concepts with the Celtic traditions of Britain, I should think that each country has its own "blend" of witchcraft, according to the historical background of its people.

No, I have no Italian connections. "Valiente" is indeed Spanish. However, I do understand a little Italian, derived in fact from my interest in *Aradia*. My family comes from the New Forest area of England, and I married a Spaniard who was a refugee from Franco's Fascist regime in Spain. (Incidentally, now the more democratic government has taken over, I understand that quite a number of Spanish witches have come out of hiding in that country.)

I would certainly like to exchange more letters with you—though, as you will realize, I am not able to be a very regular correspondent; but this is simple from circumstances and not, I assure you, from lack of interest. Thank you for offering to send me more material about your Tradition. I will look forward to reading it.

In spite of everything, I was able to spend the night with friends in a Sussex wood, celebrating the Full Moon of May. We kept it going literally until dawn! I hope you had a similar celebration. "Blessed Be..."

Sincerely,
Doreen Valiente

LETTER OF AUGUST 25, 1998

Doreen's letter is written in reply to an ongoing conversation (by phone and letter) concerning the influence that Charles Leland's writings had on the beliefs and practices of modern Witchcraft. Doreen notes the importance of Leland's material in helping to preserve "The Old Religion." My expressed stand had been that Charles Leland, and not Gerald Gardner, was the father of modern Witchcraft.

> 6 Tyson Place
> Grosvenor Street
> Brighton,
> East Sussex,
> Bn2 2JQ
>
> August 25, 1998

Dear Raven,

I'm sorry to have taken so long to write to you. I have been in poor health since I lost my partner last year, and have not been able to do very much of anything. However, I do appreciate your efforts to get the copyright matters sorted out, and wish your book every success.

I'm glad that, thanks to you, people are coming to appreciate more what a great contribution Charles Godfrey Leland made to preserving the Old Religion. His art work was quite delightful, too, and deserves to be reproduced.

Do you know that some unpublished work of Leland's' is preserved in an American University library? They also have the original manuscript of "Aradia." Someone wrote to me about this recently, but I can't find the reference at the moment.

With all good wishes, "Blessed be . . ."

Sincerely,
Doreen Valiente

Letter of May 26, 1999

In her letter, Doreen is responding to a request I sent her asking if she would like to submit a biography to be included in my *Encyclopedia of Wicca & Witchcraft*. Doreen goes on to continue a discussion we were having regarding both the authentic and the fabricated elements of Leland's Aradia material. Of interest in Doreen's letter is the mention of a *cimaruta* (a symbol of Italian Witchcraft) formerly in the possession of Gerald Gardner. This seemed significant to me when one considers that Gardner visited Italy, wrote in his books of the influence of the Roman Mystery traditions on Witchcraft, and incorporated elements of Leland's material on Italian Witchcraft into his own Tradition of Wicca.

In Doreen's letter, she mentions her amusement at being able to prove the existence of Dorothy Clutterbuck, who scholars earlier contended was an invention of Gerald Gardner's imagination and personal agenda. Doreen and I both considered it great fun to be able to pop the "bubble of correctness" that some scholars blow around themselves whenever the occasion presented itself to us.

6 Tyson Place
Grosvenor Street
Brighton,
East Sussex,
Bn2 2JQ

May 26, 1998

Dear Raven,

Many thanks for your kind letter last month, and your invitation to be an "entry" in your forthcoming "Encyclopedia of Wicca,"

However, I have thought it over, and I don't think I want to give out all these personal details. I would rather remain a woman of mystery! Nevertheless, I wish you every success with this, as with the rest of your books.

I have been reading the new translation of "Aradia", published by Phoenix Press. This is the most interesting, though it raises a number of questions. It seems to settle the question of whether or not "Maddelena," was a real person. Apparently, she may have emigrated to America, and may yet be traceable through old records. (I remember the fun I had tracing down Dorothy Clutterbuck, after people had alleged that she was just a figment of Gerald Gardner's imagination). Also, what has become of her original MSS. of the material she supplied to Charles Godfrey Leland? I only hope that some of Leland's still remaining unpublished MSS. may yet see the light of day.

The other day I had a great find in a Brighton junk shop. I found a beautiful cimaruta, the witch amulet in the shape of a spring of rue. (like the one you illustrate in "Ways of Strega."). It is silver, of course—the Moon's metal. I haven't even seen one for sale before in this country—mine, illustrated in "ABC of Witchcraft," was given to me by Heral Hardener. I wonder how on earth this on ended up where I found it? It is a rather better version than the one I already have, so needless to say, O brought it, for quite a moderate sum, as the shopkeeper evidently had no idea what it was, other than "some sort of lucky charm."

This find cheered me up, as I have been very much "under the weather." In fact, I have not been well since my partner, Ron, passed away on the Autumn Equinox of 1997. We have been having a very cold spring, and that doesn't help my arthritis. However, I have been out on the Sussex Downs with some friends, and the may-flower (the hawthorn blossom) is just wonderful this year. We go out to our famous hill figure, the Long Man, associated for many years with Sussex witchcraft.

I hope you can read my writing—I'm not up to using a word processor. All good wishes, and "Blessed Be . . ."

Sincerely,
Doreen Valiente

ℬIBLIOGRAPHY

Alexander, Hartley Burr. *The World's Rim: Great Mysteries of the North American Indians.* New York: Dover Publications, 1998 [1953].

Allen, Richard H. *Star Names: Their Lore and Meaning.* New York: Dover Publications, 1963.

Anderson, William. *Green Man: The Archetype of Our Oneness with the Earth.* San Francisco: Harper Publishing, 1990.

Ankarloo, Bengt, and Stuart Clark. *Witchcraft and Magic in Europe: Ancient Greece and Rome.* Philadelphia: University of Pennsylvania Press, 1999.

——. *Witchcraft and Magic in Europe: The Eighteenth and Nineteenth Centuries.* Philadelphia: University of Pennsylvania Press, 1999.

——. *Witchcraft and Magic in Europe: The Twentieth Century.* Philadelphia: University of Pennsylvania Press, 1999.

Ankarloo, Bengt and Henningsen, Gustav. *Early Modern European Witchcraft.* Oxford: Clarendon Press, 1993.

Bailey, Cyril. *Phases in the Religion of Ancient Rome.* Berkeley: University of California Press, 1932.

Bartel, Pauline. Spellcasters: Witches and Witchcraft in History, Folklore, and Popular Culture. Dallas: Taylore Trade Publishing, 2000.

Barth, L. "The Sectarian Attitude in Orgonomy." *The Creative Process: Bulletin of the Intersciences Research Institute* 3(2) 1961.

Baroja, Julio Caro. *The World of Witches.* Chicago: University of Chicago Press, 1964.

Bean, O. *Me and the Orgone.* New York: St. Martin's Press, 1971.

Beyerl, Paul. *A Compendium of Herbal Magick*. Custer: Phoenix Publishing Inc., 1998
——. *The Master Book of Herbalism*. Custer: Phoenix Publishing Inc., 1984.
Briggs, Robin. *Witches and Neighbors: The Social and Cultural Context of European Witchcraft*. New York: Viking, 1996.
Campbell, Joseph. *The Hero with a Thousand Faces*. Princeton: Princeton University Press, 1968.
——. *The Masks of God: Primitive Mythology*. New York: Penguin Books, 1969.
Cattler, M. *The Life and Work of Willhelm Reich*. New York: Horizon Press, 1971
Davies, Owen. *Witchcraft, Magic and Culture 1736-1951*. Manchester: Manchester University Press, 1999.
Davidson, B. "The Effects of Orgone Energy on the E.M.G. Recordings of the Frontalis Muscle." Unpublished, 1991.
Dumezil, Georges. *Archaic Roman Religion*. Baltimore: Johns Hopkins University Press, 1996.
Duncan, Malcolm C. *Duncan's Ritual of Freemasonry*. New York: David McKay Company, Inc., 1976.
Eden, J. "Reichenbach's Researches." *The Creative Process: Bulletin of Interscience Research Institute* 2(1), 1972.
Eller, Cynthia. *The Myth of Matriarchal Prehistory: Why an Invented Past Won't Give Women a Future*.
Boston: Beacon Press, 2000.
Farrar, Stewart and Janet. *The Witches' God*. London: Robert Hale, 1989.
Ferguson, Ian. *The Philosophy of Witchcraft*. London: George Harrap & Co. Ltd., 1924.
Frazer, James G. *The Golden Bough: A Study in Magic and Religion*. New York: Macmillan Company, 1972 [1890].
Gardner, Gerald. *The Meaning of Witchcraft*. New York: Samuel Weiser, 1976.
——. *Witchcraft Today*. London: Rider & Company, 1954.
Gimbutas, Marija. *The Goddesses and Gods of Old Europe: Myths and Cult Images*. Berkeley: University of California Press, 1982.
——. *The Language of the Goddess*. San Francisco: HarperCollins, 1991.
Ginzburg, Carlo. *Ecstasies: Deciphering the Witches' Sabbath*. New York: Pantheon Books, 1991.

——. *The Night Battles: Witchcraft and Agrarian Cults in the Sixteenth and Seventeenth Centuries*. London: Routledge & Kegan Paul, 1983.

Goodison, Lucy, and Morris, Christine. *Ancient Goddesses, The Myths and the Evidence*. Madison: University of Wisconsin Press, 1998.

Graves, Robert. *The White Goddess*. New York: Farrar, Straus and Giroux, 1948.

Green, Miranda J. *Dictionary of Celtic Myth and Legend*. London: Thames and Hudson Ltd., 1997.

——. *Symbol and Image in Celtic Religious Art*. New York: Routledge, 2003.

Haynes, Sybille. *Etruscan Civilization*. Los Angeles: J. Paul Getty Trust Publication, 2000.

Hall, Manly P. *The Secret Teachings of All Ages*. Los Angeles: Philosophical Research Soceity, Inc., 1973.

Heselton, Philip. *Wiccan Roots: Gerald Gardner and the Modern Witchcraft Revival*. Berks: Capall Bann Publishing, 2000.

Highet, Gilbert. *The Classical Tradition: Greek and Roman Influences on Western Literature*. New York: Oxford University Press, 1985.

Hutton, Ronald. *The Triumph of the Moon: A History of Modern Pagan Witchcraft*. Oxford: Oxford University Press, 1999.

James, E. O. *The Cult of the Mother Goddess*. New York: Barnes & Noble Books, 1994.

Johnston, Sarah Iles. *Hekate Soteira: A Study of Hekate's Roles in the Chaldean Oracles and Related Literature*. Atlanta: Scholar's Press, 1990.

Kerenyi, Carl. *Dionysos: Archetypal Image of Indestructible Life*. Princeton: Princeton University Press, 1976.

——. *Eleusis: Archetypal Image of Mother and Daughter*. Princeton: Princeton University Press, 1967.

Kingsley, Peter. *Ancient Philosophy, Mystery, and Magic: Empedocles and the Pythagorean Tradition*. New York: Oxford University Press, 1995

Lavender, Susan, and Anna Franklin. *Herb Craft: A Guide to the Shamanic and Ritual Use of Herbs*. Capall Bann Publishing, 1996.

Leland, Charles Godfrey. *Aradia: Gospel of the Witches*. London: David Nutt, 1899.

——. *Etruscan Magic and Occult Remedies*. New York City: Scribners, 1892.

Lethbridge, Thomas Charles. *Witches*. New York: Citadel Press, 1968.

Liddell, W.E. and Howard, Michael. *The Pickingill Papers: The Origin of the Gardnerian Craft*. Berks: Capall Bann Publishing, 1994.

Mackey, Albert. *The History of Freemasonry: Its Legendary Origins*. New York: Gramercy Books, 1996.

Mann, E. *Orgone, Reich and Eros*. Chicago: Horizon Publishers, 1973.

Murray, Margaret A. *The Witch Cult in Western Europe*. New York: Barnes & Noble Books, 1996 [1924].

Neumann, Erich. *The Great Mother*. Princeton: Princeton University Press, 1972.

Otto, Walter F. *Dionysus, Myth and Cult*. Bloomington: Indiana University Press, 1995.

Papon, Donald. *The Lure of the Heavens; A History of Astrology*. New York: Weiser 1972.

Pocs, Eva. *Between the Living and the Dead: A Perspective on Witches and Seers in the Early Modern Age*. Budapest: Central European University Press, 1999.

Purkiss, Diane. *The Witch in History*. London: Routledge, 1996.

Rabinowitz, Jacob. *The Rotting Goddess: the Origin of the Witch in Classical Antiquity*. Brooklyn: Autonomedia, 1998.

Ravenscroft, William. *The Comacines: Their Predecessors and Their Successors*. London: E. Stock, 1910.

Reich, W. "A Case History (1945)." *International Journal of Sex, Economy and Research: Official Organ of the International Institute for Sex, Economy and Orgone Research* 4, 1978.

———. "Thermical and Electroscopical Orgonometry." *International Journal of Sex, Economy and Orgone Research: Official Organ of the Institute of Sex Economy and Orgone Research* 3(1), 1944.

Rudloff, Robert Von. *Hekate in Ancient Greek Religion*. Vancouver: Horned Owl Publishing, 1999.

Russell, Jeffrey B. *A History of Witchcraft*. London: Thames and Hudson Ltd., 1980.

———. *Witchcraft in the Middle Ages*. Ithaca: Cornell University Press, 1972.

Scot, Reginald. *The Discoverie of Witchcraft*. New York: Dover Publications, 1972 [1584].

Stenhouse, Margaret. *The Goddess of the Lake: Legends and Mysteries of Nemi*. Rome: Press Time, 1997.

Seznec, Jean. *The Survival of the Pagan Gods: The Mythological Tradition and its Place in Renaissance Humanism and Art.* New York: Pantheon Books, 1953.

Starz, K. "The Effects of the Orgone Energy Accumulator on Air." *The Creative Process: Bulletin of Interscience Research Institute* 2(4), 1978.

Turcan, Robert. *The Cults of the Roman Empire.* London: Blackwell Publishing, 1996.

Ulansey, David. *The Origins of the Mithraic Mysteries.* Oxford: Oxford University Press, 1989.

Valiente, Doreen. *An ABC of Witchcraft Past and Present.* Custer: Phoenix Publishing Inc., 1984.

——. *Witchcraft for Tomorrow.* Marlborough, UK: The Crowood Press, 1993 [1978].

Valiente, Doreen and Jones, Evan. *Witchcraft: A Tradition Renewed.* Custer: Phoenix Publishing Inc., 1990.

West, M.L. *Hesiod: Theogony, Works and Days.* Oxford: Oxford University Press, 1999.

ꟾNDEX

G

MORE BY CROSSED CROW BOOKS

Learn more at
www.CrossedCrowBooks.com